Jayãrthashastra

Jayãrthashastra

Microeconomics Through the Lens of an Epic

Tanushree Nagaveni

Copyrights © 2022 Tanushree Nagaveni

All rights reserved. No part of this book may be reproduced, stored, or transmitted by any means- whether auditory, graphical, mechanical, or electronic-without written permission of the author. Any unauthorized reproduction of any part of this book is illegal and is punishable by law.

To the maximum extent permitted by law, the author and publisher disclaim all responsibility and liability to any person, arising directly or indirectly from any person taking or not taking action based on the information available in this publication.

ISBN: 978-93-90976-89-8

Printed in India and published by BUUKS.

Dedicated to:
My dear Subbu Thatha
You are the sutradhari (director), I am only the patradhari (actor)
How many more times will you read the Mahabharata, partner?

Table of Contents

Foreword · ix
Acknowledgements · xi
Introduction · xv

Ganapathi and Veda Vyasa in a Neutral Equilibrium · · · · · · · · · · · · · · · · 1
A Boon from Kashyapa: Vinata's Diminishing Marginal Utility · · · · · · · · 6
Pandu's Indifference Curve · 12
Krishna or Narayani Sena: A Play of Preference · · · · · · · · · · · · · · · · · · 18
Arjuna's Optimal Choice · 24
Jaratkaru's Inelastic Demand · 36
Vasukis's Elastic Demand · 43
The Substitution and Income Effect Meet Shantanu and Ganga · · · · · · · · 47
Kamyakavana: A Substitute for Dvaitavana · 53
Giffen and Veblen Goods: Karna and Indra's Exchange · · · · · · · · · · · · · 62
Ulupi's Production Function for Liberation of Arjuna's Curse · · · · · · · · 71
A Catch-22 Situation for the Jaratkarus · 84
Bhanumati's Dignity: A Profit for Karna · 91
The Root Cause Analysis for Slaying Jarasandha · · · · · · · · · · · · · · · · · · 97
Hanuman's Goal: A Determinant for the Shift in Supply · · · · · · · · · · · · 120
Yudhishtira's Inelastic Supply of Dharma · 136
The Quest For Satyavati's Supernormal Profit · · · · · · · · · · · · · · · · · · · 151
Breaking-Even in Apad Dharma · 158

Arjuna's Opportunity Cost · 168
The Stable and Unstable Equilibrium in Amba's Life · · · · · · · · · · · · · · · 174
Zero-Cost Profit for Draupadi · 198
Yaksha's Hypothesis of Independent Utility · · · · · · · · · · · · · · · · · · · 208
The Folly of Drona's Price Discrimination · 227
Knight's Theory of Profit and Arjuna's Pashupathastra · · · · · · · · · · · · · 235
The Prisoner's Dilemma and the Game of Dice · · · · · · · · · · · · · · · · · · 250
Yudhishthira's Mahaprasthana · 282

Author's Bio · 293

Foreword

The biggest trees always grow from the tiniest of seeds. This was what I felt after my first conversation with Tanushree. At a time when I was coaching many of her contemporaries who were exploring themes of teenage angst and romance as the subject of their first writing endeavours, Tanushree's idea for this book had me hooked from the first conversation itself. This was all the reason I needed to take up the role of writing coach and editor for this book.

Of course, the idea seemed simple enough, but the work that lay ahead for her as an author was a journey she saw more as an exciting challenge than an arduous task. Yes, exploring the micro-economic angle in the stories from the great epic *The Mahabharata* does sound like an interesting idea; but how does an author bring their own voice and style into a book without bleeding into the actual content? If there is something you would notice about Tanushree is her unbridled energy and drive; a keen sense of direction and authority over exactly what she wanted out of this book, and as her writing coach, all I had to do was help her move some obstacles out of the way.

I do not want to waste any more print space by heaping more laurels on an author and her work you are about to get acquainted with yourself after a few more pages. All I can say here is I'm extremely glad that I could be part of the journey and creation of this book. In fact, experiencing these stories from our fantastic past all over again after years rekindled a love for these tales, and took me back to simpler times and those summers with my grandparents; and this, I believe, would be the highlight of this book for anyone reading it: A well-crafted piece of work efficiently dovetailing classical storytelling with fact-based research. While I wish her the best for this book, I know that this is just a fantastic first step for Tanushree's writing career.

ROHIT PANIKKER
Journalist/Editor/Writing Coach

Acknowledgements

Jayarthashastra is much more than just a book for me. I look at it more like a journey; one that transformed me as an individual and reminded me that nothing is truly impossible while redefining dedication and success.

I take this opportunity to thank everybody who has helped to see this dream come true.

Firstly, I would like to express my gratefulness and gratitude to Dr. Bibek Debroy for translating the Mahabharata into English and presenting a masterpiece in the form of ten volumes to the world. His work has truly touched, enlightened, and inspired the author in me. I am truly indebted to him. It has been my utmost pleasure reading his unabridged English translation of the Mahabharata and I hope to continue reading and drawing inspiration from all his works.

Thank you, Rohit sir, for carving out ornate pieces of writing out of my manuscripts. I am eternally grateful to you. I am very lucky to have a writing coach and an editor like you. Thank you once again for leading me through this journey.

I extend my gratitude to Nirmal Das for constantly supporting and guiding me through this entire journey. Thank you for all those all-nighters and the relentless work on the trailer. You made this entire process of writing a memorable one. Thank you for guiding me at every step. I look forward to working with both of you on all my future projects. I would also like to thank the entire team of BUUKS Self-Publishing without whom this project would never have been accomplishable.

My humble pranam to my gurus: Smt Goda Gopal and Smt Prabha Sheshagiri. I am privileged to be your student and I take this humble opportunity to thank you sincerely for sowing the seeds of knowledge in me and introducing me to this divine epic *Mahabharata*. Thank you, Goda Ma'am, for nurturing my interest in Sanskrit and encouraging me in all my endeavours. Thank you, Prabha Ma'am, for awakening my latent interest in *The Mahabharata*, through those exciting mythological quizzes back in Balak Science Club.

My special thanks to my economics lecturer Lisa Cletus for introducing me to the world of economics. Thank you Ma'am for taking out time from your busy schedule and attending those Google meets, answering my silly questions, and motivating me to strive harder. This project would have been impossible to achieve without your backing and blessings. I miss your lectures back at college. How I wish I could attend those classes again.

I have always been fascinated by illustrated books and wanted my book to have illustrations. My heartfelt gratitude to my drawing teacher Swetha Mohan for having illustrated *Jayarthashastra*. Spending time with you during this project has rejuvenated my memories of grades six, seven, and eight. Thank you, Ma'am.

Thank you, Lakshmi, for believing in me that I could write and for patiently hearing me out and providing your input in all our discussions. I am truly grateful to have a friend like you. Here's to many more years of our friendship! Thank you so much.

None of this would have been possible without my family: my grandfather, my grandmother, and my mother.

Thatha, you have the epitome of wisdom, you are the personification of patience, an ocean of knowledge and experience. You are what I call life's pristine view. I love you and thank you wholeheartedly for pushing me beyond my boundaries and showering me with your tender care and affection. "Are you ready for the next project, partner?"

My profound gratitude to my grandmother for being an integral part of all my endeavours. My humble thanks to you for teaching me to embrace my failures and use them as stepping stones to leap towards success. Thank you for being my best friend and being beside me at every step of my life.

Thank you Mumma for being a pillar of strength and for converting every dream of mine into a reality. Thank you for being the backbone of my life and holding my hand and leading me through all my successes. I love you, Mumma. I am thankful to God to have a mother, friend, and mentor like you. You mean the world to me.

Introduction

Dharmecha Arthecha Kamecha Mokshecha Bharatarshabha |
Yadi Hasti tad anyatra yanne hasti na tat kutrachit ||

"In the expanse of righteousness, economics, desire, and liberation, if what is found in the Mahabharata is found anywhere else, then what is not found here will be impossible to discover anywhere else".

Two parts of this shloka have always intrigued me and given me sleepless nights: "Arthecha" and "yanne hasti na tat kutrachit". I would always ponder over the validity of what is said here. "Is it true that it is impossible to find anything that has not already been mentioned or dealt with in the Mahabharata? And why did Veda Vyasa use the word "Arthecha" in his shloka?

At this point, I must confess that as I was gearing up to find answers to these questions of mine, I was also passionately delving into introductory microeconomics (In the sense that I had then thought economics comprised only of microeconomics. Of course, I realised later that I was wrong and that economics was an ocean.)

So, I began to read, or rather, re-read all these stories and every time I reached the end of a story I asked myself a question: "How does this story relate to the microeconomics theories I learnt in grade 12?"

Tanushree Nagaveni

This exercise is what led to the creation of *Jayarthashastra*.

Now, after engaging in this extensive process of reading and trying to understand the moral core of The Mahabharata and the tenets of modern economics, you might want to ask me if I am convinced whether what is not found in the Mahabharata is impossible to be discovered anywhere else.

My answer is yes and I am sure you will feel the same way too after you finish reading this book because at the end of this journey you will realise that the Mahabharata is not just an epic or a literary masterpiece but an enigma waiting to be explored from new perspectives and point of views.

Happy reading!

Ganapathi and Veda Vyasa in a Neutral Equilibrium

Suklambhara-dharam Vishnum Shashi varnam chatur bhujam |
Prasanna vadhanam dhyaayet sarva vighnopashaanthaye ||

I bow to you, Lord Ganesha. The one who is dressed in splendid white garments, who is pervading everywhere, whose complexion resembles that of the moon, and the one with four arms. O the one with a pleasant face, I meditate on that form, please nullify all the obstacles in my path.

The Shri Mahaganapathi Temple in Malleshwaram holds a very special place in my heart. It was in this magnificent temple that I performed my maiden Bharatanatyam performance. It is the place where I find the answers to all my questions.

Above all, it is the place where I was introduced to these magical life-transforming two words, "Jai Ganesha" by Sri Satyanarayana Shastri (Gani), who crafted my journey in Bharatanatyam with his blessings.

Invoking Lord Bande Ganapathi's blessings and Sri Satyanarayana Shastri's blessings, I commence this journey called Jayarthashastra.

I dedicate this chapter humbly to Gani Thatha.

Krishna Dvaipayana Vedavyasa was the illustrious son of Sage Parashara and Satyavati. Having conceived the great epic Mahabharata, he began thinking about all the possible ways in which he could present his sacred work to the rest of the world. He then began to meditate on Lord Brahma, the creator of the universe.

Pleased with his penance, Lord Brahma appeared before Vedavyasa. At the sight of Lord Brahma, Krishna Dvaipayana Vedavyasa prostrated before him and then stood before him with his head bowed down and hands folded in obeisance to the father of the universe. Having praised the Lord, he prayed, "Lord, I have conceived an excellent work, but cannot think of one who can take it down to my dictation." Brahma extolled Vyasa and said: "O sage, invoke Ganapati and plead him to be your amanuensis." [1] Having advised Vedavyasa thus, Lord Brahma disappeared.

Vedavyasa then began meditating on Lord Ganesha. When Lord Ganesha appeared before him, Vyasa was pleased and offered him prayers as per the prescribed rites. Having paid his respects to Lord Ganesha, Vedavyasa then sought his aid. "Lord Ganapati, I shall dictate the story of the Mahabharata and I pray you to be graciously pleased to write it down." Ganapati replied: "Very well. I shall do as you wish. But my pen must not stop while I am writing. So, you must dictate without pause or hesitation. I can only write on this condition?" Vyasa agreed, guarding himself, however, with a counter stipulation: "Be it so, but you must first grasp the meaning of what I dictate before you write it down."[2]

Ganapathi smiled and agreed to Vedavyasa's conditions. Krishna Dvaipayana then began composing verses of the great epic Mahabharata. Vedavyasa would occasionally compose some complex stanzas which would make Ganapati pause a while to get at the meaning and Vyasa would avail himself of this

---

1 Mahabharata by C. Rajagopalachari.
2 Mahabharata by C. Rajagopalachari.

interval to compose many stanzas in his mind. Thus, the Mahabharata came to be written by Ganapati to the dictation of Vyasa.[3]

Neutral Equilibrium

In economics, the word "equilibrium" or "market equilibrium" refers to a situation of the market in which demand for a commodity is exactly equal to its supply corresponding to a particular price. Equilibrium may also be described as a situation where at a given price, the quantity demanded is equal to the quantity supplied. In other words, when demand=supply, the market has attained its equilibrium.[4]

---

3 Mahabharata by C. Rajagopalachari.
4 All in One Economics CBSE Class XI.

Predominantly, there are three types of equilibrium in economics

1. Stable Equilibrium
2. Unstable Equilibrium
3. Neutral Equilibrium

For the next part of our discussion, let us focus on neutral equilibrium.

Neutral equilibrium refers to the situation in which disturbing forces neither bring the equilibrium to its original position nor do they drive it from its original position. The equilibrium rests where it has been moved.

When an initial equilibrium position is disturbed, the forces of disturbance bring it to the new position of equilibrium where the system has come to rest. A ball on the billiard table if disturbed will come to rest at the new position to which it has moved. According to Prof. Pigou, *"An egg lying on its side is in neutral equilibrium."*

Thus, in the case of neutral equilibrium, the object assumes once for all a new position after the original position is disturbed.

Now, having understood the concept of neutral equilibrium, let us explore the same concept through the story of Ganesha and Vedavyasa.

In the story, the initial equilibrium is that point where Lord Ganesha appears before Vedavyasa and agrees to be his amanuensis. This initial equilibrium is disturbed by the two conditions imposed by both Lord Ganesha and Vedavyasa. These conditions resemble the disturbing forces present in a market. Although these conditions (disturbing forces) disturb the initial equilibrium, they do bring it to a new position where both the parties mutually agree to each other's conditions and the system comes to a rest.

Therefore, the two conditions imposed by Lord Ganapathi and Krishna Dvaipayana Vedavyasa neither bring the initial equilibrium to its original position, nor do they drive it away from the original position. The equilibrium between Lord Ganapathi and Krishna Dvaipayana Vedavyasa rests where it has been moved (the mutual agreement between either party to abide by their conditions).

A Boon from Kashyapa: Vinata's Diminishing Marginal Utility

I was nine years old when my acquaintance with Amar Chitra Katha began. The first comic: "Garuda" was so thrilling that it instantly transported me to the realm of mythology. The entire story came alive before my eyes. The bright red and blue hues contrasting the fading cream shade of the old paper captivated me. That day, I discovered my passion for mythology.

When I reread the story of Garuda in the Mahabharata recently, the words in the book reminded me of the same ACK comic images. It is a memory that reminds me of my childhood. What is your memory that connects you to your childhood?

Reminiscing that rainy day in my school library, I present to you the story of Garuda with a twist...

Daksha Prajapati[5] had two daughters, Kadru and Vinata. They were married to Kashyapa[6]. Kadru and Vinata served their husband with utmost devotion and joy. Kashyapa was pleased with the conduct of his wives and desired to give them a boon, each. Kadru aspired to give birth to one-thousand nagas (snakes) as her children while Vinata desired to have two sons who were mightier than Kadru's sons. Kashyapa granted both of his wives the boon of their choices and journeyed to the forest. Subsequently, Kadru gave birth to one thousand eggs while Vinata gave birth to two eggs. Following the passage of five-hundred years, Kadru's valorous sons arrived. On the contrary, Vinata's eggs showed no signs of hatching.

---

5 Daksha Prajapati is the manasaputra (a son created by the mind) of Brahma. Often depicted as a man with an obese physique and a goat's face, Daksha is an agent of creation.
6 Kashyapa is a one of the saptarishis of the Rigveda.

Vinata became restless and was eager to have a son. In haste, she broke open one of the eggs and was surprised to see her son whose upper body was formed, but the lower body was yet unformed. Vinata's son was outraged at his mother's foolish action and cursed her in a fearful voice, "O mother! Since out of avarice, you broke open this egg and didn't allow my body to be completely developed, you will be enslaved for 500 years by the woman you sought to equal. O mother! Your other illustrious son will set you free from slavery, if you wait patiently and do not break open the egg prematurely and deform his body like you have done mine. If you wish to have a son of unrivalled strength, you must patiently wait for his time of birth, for 500 years."[7] Your other son will set you free from your suppression, only if you wait patiently for his arrival." Having spoken thus to his mother, Aruna[8], abandoned her and rose to the sky.

After 500 years, the mighty Garuda[9] was born. Although, he abandoned his mother immediately after birth in search of food, true to Aruna's words, he relieved his mother from her slavery through his bravery and intelligence[10].

---

7 The Mahabharata 1 Translated by Bibek Debroy

8 The word 'Aruna' refers to the red tint in the morning sky. Aruna is the elder brother of Garuda and the charioteer of the Sun God.

9 Garuda is the eagle-bird. He is the mount (vahana) of Lord Vishnu and is the king of the birds (Pakshiraja).

10 Garuda waged a war against gods including Indra in order to bring the amritha vessels for his brothers. Having obtained the vessel, he flew back to the earth. Abiding by Indra's request of not allowing the nagas to obtain the amritha, as it would bring great trouble later, he along with Indra forged a plan. Upon reaching his brothers Garuda placed the vessel before them, and asked them to first purify themselves before drinking. While they were away purifying themselves, Indra took back the amritha vessel and returned back to the heavenly abodes.

Following the liberation of Vinata's slavery, both Garuda and Vinata retired to the forest, where he ate snakes and was honoured by all the birds.

Diminishing Marginal Utility

Satisfaction is an emotional state, in which an individual experiences the fulfilment of all needs and desires.

Have you ever asked yourself, whether this sense of gratification can be quantified?

The first concept that comes to my mind when I hear the word 'satisfaction' is 'Utility'. Satisfaction derived from the consumption of a commodity is utility. In other words, the want-satisfying capacity of a commodity is its utility. Utility can be measured in utils. Utils is a hypothetical measuring unit of utility.

There are two approaches to study utility analysis, the cardinal utility analysis (quantification of utility in cardinal numbers) and the ordinal utility analysis (allocation of ranks based on the utility derived from the consumption of a commodity). Under the cardinal utility approach, there are two measures of utility, namely the total utility and marginal utility.

Total utility is the total satisfaction that a consumer derives from consuming a given amount of any commodity. Similarly, marginal utility is the change in the total utility caused by the consumption of an additional unit of the same commodity. Now, as we consume successive units of the same commodity, the total satisfaction that we derive from the consumption of these additional units decreases, therefore the total utility initially increases and later diminishes as we continue our consumption of the successive units. Marginal utility being the utility of the additional units, decreases from the beginning of the consumption, becomes zero, and then becomes negative. This nature of the marginal utility to continually decrease from the beginning of the consumption of a product is given by the law of 'diminishing marginal utility'.[11]

---

11 NCERT Introductory Microeconomics Textbook in Economics for Class XII

According to Alfred Marshall, the law of diminishing marginal utility is defined as, "The additional benefit which a person derives from a given increase of a stock of a thing diminishes, other things being equal, with every increase in the stock that he already has."

The law of diminishing marginal utility simply states that a consumer wishes his needs to be satisfied only up to a limit. This limit is termed as maximum satisfaction in economics. Beyond the point of total satisfaction, the fulfilment of a need may harm a consumer. We can conclude that even the emotional state of satisfaction has a boundary and when the emotional state overflows this boundary, we end up in despair.

At this point, it would be useful to look at the graph below. On the x-axis, the passage of time is measured. Contrasting to this, the total utility (TU) and Marginal utility (MU) are measured on the y-axis. The black line represents the TU curve, while the grey line represents the MU curve.

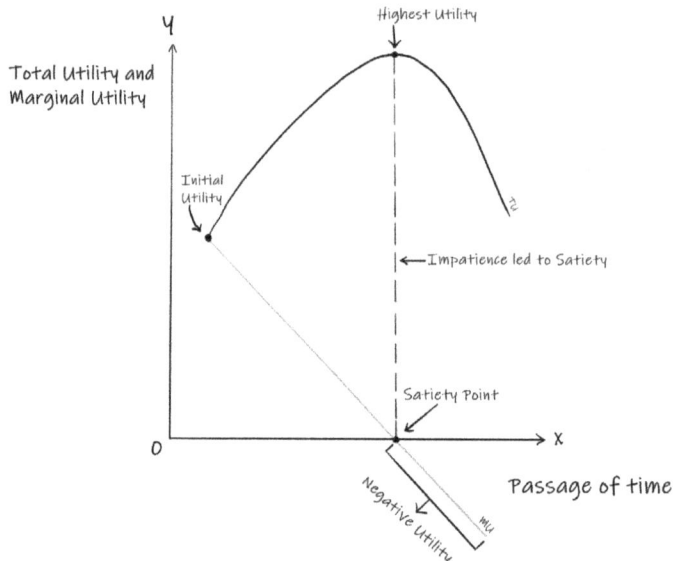

Vinata's total utility is the satisfaction that she derives when she receives the boon of her choice from Kashyapa. The moment when she receives the boon from Kashyapa is the initial utility. Total utility initially increases. This is represented by the upward rising TU. We may assume that Vinata's total utility initially increases owing to her experience of motherhood (laying of eggs and keeping them in steaming vessels). The highest utility point on the graph below represents that point in time where, out of restlessness, Vinata breaks open one of her eggs and sees her son Aruna. The TU curve from there onwards starts descending downwards because Vinata's satisfaction is transformed into despair. A feeling of devastation engulfs her as she hears the curse from her son.

The MU curve decreases from the beginning. This is because Vinata's eager anticipation for her son creates a feeling of anxiety within her. Anxiety being the exact opposite of satisfaction simply causes the MU curve to slope downwards. The Satiety point is just before Vinata realises that her son's body is deformed. Restlessness causes the MU curve to intersect the x-axis and travel into the negative quadrant, where utility becomes negative corresponding to the curse uttered by Aruna. The events that occur in Vinata's life while giving birth to her children clearly depict the operation of the law of diminishing marginal utility.

Pandu's Indifference Curve

Science or Commerce? The typical dilemma in a 10th grader's mind. Often, as a 10th grader, I received a lot of advice from everyone. It was as if their words of advice were just meant to mask the dilemma within me. However, the magnanimity of this perplexity chose to only embrace me with its power. I rattled in the beginning, not being able to contemplate the nature of my predicament. But as my proximity with this dilemma grew exponentially, I realised that it was the expression of indifference, which was truly the solution to my problem.

I loved science and commerce equally. It was simply impossible for me to differentiate my satisfaction between the two. During school days, I constantly heard one phrase, "Art keeps us connected with our past, while science takes us to the future and commerce takes care of our present needs." I had to choose between the past, present, or the future. But only one question procrastinated this game of choosing- "What if I am indifferent and love all of them impartially?"

That question reminded a story from the Sambhava Parva of the Mahabharata...

Vaishampayana[12] said, 'One day, in the great forest frequented by deer and predatory beasts, King Pandu saw a stag that was the leader of its herd mating with a doe. With five swift and sharp arrows that were decorated with golden feathers in their shafts, Pandu shot both the stag and the doe. The stag was actually the immensely energetic son of a rishi, blessed with the power of austerities. The energetic one was uniting with his wife in the form of a deer. While still united with the doe, he fell on the ground instantly and as he began to lose his senses, lamented in a human voice.

The deer said, "Even evil men who are enslaved by lust and anger, are therefore deprived of reason and are always sinful, stay away from such cruel deeds. A man's judgement does not swallow destiny. Destiny swallows judgement. The wise never sanction anything that is forbidden by destiny. O descendant of

---

12 Vaishampayana is considered the traditional narrator of the Mahabharata and is a pupil of Veda Vyasa.

the Bharata lineage! You were born in a dynasty that was always devoted to dharma. Overcome by lust and avarice, how have you lost all your reason?" Pandu replied, "O deer! In dealing with deer, kings behave no differently from enemies; they kill them. Therefore, you should not blame me in your delusion. Deer can be killed openly and through trickery. That is the dharma of kings. Since you know that, why are you blaming me? When seated at a sacrifice, the rishi Agastya[13] went on a hunt. He offered each deer in that great forest to all the gods. This is the sanction of dharma. Then why are you reproving me? According to Agastya's actions, the likes of you are offerings at sacrifices."

The deer said, "Earlier, they never unleashed arrows without considering preparedness. There is a time for this and killing at such times is praised."

Pandu replied, "It is known that killing occurs, whether prepared or unprepared, through different means—strength and sharp arrows. O deer! Why are you blaming me?" The deer responded in angst, "O king! I do not blame you because you have killed a deer or because you have caused me injury. But instead of performing such a cruel act, you should have waited until my act of uniting was complete. This is a time that is for the welfare of all beings and desired by all beings. Which learned one will kill a deer engaged in pleasure in the forest? You have rendered futile my attempt to obtain offspring.

O Kourava! O Pourava! This lineage has had rishis and is famous for its righteous acts. This act was unworthy of you. O descendant of the Bharata lineage! This greatly cruel act is condemned in all the worlds. It destroys attainment of heaven and fame and is against dharma. You are acquainted about pleasures from uniting with women. You also know the sacred texts and norms of dharma. You are the equal of a god. You should not have committed such an act, which is unworthy of reaching heaven. O best of kings! Your duty is to punish men who act cruelly, are engaged in evil acts, and have abandoned

---

13 Agastya is a revered sage and one of the saptarishis.

the three goals[14]. O best of men! O king! What have I done that you killed me? I am a sage in the form of a deer and live on roots and fruit. I always live peacefully in the forest. Since you have caused injury to me, you will certainly be injured.

Since you have been cruel to a helpless couple, when you are overcome through the pangs of desire, death will overtake you. I am a sage named Kimdama, unparalleled in austerities. Ashamed of men, I united with this deer. Assuming the form of a deer, I roamed with other deer in this dense forest. The sin of killing a Brahmana will not vest on you, since you did that unknowingly. O foolish one! But since you killed me in the form of a deer when I was overcome by desire, you will meet with the same fate that has befallen me.

Overcome by desire, when you unite with your loved one, at that very instant, you will depart for the land of the dead. The woman with whom you unite in your last moments will also go to the land of the king of the dead, inescapable for all beings. Out of devotion towards you, that best of intelligent ones will follow you. You have now brought me into grief when I was in the midst of pleasure. Like that, you will be afflicted with misery when you have just found happiness."

Having said this, in great pain, the deer gave up its life. In an instant, Pandu was also immersed in grief.'[15]

The Case Of Indifferent Utility

Have you ever been in a situation, where between two choices, you prefer both the choices equally? Think about it. Many times, when we are presented with two choices, we are simply unable to choose between them, because we prefer both choices equally. Let us try and understand this behaviour through a microeconomic dimension.

---

14 Dharma, Artha and Kama.
15 The Mahabharata 1 Translated by Bibek Debroy

We are all consumers. We decide which goods to buy based on our consumption needs. This is precisely the problem of choice. Between two goods we prefer that good which gives us the maximum satisfaction. So, what do we mean by 'prefer' in the previous sentence? Try replacing the word 'prefer' with 'like/love', you will be able to make sense of it. Preference and like are synonymous.

In microeconomics, the preference of the consumer over all the available consumption bundles, dependent on the price of the goods and the income of the consumer, may be represented diagrammatically. This approach of explaining a consumer's preference is termed ordinal utility analysis.

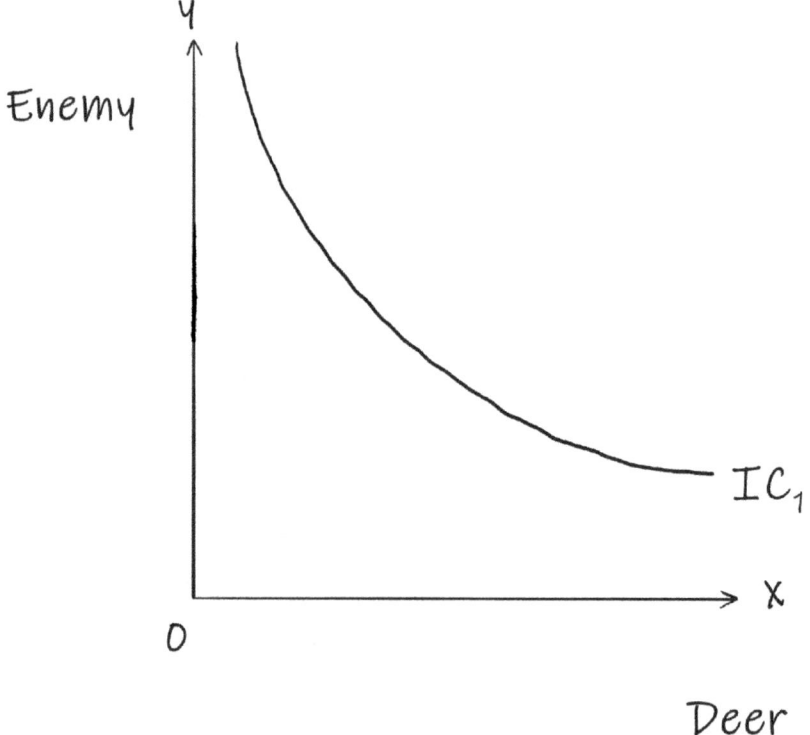

Enemy

Deer

All the consumption bundles, each comprising of two goods, can be plotted on an XY-plane. Those bundles which give the consumer the same level of satisfaction represent the indifference set. All the points, representing the consumption bundles in the indifference set, can be joined together to form a curve. This curve is called an indifference curve.

In other words, an indifference curve is defined as the locus of possible combinations of the two goods that yield the same level of satisfaction (utility).

From the story, it can be inferred that Pandu derives satisfaction from hunting deer. This abstract feeling is called utility. From his conversation with Rishi Kimdama we can understand that no matter which deer King Pandu killed, he derived the same level of utility. Similarly, from King Pandu's words, "O deer! In dealing with deer, kings behave no differently from enemies; they kill them", we can also infer that King Pandu derived the same utility from killing the deer or the enemy. In other words, he was indifferent between them.

If we assume that Pandu's consumption bundle to consist of both deer and enemies, then we plot these consumption bundles on the XY-plane. On the x-axis, we can measure the number of deer killed by King Pandu, while the number of enemies killed by King Pandu is measured on the y-axis. If all these points yield the same utility, they represent Pandu's indifference set and when these points are joined by a curve, it forms an indifference curve IC_1. At any point on the indifference curve IC_1, King Pandu derives the same utility.

Krishna Or Narayani Sena: A Play Of Preference

Season 17, Episode 5: Arjuna goes to Krishna…

My craze for Mahabharata was well-known since childhood. But, the Starplus Mahabharat series of 2014-15 seemed to have an entirely different effect on me. I was so mad about that episode where Arjuna and Duryodhana go to meet Krishna that I rewatched the same episode countless times. The dialogues were so effective and the entire episode resonated a divine feeling each time I rewatched it.

During my summer vacation, each day began with Mahabharata and ended with Mahabharata. I even dreamt about Mahabharata, sometimes imagining myself to be a character from the story… I would even mono-act a scene from the serial during my pastime, improvising the dialogues sometimes…

However, I never imagined that I would be writing the same story in my book with a new perspective.

Krishna was resting when both the princes arrived in the beautiful city of Dvaraka. Duryodhana was the first to enter the chamber where Krishna was sleeping. He made himself comfortable on a seat, which was closer to Krishna's head. After some time, Arjuna arrived there. Having seen Krishna asleep, Arjuna sat beside his feet with his hands folded together in salutation and devotion.

After some time, Krishna awoke and saw Arjuna first, but he offered hospitality to both the princes. Without wasting any opportunity, Prince Duryodhana requested Krishna to take his side in the battle since he had arrived there first. Krishna contradicted Duryodhana that he had seen Arjuna first. Duryodhana was perplexed by Krishna's response. But Krishna calmed Duryodhana by saying that he would help both of them.

Since Krishna saw Arjuna first, he offered the first choice to him. There were two choices for Arjuna — the one hundred million cowherds called Narayani Sena on one side and Lord Krishna himself on the other side, unarmed and bound by his word not to fight in the war.

Arjuna chose Lord Krishna, whereas Duryodhana chose the Narayani Sena. Once Duryodhana departed, Krishna questioned Arjuna, "O Arjuna! What is the reason for your preference?" Arjuna replied, "O Krishna. I am aware that you are capable of eliminating the enemies alone. I am skilled in destroying the enemies all by myself. Yet, your accomplishments are renowned throughout the world. I aspire to become distinguished, and thus I have chosen you. Further, it has always been my strong desire to have you as my charioteer. My desire has also been a motive for which I chose you, O Krishna!"

Krishna was pleased to hear Arjuna's humble words and he agreed to become his charioteer in the war.

Monotonic Preference

In economics, consumers are assumed to be rational and their behaviour is governed by the monotonicity of preferences. It means that a consumer will always prefer more of that commodity that offers him greater satisfaction or in other words greater utility.

Monotonic preference refers to a situation, where the consumer will prefer the combination providing more commodities than the combination providing lesser commodities.[16]

Between any two bundles of goods, which are represented here as (x1, x2) and (y1, y2), a consumer will prefer the bundle (x1, x2) if it has more of at least one of the goods x1 or x2 but no less of the other good when compared to the consumption bundle (y1, y2). These kinds of preferences are called monotonic preferences.

The concept of monotonic preferences can be further extended to the Indifference Curve Analysis. Between any two indifference curves, the customers' preference is always for the consumption bundles on the higher indifference when compared to the consumption bundles on the lower indifference curves. In other words, the higher the indifference curve, the higher is the perceived satisfaction.

As observed in the above story Arjuna behaves like a rational consumer and exhibits monotonic preference. The following explanation elaborates the reason for Arjuna's monotonicity of preferences:

- Arjuna had two choices. The Narayani Sena or Lord Krishna. While making a decision, Arjuna had to weigh both these choices in terms of their characteristics. In this process of evaluating these choices, Arjuna had to allocate preferences to both the options based on the number of attributes each one possessed.

---

16 All in One Economics CBSE Class XI

- Hypothetically, Arjuna would have considered the characteristics of both the choices presented to him.

Characteristics of Krishna	Characteristics of Narayani Sena
1. An embodiment of Dharma 2. An epitome of wisdom and knowledge 3. A close friend 4. Known for his achievements 5. A well wisher of the Pandavas	1. Experienced Warriors 2. Unparalleled in strength 3. Have fought many battles successfully 4. Equal to Krishna's strength

- Later, having compared both sets of characteristics, Arjuna allocates a preference for both. In this case, Krishna's attributes outweigh the traits of the Narayani Sena. Hence, Arjuna's inclination for Krishna would be greater than his preference for the Narayani Sena. Such a decision represents monotonic preference.

    ALLOCATION OF ARJUNA'S PREFERENCE BASED ON THE ANALYSIS OF CHARACTERISTICS

    1. Krishna
    2. Narayani Sena

- Arjuna clearly states in his conversation that the primary objective of having Krishna on his side is to acquire fame. Therefore, it is natural that Arjuna derives higher utility from Krishna than the Narayani Sena.

  Utility derived from Krishna > Utility derived from Narayani Sena

  (Krishna)>(Narayani Sena)

- Arjuna exhibits an inelastic demand for Krishna. His demand for Krishna is independent of the might of the Narayani Sena. In other words, an increase in the might of the Narayani Sena would not affect Arjuna's demand for Krishna.

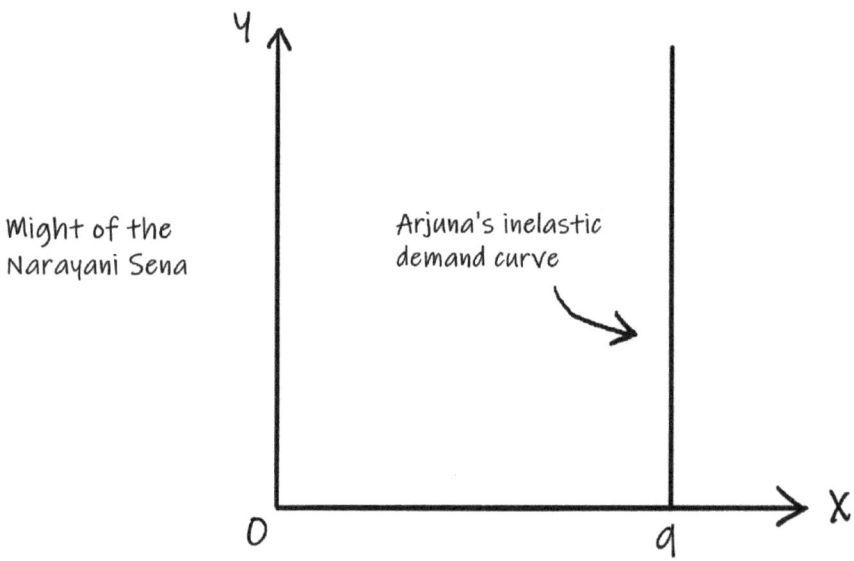

Demand for Krishna

Inelastic demand indicates a condition in which the quantity of a commodity demanded by a consumer remains insensitive to any change in the price of the commodity. In everyday life, we all exhibit an inelastic demand for essential goods.

The graph above represents Arjuna's demand for Krishna through a demand curve. Traditionally, quantity demanded is measured on the x-axis and the price for the commodity is measured on the y-axis. However, in our story, Arjuna's demand for Krishna is measured on the x-axis while the might of the Narayani Sena is measured on the y-axis. Traditionally, inelastic demand represents the situation that the quantity demanded is unaffected by the change in price. Likewise, Arjuna's demand for Krishna remains constant irrespective of the increase in the might of the Narayani Sena.

Since Arjuna's demand is insensitive to the might of the Narayani Sena, the demand curve will assume the shape of a vertical straight line. Furthermore, Arjuna's demand cannot be expressed in quantitative terms. Therefore, we can speculate Arjuna's demand for Krishna to be q.

Arjuna's Optimal Choice

yo maam pashyati sarvatra sarvam cha mayi pashyati
tasyaaham na pranashyami sa cha me na pranashyati
||Bhagavad Gita 6.30||

For the one who sees Me everywhere and sees everything in Me,
I am never lost, nor is he ever lost to Me.[17]

The beauty of the Bhagavad Gita was unknown to me until I met my two Gurus: Smt Goda Gopal mam and Smt Prabha Sheshagiri mam. Both have played a very important role in sculpting my personality from the age of three. They inspire me every day.

It gives me immense pleasure to recount that I learnt the first letter in Sanskrit and the first shloka from Smt Goda Gopal mam at Adarsha Samskruta Mahavidyalaya.

One of the best moments in the Balak Science Club was the chanting of the 12th chapter of the Bhagavad Gita. Reciting the verses from the 12th chapter in chorus along with my classmates always felt surreal.

Every time I recited those shlokas, I lost track of reality. It felt as if I was Arjuna and Krishna was teaching me the way of life.

When I think about the Bhagavad Gita, I always remember what both my gurus said, "Bhagavad Gita is the user manual of life. If one aspires to live life to the fullest, then one must start with the Bhagavad Gita".

---

17 Bhagavad Gita as it is by A C Bhaktivedanta Swami Prabhupada.

Arjuna said, "O Achyuta! Place my chariot in between the two armies, while I look at those who are desirous of battle and are assembled here. Let me see with whom I will have to fight in this war-related business. In a desire to do good to the evil-hearted son of Dhritarashtra, they have gathered here, desirous of fighting. I want to see them."

Thus, spoken to by Arjuna, Krishna placed that magnificent chariot between the two armies, in front of Bhishma, Drona and all the other rulers of the earth and said, "O Partha! Look at those of the Kuru clan who are assembled here." There, Partha saw fathers and grandfathers, teachers and maternal uncles, brothers, sons, grandsons and friends, fathers-in-law, and well-wishers in those two assembled armies.

Seeing them, all the friends and relatives assembled there, the son of Kunti was overcome with great pity. And in sadness, uttered the following words. "O Krishna! Having seen these relatives here, assembled with a desire to fight, my body is going numb and my mouth is going dry. My body is quivering and my body hair is standing up. My skin is burning and the Gandhiva is slipping from my hands. O Keshava! I cannot stand and my mind is in a whirl. The omens that I see are ill ones. I don't see any good that can come from killing one's relatives in a war. O Krishna! I don't want victory. Nor do I want the kingdom or happiness."

Saying this, on that battlefield, Arjuna sat down in his chariot. He threw away his bow and arrows, his mind overwhelmed with grief.

The lord said, "O Arjuna! From where, when we have this emergency, has this kind of weakness overcome you? This does not lead to heaven or fame and characterizes those who are not aryas. O Partha! Give up this weakness, this is not deserving of you. O one who scorches the foes! Give up this petty weakness of heart."

Tanushree Nagaveni

Arjuna said, "O Madhusudana! How will I use arrows to fight in this war against Bhishma and Drona? O slayer of enemies! They are deserving of worship. In this world, it is better to beg for alms than to kill one's respected preceptors. If I kill my elders, the wealth and other objects of desire that I enjoy, will be drenched in their blood. I don't know which is better for us, they defeat us or we defeat them. The sons of Dhritarashtra are in front of me. Those are the people we don't want to kill in order to live. My normal nature has been overtaken by a sense of helplessness. Confused about what is dharma, I am asking you. Tell me that which is decidedly best for me. I am your disciple. I have sought refuge in you. Instruct me. This grief is exploiting my senses and I don't see what will remedy that, even if I win lordship over the gods, or this earth, without any enemies and prosperous."

Having said this to Krishna, Arjuna, the scorcher of foes, then told Govinda, "I will not fight," and fell silent. To the person who was immersed in grief between the two armies, as if with a smile, Krishna spoke the following words. The lord said, "You speak as if you are wise, but you are grieving over those that one should not sorrow over. The wise don't sorrow over those who are dead or those who are alive. It is not the case that I, or you, or these kings, did not exist before this. Nor is it the case that we won't exist in the future, all of us will be there. The soul passes through childhood, youth and age in this body, and likewise, attains another body. The wise don't get bewildered by this. O Kounteya! Because of contact between senses and objects, feelings of warmth and cold, pleasure and pain result. But these are temporary and are created and disappear. O descendant of the Bharata lineage! Therefore, tolerate these. O best among men! The wise person who is not affected by these and who looks upon happiness and unhappiness equally, attains the right to immortality. That which is untrue doesn't have an existence. That which is true has no destruction. But those who know the truth realize the ends of both these. But know that which pervades all of this is never destroyed. No one can destroy that which is without change. It has been said that all these bodies inhabited by the soul are capable of destruction. But the soul is eternal, incapable of destruction and incapable of being established through proof. Therefore, O descendant of the Bharata lineage! Fight. O mighty-armed warrior! But if you think the atman to be subject to continual birth and continual death, even then, you should not grieve for this. Because death is inevitable for anyone who is born and birth is inevitable for anyone who is dead. Therefore, because this is inevitable, you should not grieve. O descendant of the Bharata lineage! Beings are not manifest in the beginning. They are manifest in the middle and are not manifest again after death. What is there to sorrow over? Some people see the atman as a wonder. Like that, some others speak of this as a wonder. And some others hear of this as a wonder. But having heard, they are unable to understand this[18]. O descendant of the Bharata lineage! In everyone's body, the atman is indestructible. Therefore, you should not mourn about any being. These great warriors will think that you have withdrawn from the war because of your fear. And those who have so far respected you will lighten their opinion of you. Your enemies will say many things that should not be said and will criticize your prowess. Is anything more painful than that? If you are slain, you will attain heaven. If you win, you will enjoy the earth. O Kounteya! Therefore, arise, deciding certainly to fight. Therefore, get ready to fight, looking upon happiness and unhappiness, gain and loss, and victory and defeat equally. And sin will not touch you. O Partha! You have just been told the wisdom that comes from knowledge of the self."

Arjuna then asked, "O Keshava! What are the signs of a person who has attained samadhi and whose intellect doesn't waver? How does he speak, how does he sit, and how does he walk?"

The lord said, "O Partha! A person is said to be unwavering in intellect when he banishes all desires from his mind. He is content within his own atman. He is not disturbed by unhappiness and he is beyond desiring happiness. He who has no control, has no thought[19]. Without thought, there is no peace. How can there be happiness for someone who has no peace? The wind rocks a

---

18 That is, it is impossible to comprehend the nature of the atman.
19 Intellect and thought about the paramatman.

boat on the water. Like that, the mind follows a sense devoted to objects and even a single sense robs him of wisdom. O, mighty-armed one! Therefore, he whose senses have been withdrawn from objects in every way, in him has wisdom been steadily established. When it is the night to ordinary beings, the controlled person is awake then. When ordinary beings are awake, the sage perceives that as night. Just as the waters enter an ocean and leave the full ocean undisturbed, like that, all sensual objects enter that person, but leave him at peace, unlike those attached to desire. A man who gives up all desire and exists without longing, without ego and a sense of ownership, attains peace. O Partha! This is the state of being established in the brahman. If one attains this, one is not deluded. Even in the end, established in this state, one attains union with the brahman."

Arjuna said, "O Janardana! If in your opinion knowledge is superior to action, then why are you engaging me in this terrible action? These mixed words seem to be confounding my intellect. Tell me that one thing that is best for me."

The lord said, "O pure of heart! I have said it before that in this world, there are two paths. There is jnana yoga for those who follow sankhya and there is karma yoga for yogis. [20]Without performing action, man is not freed from the bondage of action. And resorting to sannyasa does not result in liberation. No one can ever exist, even for a short while, without performing action. Because the qualities of nature [21]force everyone to perform action. The ignorant person who exists by controlling his organs of action[22], while his mind remembers the senses, is said to be deluded and is a hypocrite. O Arjuna! But he who restrains the senses through his mind and starts the yoga of action with the organs of action, while remaining unattached, he is superior. Therefore, do

---

20 Followers of sankhya are those who tread the path of knowledge and the word yogi is being used for those who tread the path of action.
21 Prakriti has been translated as nature. And the qualities are the three gunas of sattva, rajas and tamas.
22 That is, limbs and the like. The five organs of action are the mouth, hands, feet, the anus and sexual organs. The five senses of knowledge are sight, hearing, smell, taste and touch.

the prescribed action. Because action is superior to not performing action. And without action, even survival of the body is not possible. O Kounteya! All action other than that for sacrifices shackles people to the bondage of action. Therefore, do action for that purpose, without attachment."

"O Kounteya! Whatever you do, whatever you partake, whatever you offer, whatever you donate, whatever you meditate, offer that to me. In this way, you will be freed from the bondage of the fruits of righteous and evil action."

"The host of gods does not know of my origin. Nor do the maharshis. Because, in every way, I am the original cause of the gods and the great sages. He who knows me as without origin and without birth and as the greatest lord of the worlds, is freed from delusion among men and freed from all sins. Intellect, knowledge, freedom from delusion, forgiveness, truthfulness, control over the senses, control over thoughts, happiness, unhappiness, creation, destruction, fear and freedom from fear, non-violence, equality[23], satisfaction, austerity, donations, fame, and lack of fame—all these states of beings indeed owe their origin to me. The seven great sages, the four who came before them, and the Manus owe their origin to me and were created from my resolution. In this world, everything is descended from them. There is no doubt that he who truly knows my divine yoga is united with unwavering yoga. I am the origin of everything."

"Arjuna said, 'Out of compassion for me, the extremely secret adhyatma knowledge that you have stated has destroyed this delusion of mine. O one with eyes like lotus leaves! From you I have heard in detail about the creation and destruction of all beings, and also your eternal greatness. O supreme lord! What you have said about yourself is indeed like that. O supreme being! I wish to see your divine form. O lord! If you think that I am worthy of seeing that, then, O lord of yoga, show me your indestructible self.'"

---

23 Equality across all beings and across all sentiments.

The lord said, "O Partha! Behold my divine multi-dimensioned, multi-hued, multi-shaped hundreds and thousands of forms. O descendant of the Bharata lineage! See the adityas, the vasus, the rudras, the ashvinis and the maruts. See the many wonderful things you have never seen before. O Arjuna! In my body, in one place, see the entire universe, with all that is moveable and immovable. Also see today, whatever else you want to see. You will not be able to see me with your own eyes. Therefore, I am giving you divine sight. Witness my divine glory."

Having said this, Hari, the great lord of yoga, then showed Partha the divine and supreme form—with many mouths and eyes, with many miraculous things to see, adorned in many resplendent ornaments, with many divine weapons raised, with divine garlands and clothing, anointed with divine fragrances, extremely wonderful everywhere, resplendent, infinite, with faces in every direction. If the brilliance of a thousand suns simultaneously rises in the sky, then that brilliance can rival the brilliance of that great soul. Then Pandava saw the entire universe in one place, divided into many parts, in that great god of gods' body. Then, amazed and with his body hair standing up, Dhananjaya bowed down before the god with his head lowered and, with joined palms.

The Lord then said, "I have explained to you this knowledge, which is the most secret of all secrets. Having examined it completely, do what you wish to do. Listen yet again to my supreme words, the most secret of all secrets. You are my dearly beloved. Therefore, I am telling you what is good for you. Immerse your mind only in me, be devoted to me, worship me, bow in obeisance before me. I am pledging that you will attain me because you are my beloved. Discard all dharmas and seek refuge only in me. I will free you from all sins. Do not sorrow. You should not state this[24] to those who do not meditate[25], or are devoid of devotion or do not wish to hear. Nor to those who show me disrespect. There is no doubt that he who explains this most secret knowledge to my devotees, displays supreme devotion towards me and will attain me alone. Among men, there is no one who does greater service to me. [26]In the world, there is no one, and there will be no one, dearer to me. And he who will study this dialogue[27] of ours on dharma, my view is that he will worship me through jnana yoga. The man who only listens with faith and without disrespect, he too will be freed from sin and attain the worlds attained by those who are pure of deeds. O Partha! Have you listened to this with single-minded concentration? O Dhananjaya! Has your delusion of ignorance been destroyed?"

---

24 This knowledge and more generally, the knowledge of the Gita.
25 Also interpreted as those who do not follow their svadharma.
26 Than one who undertakes the task of explaining this knowledge.
27 The Gita again. Alternatively, this sacred dialogue, instead of dialogue on dharma.

Arjuna said, "O Achyuta! Through your blessings, my delusion has been destroyed. I have obtained knowledge about what should be done and what shouldn't be done. I am steady. I no longer suffer from doubt. I will do what you instruct."[28]

Optimal Choice Of A Consumer

A consumer's budget set consists of all the consumption bundles that are available to a consumer given his income and the price of the goods. A consumer is at liberty to choose his consumption bundle from his budget set. But on what basis does a consumer select his consumption bundle from the budget set? In economics, it is assumed that the consumer chooses his consumption bundle based on his taste and preference over all the consumption bundles present in the budget set. In other words, the consumer has a well-defined preference over all the consumption bundles present in the budget set. Between any two bundles, the consumer either chooses one bundle over the other or is indifferent between the two. [29]

In addition, it is also assumed that a consumer is a rational individual. A rational individual clearly knows what is good or what is bad for him, and in any given situation, he always tries to achieve the best for himself. Thus, not only does a consumer have well-defined preferences over the set of available bundles, but he also acts according to his preferences. From the bundles which are available to him, a rational consumer always chooses the one which gives him maximum satisfaction.[30]

At this point in our discussion let us remind ourselves that a budget set represents all the consumption bundles that are available to a consumer and that a consumer's preference over all the consumption bundles can be

---

28 The Mahabharata 5 Translated by Bibek Debroy.
29 NCERT Introductory Microeconomics Textbook in Economics for Class XII.
30 NCERT Introductory Microeconomics Textbook in Economics for Class XII.

graphically represented through an indifference map (a family of indifference curves).

Therefore, the consumer's problem can also be stated as follows: The rational consumer's problem is to move to a point on the highest possible indifference curve given her budget set.[31]

Having defined the problem of a rational consumer, let us now think about where the optimum would be located?

Given the monotonic preferences of a consumer, it is obvious that the optimum point would be located on the budget line. A point below the budget line cannot be optimum. Compared to a point below the budget line, there is always some point on the budget line which contains more of at least one of the goods and no less of the other, and is, therefore, preferred by a consumer whose preferences are monotonic.[32] Points located above the budget line in the graphic plane are not available to the consumer.

Let us now expand our understanding further by thinking about where the optimum point would be located on the budget line.

"The point at which the budget line just touches (is tangent to), one of the indifference curves would be the optimum."[33]

Why?

This is because apart from the optimum point, other points on the budget line lie on a lower indifference curve and are inferior. Consumption bundles above the budget line are not affordable. Therefore, the optimum consumption

---

31 NCERT Introductory Microeconomics Textbook in Economics for Class XII.
32 NCERT Introductory Microeconomics Textbook in Economics for Class XII.
33 NCERT Introductory Microeconomics Textbook in Economics for Class XII.

bundle is located on the budget line at the point where the budget line is tangent to an indifference curve.[34]

Let us now apply our understanding of the optimal choice of a consumer to understand Arjuna's optimal choice.

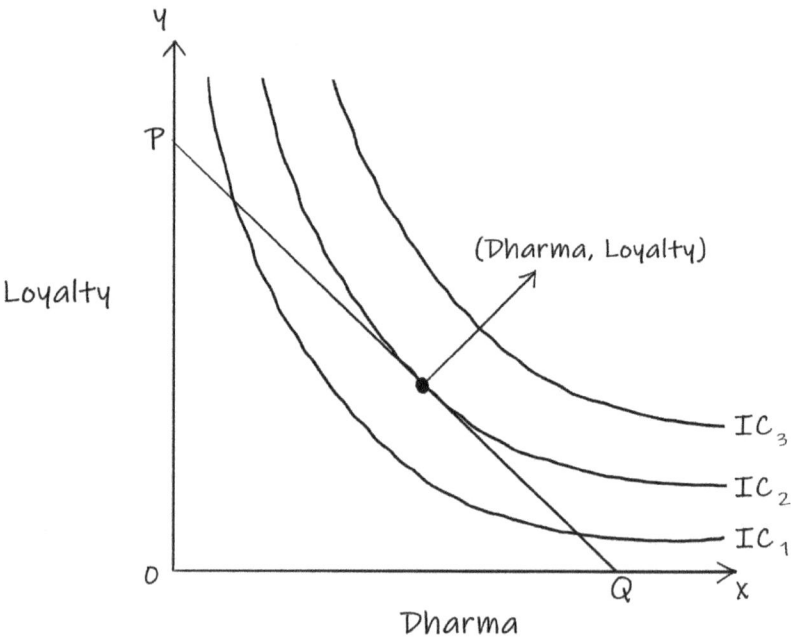

- Arjuna's budget set consists of both loyalty towards his relatives and his Kshatriya dharma to fight in the war.
- Let us indicate loyalty with the letter L and dharma with the letter D.
- Thus, the possible combinations of the consumption bundles would be: (0, L), (D, 0), (D, L)
- From the story, we know that Arjuna is indifferent between loyalty and his dharma.
- So, the consumer problem would be: How can Arjuna uphold his loyalty and not violate his dharma guided by the teachings of Krishna?

---

34 NCERT Introductory Microeconomics Textbook in Economics for Class XII.

- Arjuna's budget line PQ, in this case, is for his actions to abide by Krishna's teachings
- Therefore, Arjuna's optimum point lies at that point where his budget line is tangent to the indifference curve IC2.
- At this point, Arjuna can uphold his loyalty and follow his dharma guided by Krishna's words.
- IC1 represents a scenario where Arjuna would not fight with the Kauravas
- IC2 represents the scenario where Arjuna fights with the Kauravas while bearing in mind Krishna's words, *"O Kounteya! Whatever you do, whatever you partake, whatever you offer, whatever you donate, whatever you meditate, offer that to me. In this way, you will be freed from the bondage of the fruits of righteous and evil action."*
- IC3 represents a scenario where Arjuna does not abide by Krishna's teachings, which is not affordable for Arjuna
- So, given the three ICs, IC2 is the highest IC Arjuna can reach given his budget constraint.

Jaratkaru's Inelastic Demand

The theory of demand forms the major idea in microeconomics. Have you ever wondered how the fundamentals of demand theory can be linked to a complex epic like Mahabharata having over 100000 verses? Um… let us explore the concept of demand through the tale of sage Jaratkaru.

Jaratkaru was an exceptional sage who undertook rigid austerities throughout his life. Since Jaratkaru was engaged in such austerities, he never yearned for a wife. Jaratkaru journeyed across the earth visiting holy tirthas[35] and cleansing himself in their waters. On one such day, he encountered his ancestors in a cave. To his surprise, these people were hanging upside down in that cave, suspended from a fibre of grass. The ends of these fibres were being chewed up by rats.

Jaratkaru questioned his ancestors, "Who are you? Why are you hanging upside down, supported by a single fibre of grass? I cannot see you in this pathetic state, please tell me how I can help you."

---

35 Holy tirthas refers to a water body considered as a pilgrimage site by Hindus.

His ancestors replied, "O Brahmana! Know us to be the rishis, popular as Yayavaras[36]. We have been dislodged from the heavenly realms due to the absence of progeny. The single strand that is visible to your eyes symbolises the last progeny left in our lineage. He is a great rishi by the name Jaratkaru. But he does not have a wife or a son. O Brahmana! If you really aspire to help us, then please inform Jaratkaru about our afflicted state. Also, advise him to marry a girl and beget a son, so that we can obtain the heavenly realms again."

On hearing his ancestors' plea, Jaratkaru was filled with remorse and spoke thus to his forefathers, "I am Jaratkaru. It is because of me that you are in this predicament. In order to ensure that you obtain your rightful place in the divine abode, I shall only marry a girl who shares the same name as mine; one who is bestowed upon me as a benefaction; one who shall become my wife by her own accord; and one who does not have to be supported by me for her sustenance. If not, I shall not marry."

Having spoken thus to his ancestors, Jaratkaru roamed around the earth in search of a suitable girl. Despite his relentless search, he never found a girl, who satisfied all his conditions. Overcome by grief, he lamented in the forest, "Hear my words, O creatures of the forest. I am a rishi absorbed in fierce austerities. But my afflicted ancestors advised me to marry a girl. Abiding by their advice, I am journeying across the earth in search of a suitable girl. If any of the creatures, who have heard my grief has a daughter, then please give me her hand in marriage and relieve me of my distress. The girl must share the same name as mine; she ought to be bestowed upon me as a benefaction of her own accord; and I should not have to support her for sustenance". The snakes, who were appointed by Vasuki to look out for Jaratkaru, overheard the sage's words and immediately informed Vasuki about the sage's plea.

Vasuki was delighted at the words of the snakes and he proceeded to the forest with his sister. Vasuki, the king of the snakes offered his sister to Jaatkaru,

---

36 Yayavaras refers to a particular section of class of Brahmanas.

however, the great-souled one did not accept her immediately, thinking about whether the maiden would satisfy all his conditions. He repeated all his conditions before Vasuki and asked for the maiden's name.

Vasuki addressed the venerated rishi, "O rishi! She is my sister Jaratkaru. She is an ascetic and I promise to support her". Upon hearing those words of Vasuki, Jaratkaru accepted Vasuki's sister, who satisfied all his conditions, in marriage as per the prescribed rites.

Inelastic Demand

To understand the link between demand theory and Mahabharata, one is always encouraged to first read "what is demand?" Put simply, demand is 'the desire to have something'. Refining the words, a bit, demand is the quantity of any commodity in the market, that any consumer (purchaser) is willing to buy and able to afford with his current monetary income during a given period of time. The concept of demand comes with some alterations to match a given situation. One such major alteration is the elasticity of demand.

The words 'elasticity of demand' refers to the degree of change in demand caused by a change in any one of the economic factors of income, price of the commodity, and the price of related goods. The responsiveness of demand to the change in the price of a commodity is called 'price elasticity of demand'. Similarly, the responsiveness of demand to the change in the income of a consumer is called 'income elasticity of demand'. The responsiveness of demand to the change in the price of related goods is called 'cross elasticity of demand'. Summarising the above discussion, one can conclude that elasticity of demand effectively answers the question, "BY HOW MUCH DOES THE DEMAND CHANGE?"[37]

Price elasticity of demand is the measure of the sensitivity of quantity demanded to a change in the price of a commodity, ceteris paribus (meaning, other things being constant). Predominantly, there are three types of price elasticity of demand: elastic demand, inelastic demand, and unitary elastic demand.

The above story of Jaratkaru is an immaculate exemplification of the concept of inelastic demand. Inelastic demand indicates a condition in which the quantity of a commodity demanded by a consumer remains insensitive to any change in the price of the commodity. In everyday life, we all exhibit an inelastic demand for essential goods.

Taking a leap back to the story of Jaratkaru, one can now easily comprehend that Jaratkaru manifests a demand for a wife to ensure that his ancestors attain

---

[37] Tulsian's Business Economics and Business and Commercial Knowledge, A Self-study Textbook By PC Tulsian and Bharat Tulsian

a place in heaven. The conditions that Jaratkaru imposes for the selection of a bride make his demand more selective.

You might ponder over the thought: "How does Jaratkaru manifest an inelastic demand?" From his conditions, we can analyse that Jaratkaru will only marry someone who will satisfy all his conditions no matter how many years he has to wait. Even though the number of years (waiting period) may increase, his demand for a girl who will fulfil all the following parameters will remain unaffected:

4. She should have the same name 'Jaratkaru'
5. She should be given as a gift
6. She should marry him by her own will
7. She should be able to support herself and remain independent of her husband for survival

This means that Jaratkaru is demonstrating an inelastic demand for a wife. Therefore $|e_D|=0$.

Jaratkaru's inelastic demand can be depicted using a demand curve. The below graph represents a hypothetical demand curve of Jaratkaru. Traditionally, the demand curve measures quantity demanded on the horizontal axis and the price of a commodity on the vertical axis. But in this case, Jaratkaru's demand for a suitable girl is represented on the x-axis and the waiting period or the number of years is represented on a y-axis.

Since his demand is insensitive to the waiting period, the demand curve will assume the shape of a vertical straight line. Furthermore, Jaratkaru's demand cannot be expressed in quantitative terms. Therefore, we can speculate Jaratkaru's demand to be q.

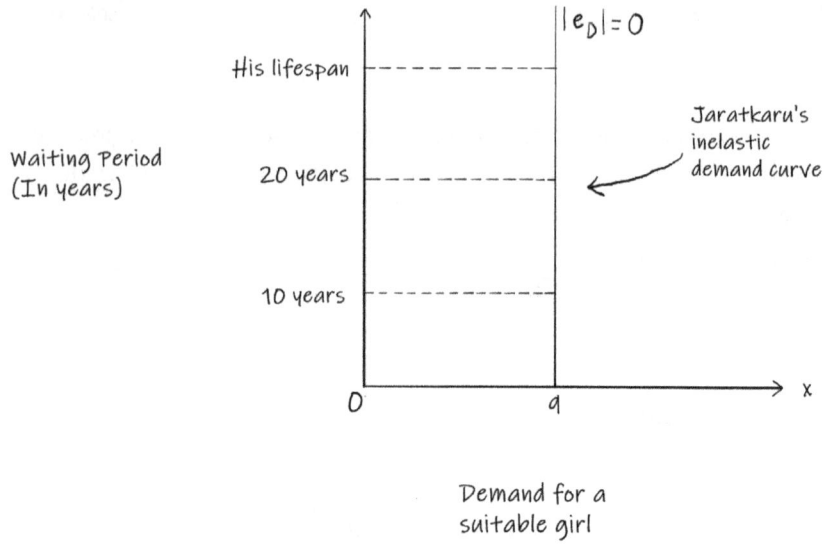

Demand for a
suitable girl

Having married Jaratkaru (the serpent princess), rishi Jaratkaru restores his ancestors to their heavenly abodes. However, after begetting a son named Astika[38], Jaratkaru leaves his wife and returns to his original place.

While Jaratkaru exhibits an inelastic demand for a wife, Vasuki exhibits an elastic demand for a groom suitable for his sister. Though they are two sides of the same story, both these parts highlight contrasting elasticities of demand…

---

38 Astika is the son of Jaratkaru. A great sage, who is credited for stopping the snake sacrifice conducted by Janamejaya.

Vasukis's Elastic Demand

Many precious elements emerged from the churning of the ocean. Among them, a magnificent horse named Ucchaihshrava emerged. Kadru[39] noticed the horse and asked Vinata[40], "Vinata, can you tell me the colour of the horse's tail?" Vinata replied that the king of horses had a white tail and suggested that they should have a wager on the same. Kadru asserted that the one who lost the bet would become a slave of the other. Furthermore, Kadru believed that the horse had a black tail. Determined to examine the horse's tail, they returned home.

Desperate to win, Kadru instructed her 1000 Naga children to cover the horse's tail to create an illusion that the horse's tail was black. But, when the snakes refused to carry out their mother's orders, Kadru cursed her children. She uttered these words in rage, "In the snake-sacrifice conducted by the Pandava King Janamejaya[41], you all shall be consumed by the fire".

When Vasuki[42] heard about his mother's curse, he called for deliberation with Airavatha[43] and all the other serpents. Vasuki cried out in distress, "O brothers! We are all aware of the curse which will befall us when King Janamejaya

---

39 Kadru is the daughter of Daksha Prajapati and the wife of Kashyapa.
40 Vinata is also the daughter of Daksha Prajapati and the wife of Kashyapa.
41 Janamejaya is the son of King Parikshit; the grandson of Abhimanyu and the great-grandson of Arjuna.
42 Vasuki is the king of the serpent, who wears a nagamani on his forehead. He is adorned by Shiva around his neck.
43 Airavatha is one of the Naga born to Kadru and the sibling of Vasuki.

conducts his snake sacrifice. To save ourselves from complete annihilation, it is important to find mitigation for our curse. I request all of you put forth your suggestions on how the race of serpents may be preserved".

Some serpents suggested, "Let us bite the king", while the others advised all the serpents to assume the form of clouds and shower rain so that the sacrificial fire could be extinguished. Vasuki was not satisfied with any of the propositions made by all his brothers and found himself in a depressed state.

Elapatra[44], who heard all the suggestions given by his siblings, recounted the story of serpents getting cursed by their mother Kadru.

He said, "When the curse was imposed, I was frightened and climbed up into my mother's lap.[45] I heard the conversation between the gods and Lord Brahma himself. The gods questioned Brahma as to why Kadru was not stopped from uttering such a cruel curse. Lord Brahma replied that the destruction of our race was essential due to a population explosion of serpents. He further specified that in the Yagna conducted by King Janamejaya, all the poisonous snakes would be destroyed. I was truly taken aback by these words of the supreme grandfather. It felt as if the destruction of all of us was certain. But, when I was engulfed by devastation, I heard Lord Brahma pronouncing a remedy for our curse. He said that in the line of the Yayavaras, a great rishi would be born who would be intelligent, austere and self-controlled, and would be known by the name of Jaratkaru. Jaratkaru would have a son named Astika, who would also be blessed by the power of austerities. He would end the sacrifice and snakes who are virtuous would escape.'. It was also mentioned that Rishi Jaratkaru will beget a son with a woman who has the same name, Jaratkaru. "O Vasuki! I see before me your sister, who bears the name of Jaratkaru. Give her as alms to the rishi of rigid vows when he comes

---

44 Elapatra is one of the sons of Kadru and the sibling of Vasuki.
45 The Mahabharata 1 Translated by Bibek Debroy

looking for alms, so that this great danger to the snakes may be pacified. I have heard that this is the means of escape."⁴⁶

Vasuki guarded his sister and appointed several serpents to keep a watch on the arrival of Jaratkaru.

Elastic Demand

Elastic demand refers to a situation in which the market price remains fixed, only the quantity demanded increases. If the price drops below that level then the quantity demanded drops to zero.⁴⁷

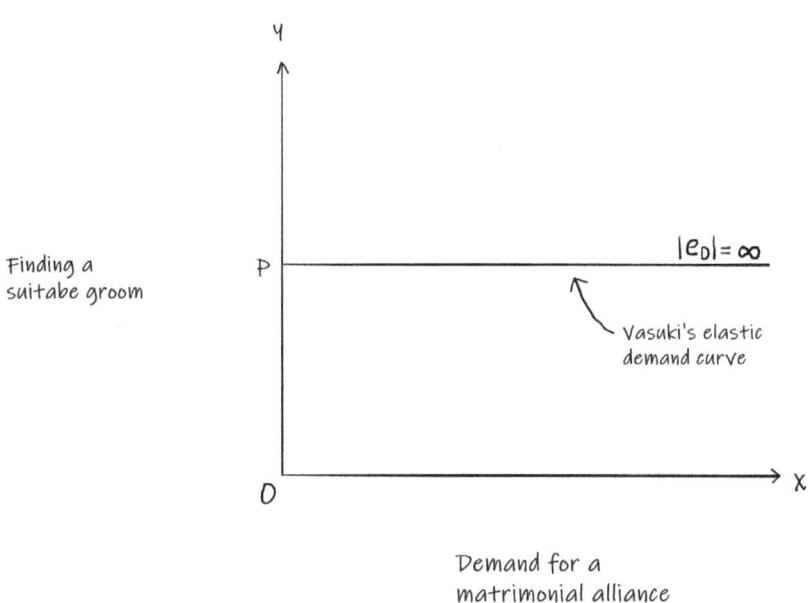

From the above story, one can easily interpret that Vasuki is exhibiting an elastic demand.

---

46 The Mahabharata 1 Translated by Bibek Debroy
47 NCERT Introductory Microeconomics Textbook in Economics for Class XII

The graph below represents Vasuki's elastic demand. On the x-axis demand for a matrimonial alliance is measured and on the y-axis, the finding of a suitable groom is measured.

Here, the demand for a matrimonial alliance increases as Jaratkaru is approaching her youth. Finding a rishi who will beget a son capable of saving the serpents from the snake sacrifice is the price p. This price remains constant. Vasuki will exhibit a zero demand for a matrimonial alliance with any other rishi apart from Jaratkaru. Therefore, $|e_D|=\infty$. Vasuki's elastic demand can be represented using a demand curve. The demand curve will be a horizontal straight line that cuts the y-axis at p, parallel to the x-axis.

The Substitution and Income Effect Meet Shantanu and Ganga

It was 2019 when my acquaintance with economics began... I remember the first day in pre-university college and the first lecture was economics. My economics lecturer Lisa Cletus entered and began the class with an introduction about herself. The energy in her voice was rather contagious. Although I was a little exhausted owing to the rigorous dance rehearsals in the morning, I felt alerted at the very instant, when I heard her voice. At that moment, it felt as though she and I had been waiting for an eternity for this acquaintance. Well, in the first year, my lecturer introduced us to the great giants, "The Indian economic development" and "Statistics for economics".

At the end of the first year, I was of the notion that economics is a simple and easy-to-understand subject... Allow me to be frank with you: This feeling didn't last for long.

And the second year began...

"Chapter 2 - Theory of Consumer Behaviour". The name might sound fascinating to read... Don't get misled by the name of the chapter. As they say, "Never judge a person by their appearance", I would like to modify it a bit, "Never judge a chapter by its title".

Precisely, the abstract dimension of microeconomics began from Chapter 2. To be able to understand something abstract, you must also enter into the realm of the

Tanushree Nagaveni

abstract and let down your guard about reality to be able to understand what is actually happening? Thanks to my lecturer, in my journey across this abstract world, she led me like a light.

Concept after concept, she very carefully broke down all the nuances of each of these concepts for us, so that we could etch them into our memory. In the beginning, I felt that maybe I could sail through this chapter holding onto the support offered by my teacher, but I surely overestimated my ability to maintain a firm grip. This realisation dawned on me the day she began with the explanation of income effect and substitution effect. She gave each one of us the opportunity to explain the terms, "substitution effect" and "income effect" in a way as we understood it. When my turn arrived, I had almost immediately declared within myself that I was going to get it wrong. Nevertheless, I gave it a try...

I said, "Ma'am, I think, the substitution effect is something related to the change in our preference for goods or services based on the change in prices of other goods and the income effect is something related to the change in our capability to be able to afford a commodity or not". Just as I was expecting my lecturer to say something about my explanation, there was some issue with the network connectivity, and the audio along with the video stalled.

Anxiety was at its peak and a network issue amplified it a thousand-fold, I waited for a few seconds with hopeless sighs. When the audio resumed, I heard her explaining the same concept again and she said, "Yes Tanushree, that is absolutely right!"

The same anxiety decided to embrace me, the day I read the story of Shantanu and Ganga. I thoroughly enjoyed the story. But, when the turn of matching the microeconomic concept arrived, I was left in a fix. I flipped the pages of my textbook and yet again, I landed on the same page of substitution effect and income effect. At first, I noticed the sticky note on the page proudly presenting the same explanation I gave on that day I first encountered the substitution effect and income effect. I was inspired and have landed here where I present to you the substitution effect and income effect from the eyes of King Shantanu.

Shantanu, the valorous son of Pratipa[48], often travelled to the forest to hunt deer and buffaloes. On one such day, while he was in the forest, he meandered along the river Ganga and arrived at a spot, frequently visited by rishis. Shantanu experienced an elevated sense of peace and calm gazing at the hues of browns and greens. As he continued to soak deeply into this feeling of serenity, he noticed a maiden at a distance. At first, he could not believe the image in front of his eyes. A beautiful lady with a slender physique, standing beside a tree... her ornaments making a soft gentle tinkle at every sway of the wind. Her garments dyed with shades of blue enchanted Shantanu. His eyes were not content at the mere sight of her. He yearned for something more. Just as a honeybee, attracted by the scent of nectar, accelerates towards the flower, Shantanu approached the maiden and uttered these words enticed by her form, "O beautiful one! Who are you? I am enraptured at the mere sight of you. Please be my wife".

The lady, who was also attracted to King Shantanu, spoke in a gratifying tone, "O king! I am Ganga. It will be my honour to be your wife. I shall always follow my dharma as your wife and shall abide by your words. But I shall only be your wife if you accept my condition. You must never question my actions, nor stop me from carrying out my actions. If you ever question my actions, then I shall leave you and go away". Intoxicated by love, Shantanu accepted the conditions of Ganga and married her.

Ganga and Shantanu were a happy couple. Shantanu always abstained from questioning any of Ganga's actions. Although they both lived happily, their glee was short-lived. In due course, Ganga gave birth to eight sons. You might wonder, what is so strange about this? Allow me to explain. The ironic part was that, as soon as a son was born, Ganga would diligently carry the baby and flung it into the river, saying, "This is for your own good".[49] Each time

---

48 Pratipa was a king who belonged to the Bharata race of Lunar Dynasty and was the father of Shantanu and grandfather of Bhishma.
49 The Mahabharata 1 Translated by Bibek Debroy.

Ganga released the infant into the water, Shantanu felt as if life was slipping away from him, little by little. Although it was painful for him to watch this episode in front of his eyes, he never mustered the courage to stop Ganga from carrying out this miserable deed. Shantanu was left weakened at the demise of every son.

When the eighth son was born, Shantanu somehow managed to gather some courage from within and was determined to stop the annihilation of his son, who would become his heir in the future. Ganga repeated the same action… She took the infant and approached the crystalline river. As she was about to drop the baby into the gushing river flowing ferociously, Shantanu interrupted and exclaimed, "Dear one! Why are you committing such a terrible act by killing our own progeny? It is inappropriate to destroy one's own child. Do not succumb to adharma dear Ganga, please protect our son". At these words, Ganga halted her action and turned around to address Shantanu with her words, which sounded like Amrutha, "O King! You have breached the promise which was made at the time of our marriage. Since you have questioned my actions, it is time for me to leave you. Your son shall carry forward the legacy of your lineage. He shall be known as Devavratha. O king! He shall remain unparalleled in strength, valour, and bravery…"

Well, for the next part of our discussion it may be useful to think of Shantanu as a rational consumer.

The Question Of Demand

King Shantanu initially exhibited a demand for Ganga. Since we already understand that demand refers to a quantity of a commodity, which a consumer is willing to buy and able to afford, given his income and the price of the commodity, we can alter the same explanation a bit to fit our story. Shantanu's demand for Ganga comes at the price of him complying with the conditions imposed by Ganga at the time of their marriage. After the initial days of their marriage, Shantanu's patience in the form of income was sufficient to pay the price of compliance with the conditions.

On the contrary, when Ganga gave birth to seven sons, the price for her companionship increased tremendously. In addition to complying with her conditions of not questioning or interfering with her actions, King Shantanu also had to suffer the loss of children. In this case, his patience or income was not sufficient to pay the price. At this point in the story, it may be useful to interpret that the fruition of their marriage had become expensive. Shantanu's income was not sufficient to pay the price. This is an income effect.

As a result, when the eighth son was born, he exhibited a demand for his son. The price for having a son was to breach the promise and consequently sacrifice Ganga's companionship. But, by having a son, the legacy of Shantanu's lineage was safeguarded. His son would become the king and rule over his affluent kingdom in the future. The price for having a son (sacrificing

Ganga's companionship and suffering separation) was less than the price for having Ganga as his wife till eternity (complying with her conditions and suffering the loss of progeny). Even though the price for having a son was lesser than that for having a wife, the satisfaction he derived from having a son was greater as the legacy of his empire was at stake. Therefore, Shantanu substituted his demand for Ganga with the demand for a son. The process of shifting his demand from Ganga to his son, Devavratha is caused by the substitution effect.

In microeconomic terms, the income effect is defined as a change in the demand for goods or services caused by a change in the consumer's purchasing power as a result of the change in his income. Substitution effect on the other hand refers to a change in the demand for goods or services resulting from the change in the relative price of that good compared to that of its substitute goods or services. It is important to note that income effects can be **direct or indirect.** For example, let us assume that you have pocket money of Rs. 10000 per month. You spend Rs. 5000 on purchase of novels and the rest Rs. 5000 on entertainment.

- Suddenly, your pocket money reduces to 6000, then you spend less on entertainment. This is because of the reduction in your funds. This behaviour occurs due to a **direct income effect.**
- Similarly, if the price of entertainment increases, even then you will spend less on entertainment because your income is simply not enough to pay the price for entertainment. This is because of an **indirect income effect.**

Both substitution effect and income effect work together. They are inseparable. The negative slope of the demand curve can be attributed to the combined working of these two effects.

Kamyakavana: A Substitute for Dvaitavana

That incident stuck with me… I was adventuring through an imaginary forest following a dark shadow of someone. There was something uncommon about that adventure. It seemed as though my intellect had switched itself off for some time and my mind was in charge of running the show. I could feel every movement of mine to the highest intensity…. The rhythmic clicking of my shoes with the marshy mud, the sound of a twig breaking due to the force of my shoes. Every tiny detail of that scene seemed to be under my control.

The pale blue sky interrupting the harmony of the brown dark bottle-greens in a perfect jigsaw-puzzle pattern was as per my imagination. Just before I could discover my purpose in following that shadow, I was awakened by the noise outside the room. I was afraid and in a dilemma as I could not contemplate what I'd just seen. The difference between a dream and the state of being awake had become insignificant. It took a few seconds before I could reboot my consciousness to fit the reality for even my senses were perplexed with their experience in that imaginary forest.

I could remember my dream completely. That day, I had acquainted myself with the dimension of lucid dreaming.

Kounteya Yudhishtira was lost in a deep slumber in the hermitage of Dvaitavana. The cool breeze entering the room through the window soothed him. However, suddenly he could hear the voices of deer from the Dvaitavana in his dream. They lamented in grief. Their quivering tone revealed the intensity of their suffering. They shuddered in fear as they stood before him in salutation. Yudhishtira, deeply touched by their sorrow, addressed them in compassion, "Who are you? What can I do to alleviate your suffering?"

Addressed by Dharmaraja[50], the deer from the Dvaitavana replied, "O King Yudhishtira! We are the last surviving members of the deer population of Dvaitavana. We humbly request you to shift your dwelling from the Dvaitavana, otherwise, our population will become extinct. Our friends and relatives have been killed by your brothers and only a few of us remain. As a King who follows Dharma, show us compassion and allow our progeny to develop. Please help us increase our numbers, O great King!"

---

50 Dharmaraja - Yudhishtira's name.

Dharmaraja was overcome by remorse as he heard the deer. As a monarch who believed in the welfare of all beings, Yudhishtira the resplendent son of Kunti[51] took an oath, "I promise you that we will safeguard your lineage by departing from this forest".

Having narrated his dream to his brothers, Yudhishtira, the benevolent one, expressed, "We have derived our sustenance from these deer. But now it is time to protect their endangered lineage. As an act of compassion, all of us need to relocate to the Kamyaka forest, located near the lake of Trinabindu[52]. We have survived on these species for one year and eight months. Let us pass the rest of our exile in the bountiful Kamyaka forest".

---

51 Son of Kunti - Referring to Yudhishtira.
52 Trinabindu - A lake in the forest of Kāmyaka.

The noble Pandavas along with the brahmanas, Indrasena[53], and other servants embarked upon their journey to the Kamyaka forest. After travelling a considerable distance, the mighty warriors caught sight of the Kamyaka hermitage inhabited by ascetics. As they entered the hermitage, they were welcomed by the brahmanas.

Substitute Goods

Since the following discussion speaks about substitute goods, it would be useful to refresh our understanding of demand and the law of demand:

Demand refers to the quantity of a commodity that a consumer is willing to buy and able to afford in the market, given the prices of the goods, the tastes and preferences of the consumer, and his income[54].

"Law of Demand states that other things being equal there is a negative relation between demand for a commodity and its price. In other words, when price of the commodity increases, demand for it falls and when price of the commodity decreases, demand for it rises, other factors remaining the same".

Let us continue our discussion on the changes in demand.

Demand is dynamic in nature and subject to changes depending on various factors. If demand changes due to an alteration in the price of a commodity, then the resultant change in demand is defined by the term "Movement along demand curve". If a change in demand results from changes in any other factors apart from the price of a commodity, then such a change is given by the term "Shift in the demand curve".

---

53 Indrasena - Yudhishtira's charioteer.
54 NCERT Introductory Microeconomics Textbook in Economics for Class XII

Movement along the demand curve has two forms:

1. Extension in demand: When the quantity demanded increases owing to a decrease in the price of goods, there is a downward rightward movement on the demand curve called extension in demand.[55]
2. Contraction in demand: When the quantity demanded decreases owing to an increase in the price of goods, then there is an upward leftward movement on the demand curve called contraction in demand.[56]

Shift in demand curve:

The demand curve shifts to a new position on the XY-plane only if the change in demand is caused by factors other than the price. We must remember that price in this case is assumed to be constant. Always under a shift in the demand curve, two demand curves are drawn to indicate the change in the position of the original demand curve.

Shift in demand curve has two forms:

1. Increase in demand: Refers to an increased demand at the same price or same demand at an increased price causing a forward or rightward shift in the demand curve.[57]
2. Decrease in demand: Refers to a decreased demand at the same price or the same demand at decreased price causing a backward or leftward shift in the demand curve.[58]

---

55 All in One Economics CBSE Class XI
56 All in One Economics CBSE Class XI
57 All in One Economics CBSE Class XI
58 All in One Economics CBSE Class XI

The factors causing a shift in demand may be understood through the table below:

Factor Name	When does this factor cause an increase in demand?	When does this factor cause a decrease in demand?
Income of the consumer	• Increase in income in case of Normal Goods • Decrease in income in case of Inferior Goods	• Decrease in income in case of Normal Goods • Increase in income in case of Inferior Goods
Price of substitute goods	Increase in the price of the substitute goods causes an increased demand for the principal good	Decrease in the price of the substitute goods causes a decreased demand for the principal good
Price of complementary goods	Fall in the price of a complementary good results in an increased demand for the principal good	Rise in the price of a complementary good results in a decreased demand for the principal good
Shift in tastes and preferences	Favourable shift	Unfavourable shift
Consumer's expectation with regard to future price	If the future prices are expected to be higher	If the future prices are expected to be lower

Note 1: In addition to the above-mentioned factors there could be many more factors that affect the change in demand

*Note 2:

- Normal goods are those goods whose demand increases complemented by an increase in the income of the consumer and vice-versa.
- Examples include: Precious metals (Gold, Diamond, Platinum, etc), daily-use appliances like computers, smartphones, etc
- Inferior goods are those goods whose demand increases when the income of the consumer decreases in an inverse proportion and vice-versa.

  Examples include Low-grade cereals, Second-hand vehicles, Instant Noodles, etc.

The quantity of a commodity that a consumer chooses to buy may increase or decrease in correspondence to the rise or fall in the price of the related goods subject to whether the good is a substitute or a complement of the primary good. In economic terms, a change in demand for a good caused by a change in the price of the related goods is called a cross-price effect. [59]

Substitute goods are alternative goods that can be used in place of the original/primary goods. A conventional example for the same would be pen and pencil. Notice that we can substitute a pen for a pencil or a pencil for a pen. Usually, when the price of a pen increases then rational consumers exhibit lesser demand for the pen and increased demand for a pencil. Similarly, when the price of a pen decreases then the same cult of the rational consumer may shift their consumption from a pencil back to a pen. Generalising our discussion, we can deduce that in case of a rise in the price of a substitute good, then the demand for the other/primary good increases and when there is a fall in the price of a substitute good, then the demand for the other/primary good decreases.

Complementary goods are those goods that are used along with the primary goods. They complete the demand for each other and are therefore demanded together[60]. An example of complementary goods would be cricket bat and cricket ball. We use both the bat and ball together. When the price of a bat increases, then consumers tend to exhibit less demand for both the bat and the ball, considering that consumption of one good is dependent on the other good. Similarly, when the price of a bat decreases, then consumers are encouraged to exhibit a higher demand for the bat's complement: A ball. Generalizing the example of the bat and ball, we can say that when the price of complementary goods decreases, then the demand for its interdependent good increases and vice-versa.

For our next part of the discussion, let us focus on substitute goods.

---

59 All in One Economics CBSE Class XI
60 All in One Economics CBSE Class XI

From the story, we can interpret that both the forests Dvaitavana and Kamyakavana are substitutes for each other. Applying the theory we learnt about substitutes, we realise that when the price for Dvaitavana increases, then the demand for the Kamyakavana increases. Let us replace the word "price" with "extinction of deer population" and reread the statement: When the extinction of deer population in the Dvaitavana increases, then the demand to relocate to the Kamyaka forest increases. Notice that the price for the Kamyaka forest remains constant irrespective of the changes to the extinction of deer in the Dvaitavana. So, what would be an ideal price for the Kamyaka forest? Well, we can assume the price to be the hardships the Pandavas face while relocating to the Kamyaka forest. Hardships may include a long and exhausting journey, dearth of food supplies, lack of proper shelter during the journey, threat from wildlife, or even natural disasters obstructing their travel.

We can represent the same discussion above using two graphical representations: One showing a contraction in demand for Dvaitavana while the other showing an increase in demand for the Kamyakavana.

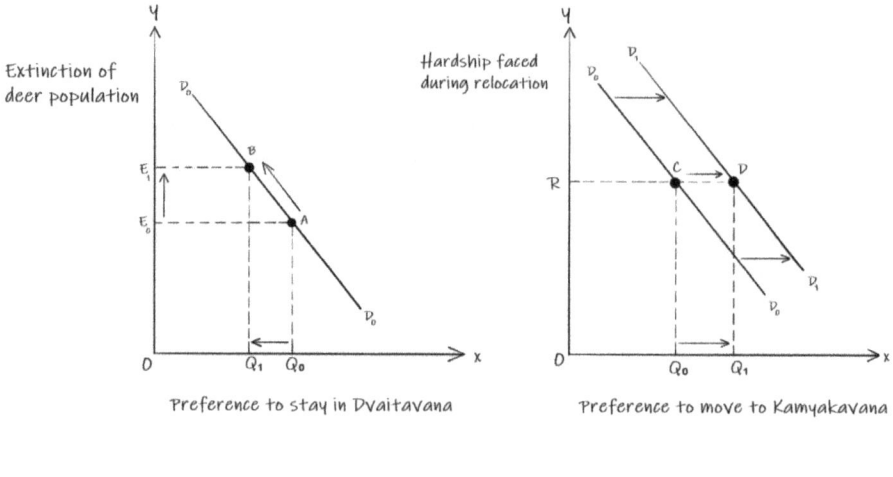

(a) CONTRACTION IN DEMAND FOR DVAITAVANA

(b) INCREASE IN DEMAND FOR KAMYAKAVANA

a. Contraction in demand for Dvaitavana
   - On the X-axis, the Preference to stay in Dvaitavana is measured
   - On the Y-axis, the extinction of the deer population is measured
   - D_0D_0 represents the demand curve for Dvaitavana
   - When the extinction of the deer population increases from E_0 to E_1 then Yudhishitra's preference to stay in Dvaitavana decreases from Q_0 to Q_1
     - ($Q_1 < Q_0$) Preference at Q_1 is weaker/lesser than at Q_0
     - Yudhishtira's preference moves from point A to point B on the demand curve

b. Increase in demand for Kamyakavana
   - On the x-axis, the preference to move to Kamyakavana is measured
   - On the Y-axis, the hardship faced during relocation is measured
   - As a result of the increase in the price of its substitute Dvaitavana, the demand for Kamyakavana increases
   - D_0D_0 represents the initial demand curve
     - D_0D_0 shifts to D_1D_1 as a result of the increased extinction of deer in the Dvaitavana
     - The preference to move to Kamyaka forest increases from Q_0 to Q_1 when the demand curve shifts from D_0D_0 to D_1D_1
     - In other words, Yudhishtira's preference shifts from point C to D
     - It should be noted that the price in the form of hardships faced during relocation remains constant

Therefore, as a ruler who embodied equality to all creatures, Yudhishtira's relocation to the Kamyaka forest helped the deer population increase their numbers.

Giffen and Veblen Goods: Karna and Indra's Exchange

"Some memories are unforgettable, remaining ever vivid and heartwarming!"

—Joseph B Wirthlin

I met Karna for the first time when I was seven years old through the Yakshagana drama "Dhana Shura Karna". The concert was nothing less than a blockbuster movie for me. The vibrant costumes, the majestic music, the fast rhythm, and the breathtaking dialogues transported me to a whole new world. The footwork of the artists made my feet tap involuntarily in sync with the rhythm. The artist who played the role of Karna truly inspired me to learn more about Karna's life.

One of the best incidents I remember from Karna's life is his act of donating his armour and earrings to Indra. From this story, I learnt the importance of sacrifice in one's life.

Once Surya appeared in the disguise of a Brahmana at the end of Karna's dream. He spoke to Karna in a voice choking with compassion, "O son! O venerable one! Listen to my advice very carefully. To safeguard the Pandavas, Indra, the king of the Gods will beg for your kundala and kavacha in disguise of a Brahmana. Being aware of your righteous nature, Indra will exploit your vow of giving anybody anything they beg for. When he asks you to sacrifice your kavacha and kundala, son, you must refuse to donate them for your welfare rests in the kavacha and kundala. Try to appease the protector of Sachi with different kinds of riches and gems. Present multiple reasons to avoid donating your armour and earrings. Karna, you need to know that the dearth of the kavacha and kundala leave you vulnerable to death. Your natural armour and earrings make you invincible and immortal. Always remember these words when the great Shakra approaches you tomorrow".

Karna, having acquainted himself with the true form of the Brahmana, replied with utmost devotion to his father, Dinakara[61], "O Father! It would be in my best interests to listen to your advice, however, if I am your beloved son, then you must not persuade me to fail my vow. It is well-known that I will even donate my life to the righteous brahmanas when they beg for it from me. I will certainly give away my kavacha and kundala when asked by Indra. Through my deeds, I wish to acquire glory, which the creator Brahma acknowledges through this shloka,

> *'In the next world, fame ensures the supreme objective for a man.*
> *In this world, pure fame extends a man's life.'*[62]

By donating the armour and earrings, which are natural components of my body, I will attain ever-lasting fame in all three worlds and the objective of my vow is to harness the fame even if it comes at the cost of my life".

---

61 Dinakara - Surya's name.
62 The Mahabharata 3 Translated By Bibek Debroy.

After hearing the words of the mighty Radheya, Vibhavasu Surya[63] spoke the following words, "O Karna! Refuse to donate your kavacha and kundala when asked for by Purandhara[64]. The brilliant Pandava Arjuna is your contender and he cannot defeat you in battle until you possess your kavacha and kundala. If you aspire to vanquish Arjuna in battle, then you must not offer your earrings and armour to Indra, O dear son!"

Karna, having patiently heard the advice of his father, replied, "O Father! Forgive me as I cannot abide by your advice. Obligated to my vow, I will certainly donate even my life if asked by the protector of Sachi[65]. Furthermore, I am capable of defeating Savyasachi[66] with the help of my might and weapons alone. The weapons I obtained from Lord Parashurama and Dronacharya are sufficient to torment Arjuna on the battlefield. O Surya! Therefore, please grant me the permission to observe my vow".

Touched by Karna's dedication towards his vow, Sahasra Kirana[67] spoke, "O Karna! If you wish to abide by your vow, then I shall not stop you from doing so. However, listen to my advice. When Purandara asks you to donate your armour and earrings to him, you must impose a condition on him that you will only give your kavacha and kundala to Shakra[68] if he gives you an invincible spear (shakti), capable of destroying thousands of enemies in the battlefield, in return.

Having advised Karna thus, the great Surya disappeared. Karna then repeated his entire dream in detail before Dinakara. When Bhaskara[69] confirmed

---

63 Vibhavasu Surya - The resplendent one; Surya.
64 Purandhara - Indra, (the destroyer of strongholds).
65 Protector of Sachi - Indra; the husband of Devi Sachi.
66 Savyasachi - Arjuna.
67 Sahasra kirana - Surya; the one with thousand rays.
68 Shakra - Indra.
69 Bhaskara - Surya.

Karna's dream, Radheya[70] patiently waited for Purandhara to arrive. Karna ignited a hope to obtain shakti within himself.

Later in the noon, after Karna had offered ablutions to the Sun, he donated several riches to the Brahmana. Having known that Karna does not refuse anything to the brahmanas, the lord of Devi Sachi, assumed the form of a noble Brahmana and approached Karna. He said, "O venerable one! Give me…". Karna immediately welcomed the brahmana and asked him, "O noble Brahmana! Please tell me what you desire: Beautiful women or villages affluent with healthy cattle. The brahmana simply said, "O venerable king of Anga![71] I do not ask for women or cattle. All that I wish for is your kavacha and kundala. If you are a man capable of adhering to your vows, then slice them off your body and donate it to me".

Karna replied, "O Brahmana! I will give you habitable land, women, cows, and rice for many years, but not my armour, together with the earrings"[72]. Karna thus tried to woo the brahmana with all other priceless gifts, but when the brahmana refused to ask for any other boon, Karna smiled and said, " O Brahmana! My armour and earrings have emerged from the amrita and it is because of them that I cannot be vanquished in the battle. Therefore, it is impossible for me to offer them to you. Instead of the kavacha and kundala, I offer you this prosperous kingdom. Please accept this kingdom with a happy mind". When the brahmana refused any other boon, Karna smiled and readdressed the brahmana, "O noble one! I am aware of your true form. You are the protector of Sachi and the king of the Gods: Indra. I am a suta not capable of blessing you with a boon. If there is anybody amongst us who is empowered to give a boon, it is you. By taking away my armour and earrings, you will make me a victim of destruction and death. My destruction will cause everyone to mock you. As a result, if you still wish to take my armour and earrings, then give me something in return".

---

70 Radheya - Son of Radhe; Karna.
71 King of Anga - Karna.
72 The Mahabharata 3 Translated by Bibek Debroy

At these words, Indra replied, "O son of Adhiratha!⁷³ Apart from the supreme vajra, you can ask me for any other weapon". Karna was delighted at the words of Indra and asked him for the invincible shakti. At Karna's plea, Indra thought for a while and then replied, "So be it. You can take the invincible shakti from me in exchange for your kavacha and kundala, but subject to one condition. When I release the shakti, it kills thousands of daityas in battle and returns to my hand. But when you use the shakti, you can only kill one powerful enemy, and once released, the weapon will vanquish your enemy and return to my hand". Karna responded, " O Indra! I only wish to kill Arjuna in the battle". Indra warned Karna that Arjuna was protected by Krishna.

Karna finally agreed to donate his armour and requested Indra to save his body from the terrible wounds resulting from discarding the kavacha and

---

73 Son of Adhiratha - Karna, the son of the charioteer Adhiratha.

kundala. Indra agreed. Karna began to cut up his whole body. At the sight of this bravery, gods and demi-gods in heaven showered flowers on him. Karna donated his armour and earrings while they were still soaked in blood and attained eternal flame. Having blessed Karna with the shakti, Indra returned to heaven.

Giffen Goods and Veblen Goods

Having already understood demand, we can now expand our understanding to demand function. As the name suggests, function refers to a relation between two variables, and demand function, therefore, refers to a relation between the consumer's demand for a good and its price.

Let us understand the operation of the demand function with the help of Giffen goods and Veblen goods.

Giffen goods: A Giffen good is a low-income, non-luxury product for which demand increases as the price increases and demand decreases when the price decreases. A Giffen good has an upward-sloping demand curve which is contrary to the fundamental laws of demand which are based on a downward sloping demand curve. Demand for Giffen goods is heavily influenced by a lack of close substitutes and income pressures.

Examples include low-grade varieties of bajra and salt. Notice that even if the prices of these goods increase, still the consumers would exhibit a demand for these goods. Therefore, these commodities can be classified under the category of Giffen Goods.

Veblen goods: A Veblen good is a good for which demand increases as the price increases. Veblen goods are typically high-quality goods that are made well, are exclusive, and are a status symbol. Veblen goods are generally sought after by affluent consumers who place a premium on the utility of the good. The demand curve for a Veblen good is upward sloping, contrary to a normal demand curve, which is downward sloping. Most often, when the price of a Veblen good goes up, the demand goes up; when the price of a Veblen good goes down, the demand goes down.

Examples of Veblen goods include designer jewelry, yachts, and luxury cars, etc. Affluent customers usually demand Veblen goods only when their prices soar up high. This is because often customers with high purchasing power consider these goods to be a status symbol and prefer to own something coveted and unique not affordable by others. Therefore, they often choose to buy those commodities which are expensive.

From the story of Karna's kavacha kundala dhana, we can look at the Shakti given by Indra to Karna as a Giffen good. This is because from Karna's perspective the value of the kavacha and kundala is higher than the value of the shakti. Therefore, we can assume that Karna perceives shakti to be a low-income non-luxury good, whose demand increases as the price increases. In this case, it is Indra's obstinacy to obtain the kavacha and kundala is the price that is rising despite Karna's attempts to persuade him with other riches.

On the contrary, from Indra's perspective, we can treat the kavacha kundala as a Veblen good because in Indra's point of view the value of shakti is less than the value of the kavacha and kundala. This is because the kavacha and kundala are unique and made from amritha. Similar to Giffen goods, Indra's demand for shakti increases as the price increases. In other words, with an increase in Karna's inclination for an exchange, Indra's demand for the kavacha and kundala increases.

The following diagrams represent the demand curves for both the shakti and the kavacha kundala.

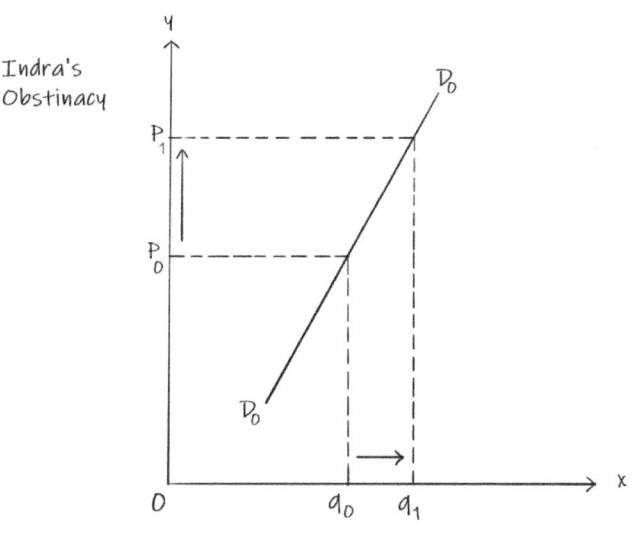

Demand for Shakti

From Karna's perspective,

- On the X-axis, his demand for shakti is measured
- On the y axis, Indra's obstinacy is measured
- Notice that unlike the traditional demand curve which is a downward sloping curve, here the demand has a positive slope
- When Indra's obstinacy to obtain the armour and earring increases from p_0 to p_1, then Karna's demand for shakti increases from q_0 to q_1.
  - p_0 represents the price level where Karna tries to woo Indra by offering him *habitable land, women, cows, and rice for many years, but Indra denies*
  - p_1 represents the price level where Karna again tries to persuade the brahmana by offering him his entire kingdom, however, Indra again denies
  - Thus when the price (Indra's obstinacy) increases from p_0 to p_1, then Karna's demand for shakti increases from q_0 to q_1.

Thus, we can consider shakti to be a Giffen good.

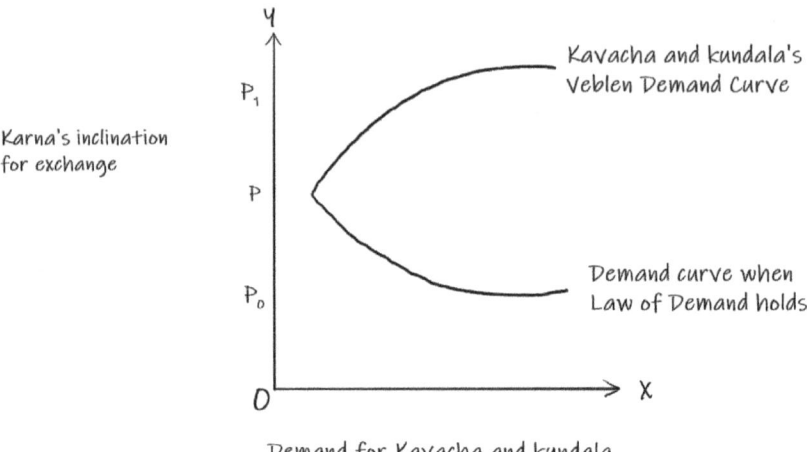

Demand for Kavacha and kundala

From Indra's perspective,

- On the X-axis demand for kavacha and kundala is measured
- On the Y-axis, Karna's inclination for exchange is measured
- Notice that the Kavacha and Kundala's Veblen Demand Curve is contrary to the traditional demand curve.
- Since Indra values the kavacha and kundala as a coveted commodity, thus as the price increases in terms of Karna's inclination for exchange increases then Indra's demand for the kavacha and kundala also increases
  - At P, Karna is telling Indra that he is not capable of giving any boon to Indra
  - At P_1, Karna proposes the exchange of shakti for his kavacha and kundala

Thus, we can consider the kavacha and kundala to be a Veblen good

Although, both the characters Indra and Karna are part of the same scenario, their individual demand for the shakti and the kavacha kundala is characterised by their distinct behaviours.

Ulupi's Production Function for Liberation Of Arjuna's Curse

While selecting stories from the Mahabharata for Jayarthashastra, one of the first stories that I selected was the story of Babruvahana. When I was asked the reason for selecting that story by my grandpa, I only said, "Dr Rajkumar".

Perhaps, Dr Rajkumar inspired me to write this chapter… Well, his magnificent acting skills in the Kannada film Babruvahana have always been a benchmark for me as an artist. Those iconic moments shared by the legends Dr Rajkumar, B Saroja Devi and Kanchana on screen have always left me speechless.

The Kannada film Babruvahana is truly synonymous to my emotions of joy and freedom. Harnessing the sprout of inspiration bestowed upon me by Dr Rajkumar's priceless acting, I narrate to you a story that is very close to my heart…

Post the great Mahabharata war, the benevolent king, Yudhishthira commenced the royal Ashvamedha sacrifice[74] at the instructions of Krishna. The horse sacrifice lasted for an entire year and as per the customs, the royal horse was left to roam any land in any direction. The horse was accompanied by the mighty army of the Kurus led by Arjuna. The Ashvamedha yagna was meant to assert Yudhishthira's primacy as the supreme emperor over those territories where the horse roamed. Arjuna, on the other hand, was entrusted with the task of challenging those rulers, who obstructed the movement of the horse. During the journey, Arjuna fought violently with the Trigartas, Vajradatta, Saindhavas and finally arrived in the country of Manipura, ruled by Chitrangada's[75] son Babruvahana.

Upon hearing about his father's arrival, Babruvahana, the king of Manipura, was stationed with brahmanas and other advisors at the palace gates, eagerly waiting for his father's arrival. However, when Arjuna saw his son waiting near the entrance, he remembered his Kshatriya dharma and was enraged. He said, "This conduct of you coming out is not in accordance with the dharma of kshatriyas. I have arrived here, protecting Yudhishthira's horse. The sacrificial animal has arrived in your kingdom. O son! Why are you not fighting with me? You are knowledgeable about the dharma of Kshatriya. O extremely evil-minded one! Shame on you. Wishing to fight, I have arrived before you and you are seeking peace. Though you are alive on this earth, no manliness exists in you. You have cast aside your weapons and have arrived here now. O worst of men! This is what your conduct has shown"[76].

---

74 The Ashvamedha was a horse sacrifice ritual followed by the rauta tradition of Vedic religion. It was used by ancient Indian kings to prove their imperial sovereignty: a horse accompanied by the king's warriors would be released to wander for a year. In the territory traversed by the horse, any rival could dispute the king's authority by challenging the warriors accompanying it. After one year, if no enemy had managed to kill or capture the horse, the animal would be guided back to the king's capital. It would be then sacrificed, and the king would be declared as an undisputed sovereign.
75 A wife of Arjuna and the warrior princess of Manipura, who was the only heir to her father, King Chitravahana.
76 The Mahabharata 10 Translated by Bibek Debroy.

Ulupi[77] appeared before Babruvahana, when she came to know of Arjuna's words. She was miserable as she saw Babruvahana standing with a bent head, insulted by his father's words. She approached Arjuna's son and spoke in a voice choked with compassion, "O son! Know me to be Ulupi. I am your mother and the daughter of a serpent. O son! Act in accordance with my words. You will then be established in supreme dharma. O scorcher of enemies! Fight with Dhananjaya[78], foremost among Kurus. There is no doubt that he will be pleased at this[79]". Babruvahana was thus instigated by Ulupi to fight with the mighty Arjuna.

Babruvahana ascended his majestic chariot abundant with arrows and other weapons. His standard depicting the golden lion, rose above the ornately-decorated chariot pole. With swift and divine horses yoked to his golden chariot, the intelligent son of Chitrangada[80] embarked towards his father, Arjuna. Within moments, Babruvahana valiantly seized the sacrificial horse of the kurus with the help of men skilled in the art of managing horses. Arjuna was delighted to behold his son adorned with a lustrous armour and helmet. He experienced an inner feeling of pride as he observed Babruvahana capturing the sacrificial horse and leading it through the palace gates. Later a fierce battle broke out between Arjuna and Babruvahana. Chitrangada's son shot thousands of sharp arrows towards Arjuna and one of those arrows penetrated Dhananjaya's shoulder injuring his shoulder-joint. Though engulfed in pain, Arjuna praised his son in these words. "Excellent. O mighty-armed one! O son! Excellent. O Chitrangada's son! On witnessing this deed, I am pleased with you. I will now shoot arrows at you. O son! Be steady in the battle[81]".

---

77 A wife of Arjuna; a serpent princess.
78 Arjuna (Since he supplied abundant quantities to his brother Yudhishthira's yagna, he is called Dhananjaya).
79 The Mahabharata 10 Translated by Bibek Debroy.
80 Babruvahana.
81 The Mahabharata 10 Translated by Bibek Debroy.

Arjuna showered a quiver of arrows towards the king of Manipura from his vajra-like gandiva. However, these powerful arrows were no match to the strength of Babruvahana. He crushed each arrow into pieces as they approached him like snakes. Arjuna was awe-struck at Babruvahana's expertise and decided to test his capabilities further. With the release of a *kshurapa* arrow, he comfortably dislodged Babruvahana from his chariot. He killed the divine horses yoked to the heavenly chariot and laughed. Babruvahana was enraged at the act of his father and began to ferociously fight with him on the ground. Arjuna on the contrary, did not wish to oppress his son excessively.[82] Thinking that his father was no longer willing to fight, the powerful one again struck him with arrows that were like virulent serpents. The young Babruvahana powerfully pierced his father's heart with a sharp arrow that had excellent tufts. In its energy, the arrow blazed like a flaming fire. O king! It severely penetrated Pandava's inner organs and caused great pain. The descendant of the Kuru lineage was severely struck by his son. O king! Afflicted and bereft of his senses, Dhananjaya fell on the ground.[83] Chitrangada's brave son also lost his senses.

Upon hearing about the fierce battle and its result, Chitrangada hurried to the battlefield and lamented over the death of her husband. Unable to digest the reality, Chitrangada fell on the ground. After a while, when she regained her senses, the divine queen of Arjuna approached the Naga princess and exclaimed in rage, "O Ulupi! Behold. Our victorious husband is lying down in the battle, slain. This is because of what you did to my young child. Are you not noble? Do you not know dharma? Are you not devoted to your husband? Because of what you have done, our husband has been killed and is lying down in the battle. Even if Dhananjaya has committed all manner of crimes towards you, I am beseeching you now to forgive him. Give him his life back. O beautiful one! You are indeed noble. You know about dharma and are famous in the three worlds. Having caused your husband to be killed by your son, why are you not grieving? O daughter of a serpent! I am not sorrowing

---

82 The Mahabharata 10 Translated by Bibek Debroy.

83 The Mahabharata 10 Translated by Bibek Debroy.

because my son has been killed. I am grieving because of my husband and because of the hospitality that has been shown to him[84]".

After speaking these words to Ulupi, Chitrangada went to Arjuna and cried out in misery, "O foremost among the kurus! Arise. O beloved! Do what brings me pleasure. O mighty-armed one! I have set this horse free. O brave one! You should indeed follow Dharmaraja's sacrificial horse. Why are you lying down on the ground? O descendant of the Kuru lineage! My breath of life depends on you and so do those of the kurus. How can someone who grants others their breaths of life give up his own breath of life? O Ulupi! Behold this praiseworthy sight of your husband having been slain in the battle. You incited the son to kill him and are not grieving. This child should sleep as he wishes. Instead, he has been killed and is lying down on the ground. O one with the red eyes! O Gudakesha[85]! It would be good if you came back to life. O extremely beautiful one! It is not a crime for a man to have many wives. Women should be like me. Their intelligence should not be like yours. This friendship[86] was ordained by the creator. It is eternal and indestructible. Know that friendship and make that relationship come true. My husband has been slain by my son now. If I do not see him alive now, I will cast aside my life. I am miserable and timid, having been separated from my husband and my son. There is no doubt that while you look on, I will fast to death[87]". Chitrangada stationed herself beside her husband, and prepared herself for fasting to death.

After a few minutes, she stopped her mourning and embraced her husband's feet. Her teardrops seemed to wash Arjuna's feet as she held them tightly. However, her attention was suddenly distracted towards Babruvahana, who regained his senses. He first noticed the plight of his mother and said these words, "My mother has been reared in happiness. What can be a greater misery than to see her seated on the ground, next to her brave and dead husband who

---

84 The Mahabharata 10 Translated by Bibek Debroy.
85 Arjuna (one who has controlled sleep).
86 Marriage
87 The Mahabharata 10 Translated by Bibek Debroy.

is lying down? He slew many brave ones in battle and was supreme among those who wielded all weapons. He has been killed by me in the encounter. It is evident that it is very difficult to die. This queen's heart is extremely firm. Otherwise, it should have been shattered. She has seen that her mighty-armed and broad-chested husband has been slain. I think it is extremely difficult for people to die until their time has come, since neither I, nor my mother, have been separated from life. Alas for the brave one's golden armour, lying down on the ground. Behold! It has been pierced by his son and he has been killed. O brahmanas! Behold. My brave father is lying down on the ground. He is lying down on a bed meant for heroes. He has been killed by me, his son. The foremost among the Kurus followed the horse and the brahmanas pronounced benedictions of peace on him. But he has now been slain by me in the battle. O brahmanas! Instruct me. What atonement should I practise now? I have slain my father in the field of battle and that is an extremely cruel sin. Having killed my father now and performed this extremely cruel deed, I should hide my face and roam around, observing extremely difficult austerities for twelve years. I should now wander around, with my father's skull affixed to my head. For the sake of my father, there is no other atonement that is possible now. O daughter of the best of serpents! Behold. Your husband has been slain by me. I have slain Arjuna in the battle and have now accomplished what is agreeable to you. I will now follow the path traversed by my father. O beautiful one! I am incapable of sustaining myself any longer. My mother and the wielder of Gandiva[88] will also be dead. O queen! Be delighted. That is the truth you have realized today". Babruvahana was afflicted by sorrow and grief. He touched water and spoke these words, "O all mobile and immobile creatures! Listen. O mother! O supreme among the serpents! You also listen. I am speaking the truth. If my father, Jaya[89], does not arise, in this field of battle, I will dry up my body. Having slain my father, I will never be able to escape. Having suffered from the act of having killed a senior, it is certain that I can visualize hell. If one kills a brave Kshatriya, one is freed by giving away one hundred cows. However, having killed my father, it is extremely difficult for me to

---

88 Arjuna.
89 Arjuna.

escape. Pandu's son, Dhananjaya, was the only one endued with great energy. He was my father and had dharma in his soul. Therefore, how can there be an escape for me?" The immensely intelligent one then touched water and was silent, having decided to fast to death[90].

Ulupi witnessed Babruvahana's agony and then thought of the *samjivanam*[91] jewel. Devoted to serpents, it presented itself. Ulupi grasped the shiny jewel gilded with ornate embellishments and spoke with a confident tone. Her words delighted the minds of the soldiers, "O son! Arise. Jishnu[92] has not been slain by you. He is incapable of being defeated by men and not even by the gods, with Vasava. For the sake of causing pleasure to your illustrious father, Indra

---
90 The Mahabharata 10 Translated by Bibek Debroy.
91 Samjivanam jewel is a jewel used to revive dead people.
92 Arjuna (because he cannot be supressed and is triumphant).

among men, I invoked the maya known as Mohini today. O son! Kaurava[93] desired to test your strength. O king! That slayer of enemy heroes came here to fight against you in the encounter. O son! It is for his sake that I incited you to fight. O son! O lord! You should not entertain the slightest bit of doubt about your having committed a sin. This man is an immensely energetic rishi. He is eternal and indestructible. O son! Even Shakra is incapable of defeating him in a battle. O lord of the earth! This divine jewel has been summoned by me. Like amrita, it always revives the Indras among serpents when they die. O lord! Place this on your father's chest. O son! You will again see that Pandava has come back to life[94]".

At these words of the serpent princess, Babruvahana immediately placed the samjivanam jewel on Arjuna's chest and within seconds, the immensely energetic one was revived. It was as if Arjuna woke up from a deep slumber. Babruvahana experienced an innate feeling of calmness as he saw his father arise. Arjuna embraced Babruvahana and inhaled the fragrance of his head. He then observed Chitrangada standing at a distance, her eyes wet and facial features communicating her misery. He addressed Babruvahana and asked him, "O slayer of enemies! Why is everyone seen to be sorrowful and miserable on the field of battle? If you know, tell me. Why has your mother come to the battleground? Why has Ulupi, daughter of Indra among the serpents, come here? I know that you fought with me because of my words. However, I wish to know the reason why the women have come here". Babruvahana's gaze shifted towards the serpent princess as he spoke in humility, "O learned one! Let Ulupi be asked"[95].

At this, Arjuna addressed Ulupi, "O delighter of the Kourava lineage! Why have you come here? Why is the mother of the lord of Manipura in the field of battle? O daughter of a serpent! I hope you do desire this king's welfare. O one with restless eyes! I hope you do wish for my welfare. O one who is

---

93 Arjuna, since he belonged to the lineage of Kuru.
94 The Mahabharata 10 Translated by Bibek Debroy.
95 The Mahabharata 10 Translated by Bibek Debroy.

beautiful to see! I hope I, or Babruvahana, have not caused you any displeasure inadvertently. O beautiful one! Has Chaitravahini Chitrangada, your co-wife, caused you any injury?"

Ulupi replied, "You, or King Babruvahana, have not committed any crime. Listen to how I have brought everything about. You should not display anger towards me. I bow down my head and seek your favours. O Kouravya! O unblemished one! I have done everything to bring you pleasure. O mighty-armed one! O Dhananjaya! Listen to everything. In the Mahabharata war, you slew the king who was Shantanu's son[96] by resorting to adharma. O Partha! My act has freed you from that. O brave one! You did not bring down Bhishma while he was fighting with you. He was slain by you while he was engaged in a duel with Shikhandi. Had you given up your life without pacifying that sin, there is no doubt that because of that wicked deed, you would have descended into hell. Through your son you have now obtained pacification. O lord of the earth! O immensely intelligent one! Earlier, when the Vasus[97] were with Ganga, I heard the Vasus talk about this, when they came to the banks of the Ganga after the king who was Shantanu's son had been slain. Having approached the great river, the gods, the Vasus, bathed there. With Bhagirathi's[98] permission, they then uttered these terrible words. 'This Bhishma, Shantanu's son, has been slain by Savyasachi[99], though he was not fighting in the battle with him. O beautiful one! He was engaged with someone else. O beautiful one! Because of that reason, we are pronouncing a curse on Arjuna.' She agreed to this. My senses were greatly afflicted and I reported this to my father. On hearing this, he was also plunged in supreme grief. For your sake, on many occasions, my father went to the Vasus and repeatedly tried to seek their favours. They eventually told him, 'O immensely

---

96 Bhishma.
97 Vasus are the attendant deities of Indra, and later Vishnu. They are the sons of Manu or Brahma Prajapati.
98 Ganga.
99 Arjuna, since he was ambidextrous.

fortunate one! The lord of Manipura[100] is young. Using his arrows, in the midst of the battle, he will bring him down to the ground. O Indra among serpents! If this is done, he will be freed from the curse.' He returned and told me about what Vasus had said. Having heard this from him, I have freed you from the curse. Even the king of the gods is incapable of defeating you in a battle. The son is said to be like one's own self and you have been vanquished by your own self. O lord! No sin attaches to me. What do you think?" Thus addressed, Vijaya was delighted and said, "O queen! Everything that you have done for me is extremely agreeable." Having said this, Jaya spoke to his son, the lord of Manipura, while Chitrangada, the daughter-in-law of the Kouravyas, heard. "Yudhishthira's horse sacrifice will take place in the next month of Chaitra. O king! With your advisers and your mothers, go there." This is what Partha told King Babruvahana. With tears in his eyes, the intelligent one replied to his father. "O one who knows about dharma! Because of your command, I will certainly go there. At the great horse sacrifice, I will serve the brahmanas. O slayer of enemies! But to show me your favours, with your wives, please enter your own city. You should not reflect about this. O lord! Without any pain, happily spend one night in your own residence. O supreme among victorious ones! Then follow the horse again."

Thus addressed by his son, Kounteya[101], the one with the ape on his banner, smiled and replied to Chitrangada's son. "O mighty-armed one! You know about the initiation I am following now. O large-eyed one! That is the reason I cannot enter the city. This sacrificial horse goes as it wills and I have to follow it. May you be fortunate. I have to depart and there is no place where I can tarry." The son of Paka's chastiser[102] was then worshipped in the proper way. Having taken leave of his wives, the supreme one among the Bharata lineage departed.'[103]

---

100 Babruvahana.
101 Arjuna, the son of Kunti.
102 Arjuna, the son of Indra.
103 The Mahabharata 10 Translated by Bibek Debroy.

Production Function

Let us recall that production is the process by which various material and non-material inputs are combined in different proportions to produce an output. In other words, production is also defined as the transformation of input into output[104].

Now, what is a production function?

The word 'function' informs us that a production function describes a relation.

Therefore, the production function of a firm is a relationship between the inputs used and outputs produced by a firm. For various quantities of inputs used, it gives the maximum quantity of output that can be produced.[105]

Production function of a firm is a functional relationship between inputs used and output produced by the firm. It expresses the maximum quantity of output that can be produced with any given quantity of inputs. Production function considers only the efficient use of inputs that helps in getting the maximum possible output.

A production function is defined for a given technology. It is the technology that determines the maximum levels of output that can be produced using different combinations of inputs. If the technology improves, the level of output attainable for different input combinations also increases.[106]

Let us understand the production function through an example.

Assume that you are a farmer, whose livelihood rests on the cultivation of rice. For simplicity, let us assume that you use only two inputs to produce rice: labour and land. A production function will tell us the maximum amount

---
104 All in one Economics CBSE Class 11.
105 NCERT Introductory Microeconomics Textbook in Economics for Class XII.
106 All in One Economics CBSE Class XI.

of rice that you can produce given the area of the land and the number of hours of labour. Hypothetically, 3 hours of labour/day and 1 hectare of land can produce a maximum of two tonnes of rice. A production that associates the relation between the above-mentioned factors and the output is called a production function.

One way to represent a production function is:

$$q = K \times L$$

Where,

- q is the amount of rice output
- K is the area of the land under cultivation in hectares
- L is the number of hours of work done by the labour in one day

The above production function gives us the exact relation between the inputs and outputs. If K or L increases, then even q will proportionally increase.

Another way to represent the production function is:

$$q = f(L, K)$$

Where,

- q is again the maximum amount of rice output
- f is the functional relationship between the inputs (L,K) and the output q
- L is the number of hours of work done by the labour in one day
- K is the area of the land under cultivation in hectares

We can also understand the breaking of Arjuna's curse as a production function.

Here, the output for Ulupi was the breaking of Arjuna's curse, which required the involvement of two factors namely: Babruvahana's valour and the samjivanam jewel.

Therefore, a production function that describes the relation between these two factors and the breaking of Arjuna's curse would be:

Liberation of Arjuna's curse = f (Babruvahana's valour, samjivanam jewel)

From the above production function, it can be easily interpreted that Ulupi was able to achieve the liberation of Arjuna's curse of the Vasus through the effective utilisation of the two factors of Babruvahana's valour and the samjivanam jewel.

A Catch-22 Situation for the Jaratkarus

The silence in the room was overpowering... However, the soft susurration of the leaves outside became a fierce rustling, loud enough to drown my concentration into the painting completely. Unaware of the gloom that was to set in, I continued to paint my abstract portrait.

The bright red violently mixed with the royal amber to portray the exquisiteness in the orange.

To quench my thirst, I reached out to the glass on the gilded brown table... On the contrary, lost in admiring the hued still life before me, unknowingly I grasped the black paint bottle. It approached me in gloomy solace.

The approaching footsteps had the sound of the clicking of the bottom of the shoes on a hard surface. In a spur of a moment, my mom lambasted my hand and shouted, "Throw away the paint bottle. Are you out of your senses? I asked you to drink water and not paint".

Overwhelmed by dread, my eyes rose to witness a perverted canvas with a black smear on it. The black smear ruined my portrait. It was all over at once. There was no escape from this. An ironic situation from which I could not flee... A catch-22 situation.

Jaratkaru, the great rishi, married Vasuki's sister, Jaratkaru. Upon their marriage, the rishi Jaratkaru entered into an agreement with his wife. He asserted, "O Jaratkaru! Please ensure that none of your actions or speech cause resentment to me. If they do, then I shall abandon you and return to the place where I belonged." Vasuki's sister was a loyal wife, who instantly agreed to her husband's conditions.

One day, Jaratkaru fell asleep on his wife's lap. As he slumbered away, the time for the sunset approached. Vasuki's sister, Jaratkaru was alarmed at the arrival of the time for agnihotra[107]. She feared the violation of dharma by her husband. Instantly, the seed of a dilemma germinated in her mind. She kept questioning herself, "How should I act so as to ensure the protection of dharma and integrity of my husband's self-esteem? Would it be appropriate to wake him from his trance? Would my action of waking him cause resentment to him? But not awakening him could possibly cause the violation of dharma."

She thought to herself, "The failure of performing evening prayers outweighs the anger of my husband. Perseverance of dharma is essential. Therefore, it is pertinent that I alert my husband about the sunset."

Retrospecting these thoughts in her mind, Jaratkaru spoke in a soft voice, "O esteemed one! Arise, the sun is descending. It is time for you to observe your evening prayers. Arise, o glorious one!"

---

107 Agnihotra refers to a simple form of homa. Agnihotra refers to the yajna of casting of ghee into the sacred fire as per strict rites, and may include twice-daily heated milk offering made by those in the Śrauta tradition.

Arising from his sleep, Jaratkaru crackled with rage from top to toe. He thus spoke in agitation, "O Jaratkaru! You have humiliated me with your words. Therefore, I will not reside with you and I will return to the place where I originally belonged. O snake! I am aware that the sun does not have the supremacy to descend while I am in a trance state!"

Vasuki's sister trembled at the words of Jaratkaru. Out of grief, she addressed him, "O venerable one! I did not wake you with a desire to insult you. I did it so that you should not face a loss in dharma."[108] It is not proper of you to abandon me like this. The purpose of our marriage remains incomplete. O rishi! Stay with me until I give birth to a son who will save my relatives from their mother's curse".

---

108 The Mahabharata 1 Translated by Bibek Debroy.

At these words of Vasuki's sister, Jaratkaru comforted her be saying, "O fortunate one! The one who is in your womb now will be a rishi who will be like the god of fire himself. He will be the best of those who follow dharma and will be learned in the Vedas and the Vedangas."[109]

Having addressed her thus, the venerated rishi departed.

The Short Run Costs

In our conversations, the words 'price' and 'cost' are often used synonymously. But, do you think there is a difference between the two words?

Yes, there is a considerable difference between the two words. In economics, the word 'cost' finds shelter in the theory of production, whereas the word 'price' relates to the theory of consumption. Cost includes all the monetary expenditure as well as non-monetary expenditure incurred by a producer in employing the factor inputs or non-factor inputs to produce a given quantity of output of a commodity.[110] Price is the amount of money that a consumer is willing to pay for a particular commodity or a service. Nevertheless, the focus of this discussion would be on the concept of cost.

Before we proceed any further with our discussion about cost, it would be useful to understand the time periods involved in production. The short run refers to a period in which the producer can alter his production by changing only the variable factors and keeping constant the fixed factors of production. On the other hand, the long run refers to a period in which the producer can vary the output by changing both the fixed as well as variable factor inputs. Let us zoom into the short run costs…

Short run costs are further classified as fixed cost, variable cost, total cost, and marginal cost. It is useful to note that total cost is the summation of fixed

---

109 The Mahabharata 1 Translated by Bibek Debroy.
110 All in One Economics CBSE Class XI

cost and variable cost. Fixed cost, denoted by FC, is the expenditure that the producer incurs to hire or purchase fixed factors of production.[111]

A producer incurs FC even if he produces zero units of output. One may ponder over this question, "If a producer does not produce anything, then why does he incur a cost?" Well, the answer to this question is quite simple. Fixed costs like payment of rent for the factory premises or payment of rent for the land or payment of salaries to full-time employees are independent of the output level. These costs have to be inevitably borne by the producer in the short run, whether he produces anything or not. So, even producing a zero level of output will incur some fixed cost to the producer.

Variable cost, denoted by VC, is the cost that the producer incurs to employ the variable factors of production such as wages to casual labourers, procurement of raw materials, electricity charges, etc. These costs are dependent on the level of output. If a producer wishes to increase his level of output in the short run, then he can increase the variable factors to yield the increased output. As mentioned earlier, Total Cost (TC) is an entirety of fixed cost and variable cost.

Having acquainted ourselves with the concept of short run cost, let us try and relate the same to the above-mentioned interesting situation of the Jaratkarus. We can assume lady Jaratkaru to be a producer, producing the output of an evening prayer by her husband. Here, the time period of the production is a short run and there are two factor inputs involved. The descending sun is the fixed factor input and her soft voice, reminding her husband of his duty is the variable factor input. Having employed these two factor inputs, lady Jaratkaru incurred costs in the forms of the wrath of her husband and their separation. The fixed cost is the fact that lady Jaratkaru is unaware of the lack of supremacy in the sun to descend while her husband is asleep. The words "I will not reside with you and will return to the place where I originally

---

[111] All in One Economics CBSE Class XI

belonged", become the variable cost. The total cost, being a totality of both FC and VC, is the separation that the wife suffers from rishi Jaratkaru.

The fixed cost, variable cost, and total cost can be sketched as a group of curves. The diagram represents all three cost curves. Notice that the x-axis is labelled with evening prayer, while the y-axis is labelled with the wrath and separation of Jaratkaru. Having already specified that the fixed cost is independent of the output level, the FC curve is a straight horizontal line, parallel to OX. The VC curve emerges from the origin, since VC=0 when output=0. The TC curve emerges from above the FC curve because the TC curve is a vertical summation of the FC and VC curves.

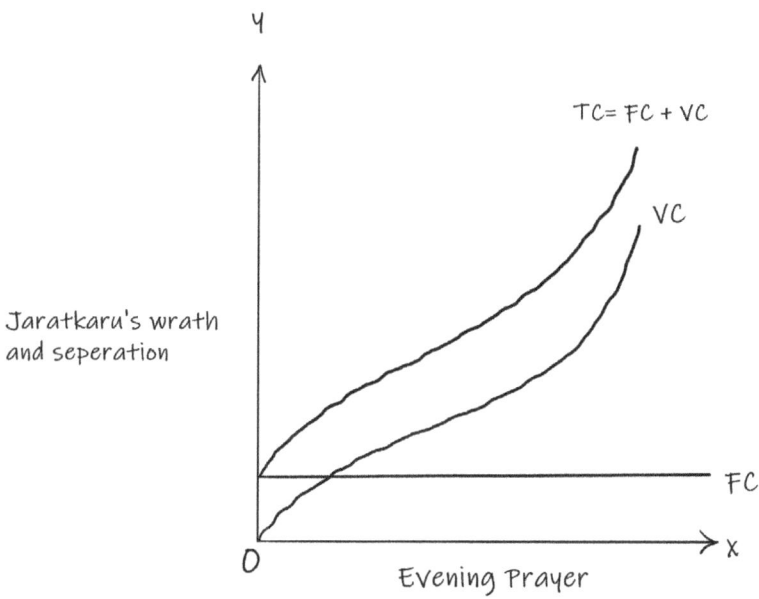

A Catch-22 Situation

Coined by Joseph Heller, in his famous novel Catch-22, the term 'a catch-22 situation' refers to an ironic situation, from which an individual cannot flee, due to the presence of antagonistic norms.

Is there a catch-22 situation in this story?

The *Astika Parva* of the Mahabharata elaborates this incident, suggesting that Jaratkaru's fundamental purpose of marrying a girl was to expand his lineage through the birth of his son, Astika. Once Jaratkaru had accomplished this goal, then he would depart from his wife.

It can be inferred that the separation of Jaratkaru from his wife was destined to happen, therefore whether or not lady Jaratkaru awakened her husband, their being apart was certain. This is a catch-22 situation. Vasuki's sister Jaratkaru cannot flee from the reality of their parting due to the presence of an agreement between Vasuki and rishi Jaratkaru where Jaratkaru agrees to marry Vasuki's sister on several conditions. One of these conditions was that Jaratkaru would not support his wife for sustenance.

Bhanumati's Dignity: A Profit for Karna

The dominance of a few words like "profit", "loss", and "money" in everyone's daily vocabulary is undisputed. Profit has become the measuring tool of success in a business, and loss a magnet attracting sympathy. We observe that these words often are associated with an emotion such as joy or jealousy for profit and sorrow for loss. But when we actually hear the word 'profit' or say it out loud, do we think about it as an incentive for an entrepreneur or as a financial gain?

Besides, we also sub-consciously categorise the words used in conversations under particular domains. This happened to me! Until I was formally introduced to commerce, I had made up an assumption in my mind. Whenever I heard the word profit or loss or even money, my mind would simply categorise these words as 'something related to a business'.

As I explored commerce, it became evident that 'profit' belonged to economics, business studies, and even accountancy. The surprising part was that in economics there is even a formula for profit.

Would you be surprised if I tell you that the formula "Profit= Total Revenue - Total Cost" could be explained through an incident from the Mahabharata? The first question appearing in your mind would be "How?"

Indeed.

Karna and Duryodhana were known for their close friendship and trust in each other... Since Duryodhana was the crown prince of Hastinapura before the great war, he had to perform several duties, which required him to travel to all the kingdoms under the sovereignty of Hastinapura.

One day, when Duryodhana had to embark upon a journey to a distant land, he assigned Karna with the responsibility of taking care of his newly-wed wife, Bhanumati. She was a new member of the Kauravas family, who had acquaintance only with her mother-in-law Gandhari, her husband Duryodhana and Karna. She had been forcefully abducted from her *swayamvar*[112] by Duryodhana with the help of his ally Karna. Bhanumati, the daughter of King Chitrangada, was petrified at this act of Duryodhana and always feared that his family would also be a replica of his personality. Furthermore, the Kalinga princess was not accompanied by her handmaidens or servants, which added to her insecurity and isolation. Therefore, she often preferred silence and did not prefer to mingle with all the members of the family, until she was convinced of their true personalities. Karna was however an exception. His genuine loyalty and respect for Duryodhana made him trustworthy.

Duryodhana was aware of Bhanumati's feelings and acted accordingly by assigning Karna the responsibility of taking care of his wife. After he left for his expedition, Bhanumati and Karna spoke to each other like old friends. Subsequently, they decided to play the pachisi (the game of dice) to pass time. It was only a matter of few minutes before the game became so interesting that both the players became engrossed in the game. Besides, the material stakes were also quite high. Bhanumati and Karna began chattering with each other as though they knew each other for centuries. It seemed obvious to Bhanumati that Karna was winning the game. She accused him, "O Karna! You are cheating!" Karna replied, "Dear sister-in-law! I am not cheating. I do

---

112 Svayam means "self" and vara means "groom". Swayamvara was a practice in ancient India, in which a girl of a marriageable age would select her groom from a group of suitors.

not need to cheat because I am an exceptional player. You are simply charging me of cheating because you are losing the game, dear Bhanumati".

As they continued with their game, Duryodhana entered the room, where Karna and Bhanumati were playing pachisi. Bhanumati, who was facing the door, noticed the arrival of her husband and immediately stood up as a sign of respect. Karna, on the other hand, faced Bhanumati and could not see his friend's arrival. He did not stand up. In fact, he misunderstood Bhanumati's action of standing up as her attempt to leave the game since she was losing.

To stop her from leaving the game, Karna grasped her pearl-embellished shawl and accidentally dragged the fabric so hard that the pearl embellishment tore apart from the rest of the shawl and all the pearls scattered on the floor. Since the shawl was attached to the pallu, when Karna pulled the shawl, even the pallu fell and Bhanumati was left half-dressed. Duryodhana stood near the door and observed the entire scene before his eyes. Bhanumati was embarrassed by the situation and frightened at the thought of her husband's reaction to the same. She froze and stood cold like a statue without uttering a word.

Karna held Bhanumati's shawl in his hand, but he noticed the sudden change in the expression on Bhanumati's face. He carefully observed the movement of her eyes towards the door and back towards him. He sensed the anxiousness in Bhanumati's stance. Her glance towards the other end of the chamber left Karna in a dilemma. He was at first scared and even worried. Following her eyes, he slowly turned around in apprehension to see his friend standing beside the door. Karna was shocked and ashamed at the sight of his friend. He thought to himself, "Surely, Duryodhana would have assumed that I have misbehaved with his wife. He is bound to punish me for this accidental act of mine. Any justification from my end would worsen the situation and harm my sister-in-law's dignity. It is best to remain silent now..." Contemplating this thought, Karna stood silent.

On the contrary, Duryodhana looked at Karna with an expression that said nothing, which confused him. To Karna's surprise, Duryodhana shifted his gaze to his wife, and asked her, "Dear, would you like me to just collect your pearls, or string them as well?"

Both, Bhanumati and Karna were awe-struck by Duryodhana's question. They had misjudged his trust in them. They looked at each other in humiliation. Duryodhana was able to read their action and instantly laughed. He added, "O Karna! I trust you, my friend. I am aware that nothing matters more to you than your loyalty and devotion for our friendship. I can never doubt you, my friend".

Ultimately, Duryodhana's trust in Karna saved Bhanumati's dignity.

Determining Karna's Profit

Now, let us analyse the above situation through the concept of profit. At this point, it may be useful for us to recollect that a firm's profit is the difference between its total revenue and its total cost of production. Total revenue usually denoted by TR is the total amount that a firm earns from the sale of its output. Total cost, on the other hand, denoted by TC is the total of the fixed cost and variable cost of production. When the total revenue earned exceeds the total cost of production, the excess of total revenue is termed as profit.

In economics, profit is denoted by the symbol π. Therefore, we can symbolically represent profit as, π= TR- TC.

Here, Karna takes the place of a firm and his profit can be interpreted in the following manner:

- Karna's total revenue is Duryodhana's infinite trust in their friendship. Karna had earned his total revenue from his loyalty and devotion towards Duryodhana.
- Karna's total cost on the other hand is his act of not justifying his actions through his speech. It is surprising to note that his silence had become his cost. Due to his silence, Karna experienced misery for a brief period. He felt scared and insecure about the reaction of his friend towards his action. He had also mentally prepared himself to accept the punishment, which would be announced by Duryodhana
- But, Duryodhana's unexpected question to his wife, shattered Karna's conclusions. In this case, Karna's total revenue exceeded his total cost, or in other words, Duryodhana's trust in Karna won over Karna's misjudgement.
- Karna had comfortably earned a profit. Along with the integrity of his trust maintained, he successfully maintained the dignity of Bhanumati.
- Bhanumati's dignity was a profit for Karna.

The below diagram summarises our discussion so far.

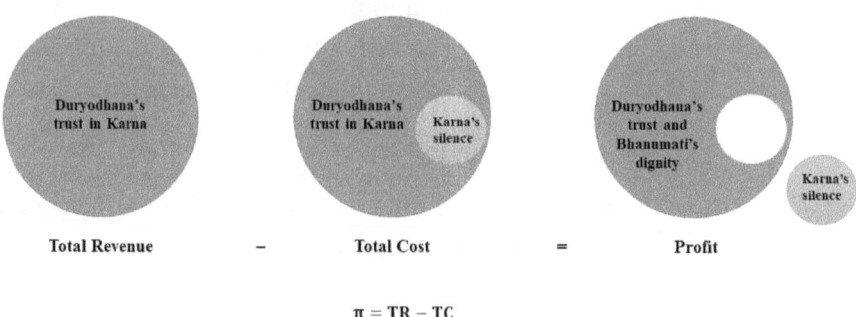

$$\pi = TR - TC$$

From the sphere of Duryodhana's trust, if you subtract Karna's silence, Karna gains a profit in the form of Bhanumati's dignity upheld.

The Root Cause Analysis for Slaying Jarasandha.

When I first heard my mother mentioning the 'fishbone diagram' in her presentation, it seemed amusing to me. I always wondered why they termed a flowchart as a fish bone.

More than a cause-and-effect diagram, the fishbone diagram appeared like a piece of art to me. I consider the fishbone diagram as a reflection of creativity as it effectively communicates the root-cause analysis of a problem.

Fishbone diagrams also serve as an advantage for visual thinkers because they can be employed for brainstorming activities.

Perhaps, back during the days of the Mahabharata, the concept of root cause analysis never prevailed and Yudhishtira was not aware about the existence of a fishbone diagram. But, what if he used one…

Vaishampayana said, 'O Janamejaya! O descendant of the Bharata lineage! Having heard the words of the rishi Narada[113], Yudhishtira sighed and thinking about performing Rajasuya, could find no peace. He had heard about the glory of the great-souled rajarshis and had learnt that they had attained the pure worlds through their deeds and sacrifices. In particular, he thought about rajarshi Harishchandra, who had performed the sacrifice, and thought about performing Rajasuya. Having honoured all those who were present in his sabha, and having been honoured by them in return, he consulted them about the sacrifice.

The lord of kings and bull among the Kuru lineage, after reflecting a great deal, made up his mind to perform Rajasuya. King Yudhishtira, protector of dharma, supreme among those who know all dharma, attentive to his subjects and always acting for the welfare of everyone without distinction, extraordinary in his energy and power, reflected on what would bring welfare to all the worlds. Having thus conducted himself and having thus reassured everyone like a father, no one could be seen who hated him and he came to be known as Ajatashatru[114].

That supreme among eloquent ones assembled his advisers and brothers and repeatedly asked them about Rajasuya. Having been thus asked by the immensely wise Yudhishtira, who was eager to perform the sacrifice, the advisers then uttered words that were deep with meaning:

"A consecrated king who wishes to achieve the characteristics of an emperor and attain the traits of Varuna, performs this rite, even though he is a king. O descendant of the Kuru lineage! You are worthy of the status of an emperor and all your well-wishers think that the time has come for you to perform

---

113 In the Sabha parva of the Mahabharata, Rishi Narada visits the Pandavas in their capital city, Indraprastha. After rhetorically explaining state craft of kings to Yudhishtira and describing the design, architecture and assembly halls of Yama, Varuna, Indra, Kubera and Brahma, Narada advises Yudhishtira to perform the Rajasuya yagna.
114 One without enemies.

Rajasuya. The time for the sacrifice, in which priests rigid in their vows establish six fires[115] to the chants of sama, is free and depends on kshatriya riches[116]. At the completion of the sacrifice, after offering all the oblations, the performer is consecrated as a universal emperor. O mighty-armed one! All of us serve you and you are capable. O great king! Do not reflect anymore and set your mind on the Rajasuya."

Separately and together, thus did his well-wishers speak. Having heard these words, full of dharma, bold, pleasant, and supreme, the Pandava accepted them in his mind. "O descendant of the Bharata lineage!"[117] Having heard the words of his well-wishers and knowing himself to be capable, he repeatedly reflected in his mind about Rajasuya. The wise one again consulted his brothers, great-souled priests, and advisers like Dhoumya and Dvaipayana.

Yudhishtira asked, "How can this great Rajasuya, worthy of an emperor and one I wish to perform, be accomplished?" Having been thus asked by the king, they then spoke these words to Yudhishtira, with dharma in his soul. "O king! You are learned in the ways of dharma. You are worthy of performing the great sacrifice of Rajasuya." When the priests and sages uttered these words, his advisers and brothers applauded them. The immensely wise and self-controlled Partha[118], always desirous of the welfare of the worlds, thought again. A wise one who considers his powers, capacity, time, place, income, and expenditure and acts with complete deliberation, never perishes. He thought that a sacrifice begun only with his one desire might bring ruin. Carefully bearing the weight on his shoulders, his thoughts went out to Krishna Janardana, as the right person to decide the course of action. Hari, supreme in all the worlds, is immeasurable, mighty-armed, and without birth, born

---

115 The six types of sacrificial fires are named agnishtoma, kshatradhriti, vyushti, dviratri, saptapeya and saptadashapeya.
116 That is, there is no need to wait for any prescribed date. Depending on one's powers, the sacrifice can be started immediately.
117 We must note that Vaishampayana is addressing Janamejaya.
118 Yudhishtira.

among men only because of his own wishes. His feats rival those of the gods and there is nothing that is not the consequence of his deeds. There is nothing that he cannot bear. Thus it was that Yudhishtira thought of Krishna. Having arrived at this conclusion, Partha Yudhishtira swiftly sent a messenger to one who was like his preceptor and the preceptor of all beings.

Riding a swift chariot, the messenger soon reached the Yadavas and the Dvaraka-residing Krishna in Dvaravati. Hearing that Yudhishtira was eager to see him, Krishna was also eager to see him and went to Indraprastha with Indrasena[119]. Travelling through many countries on the swift mounts, Janardana reached Partha in Indraprastha. Dharmaraja showed him homage in his house, like to a brother. So did Bhima. With a gladdened heart, Krishna then went to see his father's sister Kunti. After that, he sported himself with his beloved well-wisher, Arjuna, and like a preceptor, was worshipped by the twins. After he had rested himself in that pleasant place for some time and was refreshed, Dharmaraja came to him and told him about his plans. Yudhishtira said, "O Krishna! I wish to perform Rajasuya. But it cannot be performed merely through my wishing it. You are omniscient. You are the one in whom everything is possible and you are the one who is worshipped everywhere.

---

119 Yudhishtira's charioteer and clearly the one who was sent as a messenger.

Jayarthashastra

The king who is the lord of everything can perform Rajasuya. O Krishna! My well-wishers have said that I should perform it. But my final decision will certainly align with what you say. Out of friendship, some do not notice faults. Out of a desire for riches, some say that which is pleasant to hear. Some consider that to be the best course of action which brings them self-gain. It is often seen that people's advice is like this. You alone are above all motives, beyond desire and anger. You should tell me that which is supreme, for the welfare of the worlds."

Krishna said, "O great king! Because of all your qualities, you are capable of performing Rajasuya. O descendant of the Bharata lineage! Though you know everything, I shall tell you something. Those who are known as kshatriyas in this world are remnants from kshatriyas who were exterminated by Jamadagni Parashurama. O lord of the earth! O bull among the Bharata lineage! You know about the rules and the authority of words those kshatriyas established to decide lineage. All the kings and all the hierarchies of kshatriyas on this earth claim descent from Aila[120] and Ikshvaku[121]. O king! O bull among the Bharata lineage! Know that the kings from Aila's lineage and those from Ikshvaku's lineage constitute one hundred and one dynasties. O great king! The descendants of Yayati[122] and Bhoja[123] are also great in number and qualities and extend in the four directions. They and their prosperity are worshipped everywhere by the kshatriyas. "However, after having enjoyed the middle kingdom[124], a king named Chaturyu[125], one of the one hundred and one dynasties, wished to create dissension among them. Jarasandha has inherited the empire by birth and that king's influence extends everywhere. O king! O great king! The powerful Shishupala has gone to him like a disciple and has become his general. Vakra, the immensely strong king of Karusha, who fights with the powers of Maya, and many other immensely valorous and great-souled ones, are also under his protection. The illustrious Hamsa[126] and Dibhaka are also with the immensely valorous Jarasandha. And there are

---

120 Puruvara, the son of Ila and Budha, the first king of the lunar dynasty.

121 Son of Vaivasvata Manu and the first King of the solar dynasty.

122 A Chandravanshi king, who is considered to be the one of the ancestors of the pandavas and the yadavas.

123 A monarch from the Paramara dynasty.

124 The region around Mathur. Mathura was the land of the Yadavas and Jarasandha laid siege to it on eighteen occasions.

125 Jarasandha. Since chatura means clever, chaturyu maybe a reference jarasandha's wiliness. Jarasandha was the son of Brihadratha. He was born in two halves that were united by a she demon named Jara. Thus, the child came to be known as Jarasandha, the word sandhi meaning to join.

126 Brahmadatta, King of Sālva, had two wives. No children were born to them for several years. Brahmadatta's minister, Mitrasaha, also had no children. Mitrasaha was a brahmin and a scholar. On his advice, Brahmadatta, with his wives, went to Kailāsa and performed tapas to please Shiva to get children. As a result of ten years of rigorous tapas Shiva was pleased and blessed him that with two sons. Later his wives gave birth to two sons. The son of the eldest queen was named Hamsa and that of the second queen was named Dibhaka. At this time a son was also born to Mitrasaha, the minister by the blessing of Vishnu. That child was named Janardana.

Dantavakra[127], Karusha[128], Kalabha[129] and Meghavahana[130]. O great king! O descendant of the Bharata lineage! Bhagadatta[131] was your father's old friend. On his forehead, he wears a divine gem that is known as the supreme gem on earth. He is the one who punished the two Yavana[132] kings Mura and Naraka and now, with unlimited powers like Varuna, is the king of the west.

Though he has lowered his head[133] through his speech and especially his deeds, his heart actually holds affection for you, like a father does. Your brave maternal uncle, Purujit, the extender of the Kuru lineage and the scorcher of his enemies, rules in the south-west extremities of the earth and is the only king who is affectionately loyal to you. Likewise, the evil king of the Chedis[134], whom I did not kill earlier, has also gone over to Jarasandha. He is known in the world as the supreme being and out of delusion, always bears my signs[135]. There is also a king powerful in Vanga[136], Pundra, and Kirata[137], known as Vasudeva of Pundra. O great king! There is also the powerful Bhishmaka Chaturyu[138] of Bhoja, a friend of Indra's and a slayer of enemies. Through his learning and strength, he has conquered Pandya[139] and Krathakaishika. The

---

127 King of the Adhirajas.
128 Probably Vakra being repeated.
129 The name of a king.
130 Meghavahana is the king of kashmira mentioned in the Mahabharata.
131 Bhagadatta was the king of Pragjyotisha and the son of Narakasura.
132 Greek. More correctly, Ionian.
133 To Jarasandha.
134 Shishupala.
135 There was a Vasudeva of Pundra who was known as Vasudeva and also sported Krishna's signs. He is referred to a little later. In the text, Vasudeva of Pundra's crimes are ascribed incorrectly to Shishupala, though the commonality is that both were Krishna's enemies.
136 The eastern part of Bengal.
137 Kiratas are mountainous tribes who lived through hunting.
138 This is not Jarasandha (Jarasandha was referred to as Chaturyu previously), but a different Chaturyu.
139 A kingdom in South India, which is located near Tirunelveli today. The kingdom was located near the mountain Malaya and the river Tamraparni.

valorous Ahriti is his brother and is like Jamadagni Rama in battle. They also serve the king of Magadha[140]. We are his relatives[141] and always do what is agreeable to him. But though we honour him, he doesn't honour us and always does what is disagreeable to us. O king! Without bearing in mind his lineage and his strength, he has only seen Jarasandha's blazing fame and has placed himself under him. O lord! Out of fear for Jarasandha, the eighteen branches of the northern Bhojas have fled to the west and so have the Shurasenas, the Bhadrakaras, the Bodhas, the Shalvas, the Patachcharas, the Sustharas, the Sukuttas, the Kunindas, and the Kuntis. The kings of the Shalveyas, together with their brothers and attendants, the southern Panchalas, and the eastern Koshalas from the Kunti region have also fled. Out of oppressive fear for Jarasandha, the Matsyas and the Samnyastapadas have left the north in terror and fled to the south. All the Panchalas have abandoned their own kingdoms and fled in all directions. "'Sometime earlier, Kamsa[142], mindless in folly, oppressed his relatives and married the two daughters of Brihadratha's son[143], making them his queens. They are named Asti and Prapti and are Sahadeva's younger sisters.

Strengthened by this alliance, that foolish one oppressed his relatives and became superior to all of them, though this brought him great ignominy. The evil-hearted one then oppressed the elders among the Bhoja kings and in a desire to save their relatives,they concluded an alliance with us. I served my relatives by marrying off Ahuka's daughter, Sutanu, to Akrura[144]. Then, with Samkarshana[145] acting as my second, I killed Kamsa and Sunama, with Balarama's assistance. O king! Though that immediate danger was averted, Jarasandha rose up in arms against us. The eighteen branches of the Yadavas

---

140 This is Jarasandha. Magadha is the present day southern part of Bihar.
141 Bhojas are a line of the Yadavas.
142 Kamsa is the king of Mathura and the son of Ugrasena. Devaki, his cousin is the mother of Krishna.
143 Kamsa married Jarasandha's two daughters.
144 Akrura is Krishna's uncle.
145 Balarama is Samkarshana.

consulted among themselves. Even if one killed with mighty weapons that can kill a hundred at a time[146], one would not be able to kill him in three hundred years, because he had two supreme warriors named Hamsa and Dibhaka.

They were the strongest of the strong, with power like that of the immortals. When the valorous Jarasandha was united with these two brave warriors, there was no one in the three worlds who could vanquish them. Such was my view. O supremely wise among wise ones! This was not only my view. It was the view of all the kings who exist. O king! The great king famous as Hamsa was engaged in battle for eighteen days. O descendant of the Bharata lineage! A rumour spread that Hamsa had been killed. On hearing that Hamsa had been killed, Dibhaka decided that he could not continue to live in this world without Hamsa. He drowned himself in the Yamuna and, in this way, met his death. When Hamsa, the vanquisher of enemy cities, heard the news about Dibhaka, he too immersed himself in the Yamuna and drowned. O bull among the Bharata lineage When King Jarasandha heard about their deaths in the water, he left Shurasena[147] and returned to his city.

When that enemy-killing king retreated, we were delighted and began to live happily in Mathura again. But the lotus-eyed wife of Kamsa, Jarasandha's daughter, went to her father, the king of Magadha. O lord of kings! O destroyer of enemies! She repeatedly urged him to kill her husband's killer. O great king! We remembered the advice we had given ourselves at the earlier council. O lord of men! Distracted at heart, we fled. O king! We divided our great riches into small portions and out of fear for him, fled separately, with our riches, kin, and relatives. After thinking about this, we sought refuge in the western directions. O king! There is a beautiful city known as Kushasthali[148], adorned

---

146 The text uses the expression shatadha, which is a weapon that can kill a hundred at a time. More common is the expression shataghni, which is also a weapon that can kill a hundred (shata) at a time.
147 One of the names of Mathura.
148 Dvaravati.

by Mount Raivata[149]. We began to live there. We repaired its fortifications so that it became impregnable even to the gods. It was not just the bulls among the Vrishnis, even the women were capable of fighting from there. O killer of enemies! Without any fear, we now live there. O tiger among the Kuru lineage! When we look at the entry to that mountain, known as Madhavitirtha, we Madhavas have found supreme happiness[150].

With our strength, we were capable of withstanding Jarasandha's oppression.

But we have resolved to seek refuge with you. Our habitation is three yojanas deep and extends for three yojanas. At intervals of one yojana, there are one hundred gates and the portals are guarded by brave and valorous kshatriyas from the eighteen branches[151]. There are eighteen thousand warriors in our lineage. Ahuka has one hundred sons and each of them has three hundred more. Charudeshna and his brother[152], Chakradeva, Satyaki, I myself, Rohini's son[153], Samba who matches Shouri[154] in battle—these are the seven atirathas[155]. O king! Now listen to the others—Kritavarma, Anadhrishti, Samika, Samitinjaya, Kahva, Shanku, and Nidanta, these seven are Maharathas. The old king Andhakabhoja and his two sons make ten[156]. They are brave, capable of destroying the worlds, valorous, and endowed with immense strength. They have now remembered the middle country[157] and live there, among the Vrishnis. O supreme among the Bharata lineage! O descendant of the Bharata

---

149 Raivata is also known as Raivataka.
150 The Yadavas are descended from Madhu and are known as Madhavas. Madhavitirtha is the same as Raivata and probably means the tirtha of the Madhavas, though Madhavatirtha would have been more appropriate.
151 The eighteen branches of the Yadavas.
152 Pradyumna, the son of Rukmini and Krishna.
153 Balarama.
154 Both Krishna and Balarama are referred to as Shouri. Since, Krishna is the speaker, Balarama is being addressed here.
155 An warrior who is unrivalled in battle.
156 There are thus ten maharathas.
157 The middle country is the region around Mathura.

Jayārthashastra

lineage! You alone possess the qualities of becoming a universal emperor. You are capable of becoming the sovereign of the kshatriyas.

O king! But in my view, you are incapable of performing the Rajasuya as long as the immensely powerful Jarasandha is alive. He has conquered and imprisoned all the kings in Girivraja[158], the way a lion imprisons giant elephants in a cavern in that king of mountains[159]. That king Jarasandha wishes to sacrifice the lords of the earth. It was after worshipping Mahadeva that he defeated the kings on the field of battle. After having defeated the vanquished kings and their followers, he took them in fetters to his city and built a prison for men. Out of fear for Jarasandha, we too have had to abandon Mathura and have fled to the city of Dvaravati. If you wish to perform the sacrifice, seek to set them free and kill Jarasandha. O descendant of the Kuru lineage! Without this, your sacrifice cannot commence. This alone can lead to Rajasuya. This is my view. Do you think otherwise? After reflecting on everything yourself and on cause and effect, tell us what is appropriate."

Yudhishtira said, "Because you are wise, you have said what no one else could have said. No one can be seen on earth who dispels doubts the way you do. In each and every household, there are kings who do that which is for the welfare of their own. But none of them has attained the status of emperor, because the title of emperor encompasses everything. One who knows the power of others does not praise himself. He who is praised in comparison with others is worshipped. The earth is large and extensive and covered with many gems. It is by travelling far that one gets to know what is best. I consider tranquillity to be supreme, because from that freedom follows. I do not think the highest goal can be attained if I begin this rite. The wise ones who are born in every lineage know this. Sometimes, one among them will become supreme."

Bhima said, "A king who has no enterprise is like an anthill. One who tries to rule a stronger one without a plan is weak. But if the plan is right, even a

---

158 Jarasandha's capital in Maghadha.
159 In this context, the Himalayas.

weak and enterprising king can defeat a strong enemy and attain goals that bring one's welfare. There is a plan in Krishna, strength in me, and victory in Partha Dhananjaya. Like three sacrificial fires, we will consume Magadha[160]."

Krishna said, "A child grasps, without understanding the consequences of the action. Therefore, an enemy of immature understanding is not tolerated. We have heard that five have become emperors—Youvanashva by eliminating taxes, Bhagiratha through protection[161], Kartavirya through the power of his austerities, the lord Bharata through his power, and Marutta through his wealth. Know that in accordance with the principles of dharma and artha, Brihadratha's son Jarasandha is now the one to be punished. One hundred and one dynasties of kings have failed to accept his suzerainty and he, therefore, claims his empire through force. Kings who possess jewels offer him homage. Since he has been evil from childhood, he is not content even with that. He uses force to conquer foremost men and kings who have been anointed. Not a single man can be seen who does not offer him tribute. Thus has he brought under his power those kings, who number almost one hundred. How can a weaker king advance on him with hostile intent? How can those kings, who have been cleaned and washed like animals in Pashupati's house[162], be happy with their fate? It has been said that a kshatriya is honoured when he is killed by weapons. Why should we then not collectively oppose the Magadha? Jarasandha has already brought under his sway eighty-six kings and waits for the others to complete his cruel act[163]. He who obstructs him from accomplishing this will obtain blazing fame. He who defeats Jarasandha will certainly become emperor."

---

160 Jarasandha, the king of Maghadha.
161 That is, through protecting his subjects.
162 Pashupati is Shiva, the lord of animals. The sense is that the imprisoned kings have been prepared like sacrificial animals.
163 Jarasandha is waiting for the tally of imprisoned kings to become one hundred, which is when he will sacrifice them.

Yudhishtira said, "Intent on my selfish interest of becoming an emperor, how can I force you to go out, depending on strength and courage alone? Bhima and Arjuna are my eyes and you, Janardana, are my mind. What kind of life will be left for me without my eyes and my mind? When you have met Jarasandha's invincible and valorous forces, exhaustion alone will defeat you. What will your efforts serve? There is disaster if the opposite of what is intended becomes the outcome. Listen to my thoughts. I think it best to always refrain from this course of action. My heart is against it. The Rajasuya is too difficult to accomplish."

Vaishampayana said, 'Partha[164], who had obtained the supreme bow, the two inexhaustible quivers, the chariot, the pennant, and the sabha[165], now spoke these words to Yudhishtira. "O king! I have obtained the bow, weapons, arrows, valour, allies, land, fame, and strength. Though they are desired, it is difficult to achieve them. Those who are learned always praise the greatness of noble lineage. But nothing equals power and nothing pleases me as much as valour. What purpose is served if one is born in noble lineage, but has no valour? A kshatriya's livelihood is always defeat[166]. He who has valour, but lacks all other qualities, will still vanquish his enemies. What purpose is served if one possesses all the qualities, but lacks valour? All qualities exist in nascent form in valour. Mental concentration, enterprise and fortune are the causes of victory. One who possesses the forces, but is careless, does not succeed and is not favoured by fortune. It is because of this that a powerful one perishes when confronted with his foes. Misery encompasses those without strength and also strong ones who are deluded. A king who wishes to attain victory must forsake both these routes to destruction. There is nothing that can surpass the act of destroying Jarasandha and freeing the kings when achieving the sacrifice. If we do not attempt this, we will certainly be regarded as bereft of all qualities. We certainly possess the qualities. Why do you doubt our

---

164 Arjuna.
165 Arjuna obtained the sabha in the sense that it was because of him that Maya built the assembly hall.
166 Of his enemies.

qualities? Red garments are easily available to those who later wish to obtain peace of mind[167]. But wishing to see you emperor first, we will therefore fight with the enemy."

Vasudeva said, "Arjuna has exhibited the mind of one born in the Bharata lineage, especially of one who is Kunti's son. We do not know the time of our death, whether it will be night or day. Nor have we heard of anyone attaining immortality by avoiding battle. For any man, the act that pleases the heart is one of attacking enemies in accordance with principles that are laid down. Any encounter guided by good policy attains success. However, if both sides are equal, there is uncertainty[168]. But equality between the two never happens. If that is the case, why should we not adopt a policy to approach the enemy and destroy him like a river destroying a tree? We will cover our weaknesses and exploit those of the enemy. It is the policy of the intelligent not to attack stronger enemies with battle formations and armies. This appeals to me too. If we can enter the enemy's abode without armies, attack him, and attain our objective, we will not be blamed. He alone enjoys eternal royal fortune, like the soul of all beings. But if he perishes, his forces perish. Desiring to free our relatives, even if we are killed by his survivors after we have killed him in battle, we will attain heaven."

Yudhishtira asked, "O Krishna! Who is this Jarasandha? What is his valour and his prowess that he has not been burnt up when he touched you, like a moth before a flame?"

Krishna replied, "O king! Listen to Jarasandha's valour and prowess. Learn why he has been spared by us, though he has caused us displeasure in many ways. There was a king named Brihadratha. He was the powerful ruler and lord of Magadha. He was proud in battle and had three akshouhinis[169]. He was

---

167 By becoming ascetics.
168 That is, if both sides are guided by good policy.
169 An akshouhini is an army and consists of 21,870 chariots, 21,870 elephants, 65,610 horses and 109,350 infantrymen.

handsome, valorous, fortunate, and extremely powerful. His body always had sacrificial marks and he had the appearance of a second Shakra. He was like the sun's energy, like the earth in forbearance, like the destroyer Yama in his anger, and like Vaishravana[170] in prosperity. Like the rays of the sun, the entire earth was covered by qualities his noble lineage brought. That immensely valorous one married the twin daughters of the king of Kashi, blessed with beauty and riches. That bull among men had a contract in the presence of his wives that he would love them equally and not show preferences. This king then shone with his beloved and suitable wives, like an elephant with two she-elephants.

Between them, the lord of the earth was resplendent, like the embodied ocean between the Ganga and the Yamuna. His youth passed away, immersed in pleasures. But no son was born to him to carry forward his lineage, though he performed many auspicious rites, oblations, and sacrifices, to obtain a son. But the best of kings did not obtain a son to extend his lineage. One day, he heard that Chandakoushika, the son of the great-souled Kakshivat, descended from Goutama, had become tired of ascetic pursuits. Roaming as he willed, he had come and had sought shelter under a tree. The king and his wives satisfied him with offerings of all kinds of jewels. That supreme among rishis was always truthful and devoted to the truth.

He spoke to the king thus. 'O king! I am satisfied with you, you who are devoted to your vows. Ask for a boon.'

Brihadratha and his wives bowed down before him. In a voice choked with tears of despair, since there was no prospect of setting eyes on a son, Brihadratha said, 'O illustrious lord! I am about to give up my kingdom and depart for the austerities of the forest. I am unfortunate. What will I do with a boon or with the kingdom?' On hearing this, the sage, seated under the shade of a mango tree, controlled his senses and began to meditate.

---

170 Son of Vishrava. In this context, Kubera.

A mango fell into the lap of the seated sage. It was whole, without holes and without being touched by the beaks of birds. That supreme among sages picked it up, and pronouncing a mantra over it, handed the king that unblemished fruit, as means of obtaining a son.

The immensely wise great sage spoke to the king. 'O king! Depart. Your wish has been fulfilled. O lord of men! Return. O bull among the Bharata lineage!'

Remembering the contract, that supreme of kings gave the single fruit to his two wives. Dividing the fruit into two equal parts, the beautiful ones ate it. The sage always spoke the truth and what he had said was certain. They both conceived as a result of eating the fruit. On seeing them, the king became extremely happy. After some time, when the appropriate time arrived, the two queens gave birth to two half-bodies. Each had one eye, one arm, one leg, half a stomach, half a face, and half a buttock. At the sight of these half-bodies, the two of them were miserable and trembled. The anxious sisters consulted each other. In great misery, they abandoned the two half-bodies, though they had life in them. The two midwives carefully wrapped up those imperfectly born half-bodies and left the inner quarters through a back gate.

Discarding them, they returned in haste. 'O tiger among men! There was a rakshasa woman named Jara and she noticed them, where they had been thrown at a crossroad. She lived on flesh and blood.'

Driven by destiny, that rakshasa woman united the two bodies, as it would become easier to carry. As soon as the two halves were united, they became one body and a brave child emerged. The rakshasa woman's eyes widened in amazement. She was no longer able to carry the child, whose body was as hard as a vajra. The child balled his copper-red hands into fists, inserted them in his mouth, and began to roar, like a monsoon cloud heavy with rain. Extremely alarmed at this sound, the inmates of the inner quarters rushed out, together with the king. Weak and jaded, though their breasts were full of milk, the two queens suddenly came out and reclaimed their son.

On seeing them in that condition and on seeing the king, who was so desirous of obtaining a son, and also on seeing the strong child, the rakshasa woman reflected, 'I live in the kingdom of a king who desires to obtain a son. Therefore, I should not carry off this small child, like a strip of cloud hides the sun.'

Assuming human form, she spoke to the lord of men. The rakshasa said, 'O Brihadratha! This is your son. Accept him from me as a gift. He was born in the wombs of your two wives, as a result of the boon granted by the brahmana. He was abandoned by the midwives, but has been saved by me.'

At that, on obtaining the son, the beautiful daughters of the king of Kashi sprinkled him with the milk that was gushing out. Having seen all this and understood, the king was delighted. In human form, with a complexion like that of pure gold, the rakshasa woman did not look like a rakshasa at all. The king asked, 'Who are you, as golden as the womb of a lotus? You have given me my son. O fortunate one! You appear to me like a goddess. Please speak.'

The rakshasa said, 'O lord of kings! O fortunate one! I am a rakshasa woman named Jara, who can assume any form at will. Worshipped by everyone, I live happily in your habitation. O righteous one! O king! Therefore, I have always thought about offering you a favour in return. It so happened that I saw the two half-bodies of your son. On my accidentally uniting them, the son surfaced. O great king! This was because of your good fortune. I was only the instrument.'"

Krishna said, "Having said this, she disappeared, then and there. The king picked up the boy and entered his own house. The king then performed all the necessary rites for the child. He commanded that a great festival should be held in Magadha in honour of the rakshasa. The father was the equal of Prajapati[171] and bestowed a name on him. Since he had been united by Jara, he

---

171 Brahma.

came to be known as Jarasandha[172]. The son of the king of Magadha grew up and became endowed with great energy, large and strong like a fire into which oblations have been offered.

After some time had passed, Chandakoushika once again came to Magadha. Delighted at his arrival, Brihadratha went out with his advisers, subjects, wives, and son. The king showed him homage with water for washing the feet, gifts due to a guest and water to wash his mouth. Then he offered him his son and his kingdom.

The illustrious rishi accepted the king's worship and with a happy heart, told the one from Magadha[173], 'O king! Everything is known to me through my divine sight. O Indra among kings! Listen to what will happen to your son. No king will be able to equal this valorous one in valour. Like the currents of rivers make no impression on mountains, weapons hurled by the gods will cause him no pain. He will blaze forth over the heads of all those who have been consecrated and rob their light the way the sun shines over the lights of stars.

Like moths to a flame, kings who possess large armies and mounts will meet their destruction before him. Like the lord of rivers and rivulets receives swollen river water during the monsoon, he will seize the combined prosperity of all the kings. Like the earth, the abode of all crops, extensively supports good and evil, with immense strength, he will justly uphold the four varnas. All the rulers of men will be under his subjugation, just as all beings are subservient to the breath of life in their bodies. This Magadha, immensely stronger than everything in all the worlds, will witness with his own eyes Rudra Mahadeva Hara, the destroyer of Tripura[174].'

---

172 The root sandha (as in sandhi) means union or junction.
173 Brihadratha. A few lines later, Magadha will also be used for Jarasandha.
174 Rudra, Mahadeva and Hara are different names for Shiva. Tripura was a collection of three (tri) cities (pura), constructed by Maya for the demons. Tripura was in the sky and the three cities were made out of gold, silver and iron. Shiva

Having said this, the sage thought about all the acts he had to perform and dismissed King Brihadratha. The ruler of Magadha returned to his city and instated Jarasandha.

After instating Jarasandha, King Brihadratha, followed by his two wives, then left for the forest to lead a life of austerities. After his father and two mothers had retired to the forest for austerities, Jarasandha subjugated the kings with his valour. After a long time of austerities in the forest, King Brihadratha and his wives attained heaven by virtue of their austerities. He had Hamsa and Dibhaka, incapable of being killed with any weapons. They were best among the intelligent in their counsel and skilled in the art of war. I have already told you about these mighty ones earlier. My view is that these three were more than a match for the three worlds. Such is the one whom the powerful Kukuras, Andhakas, and Vrishnis[175] ignored because that was the right policy."

Vasudeva said, "Hamsa and Dibhaka have fallen. Kamsa and his advisers have been killed. The time has therefore arrived for Jarasandha's killing. He is incapable of being defeated in battle by all the gods and the demons. But we understand he is capable of being vanquished in a battle of breath. Policy exists in me. Power exists in Bhima. Valour exists in Arjuna. We will overcome him like three fires. If that lord of men is confronted by the three of us alone, there is no doubt that he will engage one of us in a duel. Out of contempt for the worlds and his pride in himself, he will certainly challenge Bhimasena to a duel. The mighty-armed and immensely strong Bhimasena is his match like death is of the worlds that confront their destruction. If your heart knows and if you have confidence in me, then, without losing any more time, entrust Bhimasena and Arjuna to me."

---

burnt them down. Tripura is also the name of the demon-king who ruled over these cities.

175 All names of Yadava tribes.

Vaishampayana said, 'Having been thus addressed by that illustrious one and on seeing Bhima and Partha standing there with smiles on their faces, Yudhishtira replied, "O Achyuta! Do not speak to me in that fashion. You are the lord of the Pandavas. We seek refuge with you. O Govinda! Everything that you have said is right. You never lead those whom Lakshmi has forsaken. As I follow your instruction, Jarasandha is dead. The kings have been set free. I have achieved the Rajasuya. O supreme among men! You are the one who acts fast. Act so that I can accomplish this task for the world. Like a miserable and diseased man and like one without dharma, kama, and artha, I have no incentive to live without the three of you. There is no Partha without Shouri and there is no Shouri without Pandava. It is my view that there is nothing in the world that cannot be conquered by the two Krishnas.

This handsome Vrikodara is supreme among all strong ones. What can this immensely famous and valorous one not accomplish when he is with the two of you? When led properly, forces perform supreme deeds. The learned say that forces without skilled leadership are blind and benumbed. The wise always conduct water to places that are low. Those who are wise always lead their forces to places where there are holes. For accomplishing our task, we will therefore seek refuge with Govinda, who is a man famous in the worlds and is knowledgeable about policy. Krishna's strength comes from his wisdom and he knows the method and the means. If one wishes to accomplish one's objectives, one should place him at the forefront. For the accomplishment of our objective, let Partha Arjuna follow Krishna, the best of the Yadavas, and let Bhima follow Dhananjaya. Policy, victory, and strength will find success in valour." Having been thus addressed, the three brothers, Varshneya and the two Pandavas left for Magadha.[176]

Root Cause Analysis And The Ishikawa Diagram

Root cause analysis (RCA) is the derivative process of arriving at the root cause of a problem to thus identify appropriate solutions. RCA is effective because it seeks to systematically prevent and solve underlying issues rather than just treating ad hoc symptoms and putting out fires. RCA can be performed with a collection of principles, techniques, and methodologies that can all be leveraged to identify the base reason behind an event or trend. Looking beyond superficial cause and effect, RCA can show where processes or systems failed or caused an issue in the first place.

A fishbone diagram is a visualisation tool to categorise the potential causes of a problem. Typically used for root cause analysis, a fishbone diagram is represented visually with the problem in the middle of the diagram (the spine of the fish skeleton), then the several categories of causes are laid out in off-shooting branches from the main line (the rib bones of the fish skeleton). These

---

176 The Mahabharata 4 Translated by Bibek Debroy

causes are further broken down into potential sub-causes until the source of the issue is found.

From the story, the problem faced by Yudhishtira is mentioned on the spine of the fish. In this case, Jarasandha is the problem. Later all the causes for the problem faced by Yudhishtira are written on the rib bones of the fish skeleton. The rectangular boxes at the edge of the rib bones depict the main causes. The branches from the main causes depict the sub-causes.

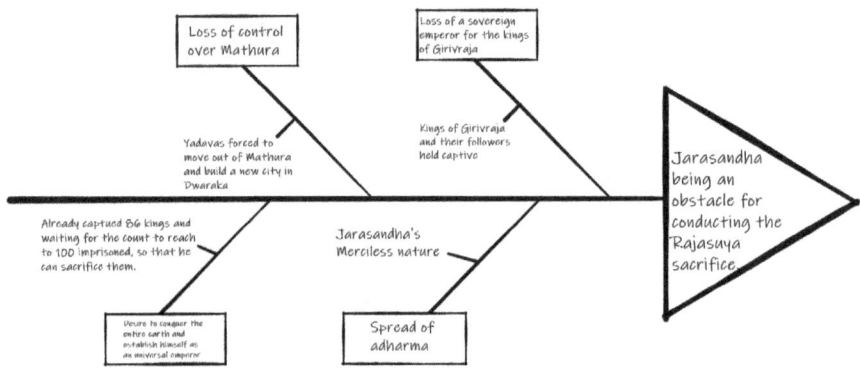

Note: Read the problem statement in the head of the fish, and asking yourself the question of, "Why is Jarasandha a problem?", now read the main causes and then analyse the sub causes to arrive at a solution. Try to predict your own solution to Yudhishtira's predicament before reading the next part of this chapter.

Based on the root cause analysis, the following solution was proposed to deal with Yudhishtira's predicament.

Solution:

PROBLEM	CURRENT CONTROL	RECOMMENDATIONS
Jarasandha is an obstacle for performing the Rajasuya.	Krishna advises Yudhishtira to systematically analyse the predicament of Jarasandha and reflect upon the subsequent causes and effects. The objective of this systematic analysis is to arrive at an appropriate decision.	Krishna strongly recommends the slaying of Jarasandha to eliminate the obstacle for the Rajasuya sacrifice.

Hanuman's Goal: A Determinant for the Shift in Supply

'Sattva Pareeksha (The test of goodness)'… the fourth lesson in I PUC Sanskrit

As my teacher began the lesson, I was instantly transported to a childhood memory. It was a rainy night and I was struggling to sleep. The thunder kept frightening me with its rageful rumbling. Each time I tried to sleep, the sound disturbed me with its chaotically-spaced recurrences. My grandpa, as a mute spectator observed the cold war between my sleep and the merciless thunder outside… he decided to narrate a story. The story acted as a means to efficiently divert my attention from the thunder.

He began by saying, "Once, Draupadi saw a beautiful flower. It was called the Saugandhika Pushpa…" As I heard my teacher explaining each shloka in the chapter, every tiny detail of my grandpa's narration came alive before my eyes.

I fell in love with the story again… Even though I knew every inch of the story in magnanimous detail, the feeling of curiosity persisted. 'Sattva Pareeksha' was indeed a passage to my childhood.

The Pandavas visited many holy tirthas[177] during their twelve years of exile. As part of their journey, the Pandavas visited the holy kshetra[178] of Badari. They spent six nights in the ashrama[179] of Nara and Narayana[180]. The hermitage of Nara and Narayana lodged many ecstatic trees and flowers. Once, Draupadi noticed a divine lotus with one thousand petals touching the ground carried by the northeast wind. The flower seemed to embrace the ground in perfect synchrony. As the fragrance of this divine flower wafted in the air, Draupadi was instantly captivated by its redolence and she propelled towards the lotus. As she moved closer towards that flower, the redolence kept intensifying. Now, all that Draupadi's senses could contemplate was the fragrance and the intricate layers of petals of the flower. As she was in close proximity to the flower, her shadow caressed the flower first followed by her hand. She picked up the flower gently without disturbing the sophisticated feather-like petals. The delicate flower settled in her hand as she approached Bhima.

With a natural smile painted on her face, owing to the fragrance and the touch of the flower, Draupadi exclaimed, "O Bhima! Look at this beautiful flower. It has seduced me with its heavenly fragrance. I desire to present this to Yudhishtira as a token of my love and affection for him. O benevolent one! If you consider me to be your beloved, then bring me this flower in large numbers, so that I can take them back to our hermitage at Kamyaka[181]".

At Panchali's[182] request, Bhima promptly journeyed in the direction of the northeast wind, hoping to find many more flowers for Panchali, whom he loved immensely. Holding a mace and a bow decorated with gold patterns

---

177 Holy tirthas - Pilgrimage sites
178 Kshetra - Area
179 Ashrama - Hermitage
180 Nara and Narayana - A Hindu deity pair considered to be a twin-brother avatar of Lord Vishnu entrusted with the task of protecting dharma.
181 Kamyaka - Name of a forest where the Pandavas spent their exile.
182 Panchali - Name of Draupadi since she belonged to the kingdom of Panchal.

and venomous arrows, Vrikodara[183], the extremely powerful one climbed the mountain of Gandhamadana[184]. The peaks of Gandhamadana were sacred and frequently visited by Kinnaras[185]. Densely covered with trees, creepers, and foliages of all kinds complementing the humming of the honeybees and cuckoos, the woods of Gandhamadana enchanted Bhima. He experienced fatigue, owing to his long tiresome journey through the dark yet enticing grooves. However, at intervals, the cool breeze, his father rejuvenated him and he navigated through regions populated by the yakshas[186], gandharvas[187], gods, and brahmarshis. As he sped through this region, the wives of the yakshas and the gandharvas stared at him in complete awe as though they had witnessed Lord Indra himself searching for his wife Sachi in these woods of the great mountain of Gandhamadana. Kounteya Bhima continued his desperate search for the flower.

After hours of wandering in the forest, Bhima suddenly recounted the misery caused to his family by the evil-minded Duryodhana to himself. As he reminded himself of the terrible incidents that had unfolded in their lives, a feeling of apprehension distracted him. He thought to himself, "Arjuna is in heaven, while I am on the lookout for this flower. Yudhishtira is all alone with the twins and Krishna. Succumbing to his affection for Nakula and

---

183 Vrikodara - Vrika means wolf and Udara means belly. Since Bhima was an insatiable eater he is called a wolf-eater.
184 Gandhmadana - Name of the mountain.
185 Kinnaras - The attendants of Kubera. They are represented as mythical beings with a human figure and the head of a horse or with a horse's body and the head of a man. They are described as celestial choristers and musicians who dwell in the paradise of Kuvera on Kailāsa. They are called Aśvamukhas, Turaṅgavaktras, "horse-faced" and Mayus.
186 Yakshas - A broad class of nature-spirits, usually benevolent, but sometimes mischievous or capricious, connected with water, fertility, trees, the forest, treasure and wilderness.
187 Gandharvas - Male nature spirits and husbands of the Apsaras. Some are part animals, usually a bird or horse. They have superb musical skills. They guard the Soma and play beautiful music for the gods in their palaces. Gandharvas are frequently depicted as singers in the court of the gods.

Sahadeva, Yudhishtira will not send them to search for me. I need to complete Panchali's task at the earliest and return to the hermitage to protect my wife, brothers, and the noble brahmanas".

Holding onto this thought, Vrikodara stormed through the foliages of the mountain at the speed of Garuda[188]. The entire forest trembled at the speed of the Vayuputra[189]. His feet stamped the earth with immense force as he continued his journey. The birds, lions, tigers, and elephants fled in all directions alarmed by Bhima's elephant-like steps.

Having reached the slopes of the peak, Bhima caught sight of a plantain grove. The grove housed golden tinted plantain trees romancing with the sun rays forming canopies of warm yet escapes of sunlight. Bhima inevitably tore across this heavenly grove, frantic to find that flower. His patience wore out ounce by ounce. His thumping footsteps encouraged the rage in him. With one angry roar, Bhima frightened thousands of birds, which rose to the sky in groups, flapping their wings to drain the extra water. As the drops of water touched Bhima's face, it seemed as though these drops evaporated due to the heat of his anger. However, Bhima followed these birds and discovered a water-body hidden between the groves of plantain trees.

The still waters adorned with beautiful lilies calmed Bhima's anger. As he entered the waters, Bhima's anger seemed to drain into the waters of that lake. Having relaxed in the lake for a while, Bhima hurried into the forest. As he entered the forest, Kounteya Bhima, overcome by immense rage, blew his conch shell. The sound of his conch shell accompanied by his roar echoed throughout the forest of Gandhamadana. The echo frightened the sleeping lions and elephants.

---

188 Garuda - The mount of Vishnu.
189 Vayuputra - Name of Bhima. Bhima is called Vayuputra because he is the son of the Wind-God.

Amid the plantain trees, Hanuman, the brother of Bhima, was asleep. Upon hearing the majestic sound made by his brother, Hanuman simply yawned. He whipped the earth below him with his long tail. The sound was as powerful as the vajra of Indra. Just like the tremor of the vajra spread in all directions, the sound made by Hanuman's tail reverberated throughout the mountains of Gandhamadana. As Bhima felt the reverberation, he was eager to find the source. He wandered around the maze-like plantain grove and finally encountered a large monkey lying in the middle of the plantation.

He was difficult to look at, like a flash of lightning. He was yellow, like lightning. His short and stout head rested on the crook of his arms. Because his shoulders were so large, the waist above his hips seemed to be slender. His tail was bent at the end and covered with long hair. It was erect and dazzling, like a banner. His lips were red and his tongue had a complexion of copper. His ears were red and his brows moved. His face was like the moon with its beam and his teeth were round and sharp. Above it, the extensive mane looked like a mass of Ashoka flowers. The immensely radiant one was lying down amid golden plantain trees. His form was resplendent as blazing fire and he looked fearlessly with eyes that were as yellow as honey.[190]

Bhima advanced towards the monkey and roared with all his effort to warn him of his powers. The monkey, however unafraid of the Kounteya's[191] ghastly roar, partly opened his eyes and smiled mockingly. He addressed Bhima in a gravelly tone. He said, "O powerful one! I am old and ill. I was resting in this plantain grove, embracing the warmth of the sun. Why did you wake me up with your atrocious roar? Is it because of your limited intelligence that you do not consider it your dharma to respect all beings? Tell me, who are you? Why have you volunteered to a terrain shunned by your kind? From here onwards, the forest is impenetrable and only accessible by siddhas[192]. You

---

190 The Mahabharata 3 Translated by Bibek Debroy.
191 Kounteya - Bhima, the son of Kunti.
192 Siddhas - Refers to a being who has achieved a high degree of physical as well as spiritual perfection or enlightenment.

cannot survive in that forest. I am amicably advising you to treat yourself to the delicious fruits and roots here and return to the place from where you have come".

Bhimasena replied, "Who are you? I am certain that you are not an ape? Tell me the reason for your disguise. I am Pandava Bhima, son of Kunti and Pandu, born from the blessing of the wind-god Vayu". The monkey smiled and said, "I am a monkey and I request you not to journey beyond this point for your wellbeing. However, if you wish me to give you the way, then I shall". Bhima raised his voice and exclaimed, "O Monkey! I am not asking for your suggestion and opinion about my well-being. I command you to get up and grant me the right of way. If you fail, then you shall face destruction at my hands".

Hearing Bhima's warning, the ape innocently replied, "O powerful one! I am old and ill. If you wish to enter the forest, then you can jump over me and continue your journey". Bhima, after much thought, said, "O Monkey! I have learnt that the Paramatma resides in your body and to jump over it would be a sin against Him. If this was not the case, then I would have definitely jumped over your amber-yellow body, just like how my brother Hanuman crossed the ocean". The monkey turned his head slightly towards Bhima with a blank expression and asked, "O brave one! You mentioned someone named Hanuman. Who is he? Do you know him? Please enlighten me". Bhima remarked, "Hanuman is my brother. He is the best among the monkeys, an embodiment of immense intelligence, strength and valour. He is my brother and I am equal to him in his strength. Therefore, grant me the path or prepare yourself for a journey to Yama's abode".

Hanuman, who was in the form of the ape, laughed to himself. He requested, "O Kounteya! I am old and devoid of power to stand erect. It is your dharma to show compassion towards the old. Please move my tail aside". Bhima, expressing contempt for the monkey, held its tail in his left hand and tried to move it. His attempt failed. Then he tried with both his hands, but he failed.

Knitting his eyebrows, he applied his maximum strength to dislodge the tail. But, his body precipitated, his eyeballs dilated and he had failed again. Ashamed of his actions, Bhima bowed before the monkey and said, "O Noble one! Please forgive me for all my words. Reveal to me your original form. Are you a siddha, or a god, or a gandharva, or a guhyaka[193] in the form of an ape? I wish to know. Please tell me".

Hanuman replied, "I am the son of Kesari[194], the one who leapt over the ocean. Know me to be that ape called Hanuman. O brother! This forest is out of reach for mortals like you. I have therefore restrained your path. It is

---

193 Guhyakas - Described as attendants of Kubera, the god of wealth, they protect his hidden treasures. Guhyakas are believed to live in mountain caves; thus their name, "hidden ones".

194 Kesari - Kesari was a male vanara who was brave and inquisitive by nature–and a chief. He was the father of Hanuman and husband of Anjana.

in my interest for you not to be cursed by the divine beings, whose abode is this forest. However, the lake you came searching for is close-by". Bhima humbly prostrated before Hanuman and addressed him with devotion, "O Hanuman! My life is blessed as I have witnessed your original form. But, I desire for more. Please bless this brother of yours by showing that gigantic form, which you adopted to leap over the ocean". Hanuman said, "O son![195] I took that form in Tretha Yuga, but in Dvapara Yuga my body decays and it is not possible for me to take back that form".

---

195 Since Bhima is the younger brother of Hanuman, he is exhibiting paternal feelings towards him by referring to him as son.

Bhima repeatedly pleaded, "O Vayu-Putra! If you are pleased with me, please reveal your gigantic form". The best one among the monkeys smiled and assumed his gigantic form. He grew as tall as a mountain and Bhima was astonished to see his brother. Hanuman's gigantic form was so radiant that Bhima closed his eyes. He was also repeatedly delighted to see his brother's form. Hanuman then smiled and told his brother, "O Bhimasena! You can only see my gigantic form up to this limit. My body can grow infinitely as per my wish".

Although Bhima was pleased to behold his brother's gigantic form, at the same time he quivered. He folded his hands in salutation to his brother and said in a humble tone, "O Hanuman! I am fortunate to have witnessed your enormous form. But I am unable to view this feat of yours anymore as you appear like the sun. I request you to return to your original size, dear brother". Having heard his brother's request, Hanuman, the son of Kesari replied, "O Bhima! You are a strict follower of dharma. Therefore, secured by Pavana[196], you may continue your journey. That path that traverses the plantain grove will lead you to the Saugandhika forest[197], where you will find the flower. Beware! The Saugandhika forest also houses a grove of Kubera[198] under the supervision of the yakshas and rakshasas[199]. Do not commit the sin of plucking any flower yourself".

Then, the best among the monkeys shrank his body to normal size and embraced Bhima. Bhima's exhaustion was destroyed and everything was at ease. With tears in his eyes, the ape once again told Bhima in a voice that was choked and affectionate, "O brave one! Return to your abode. Do not tell anyone that I am here. Because of our brotherhood, ask for a boon. If you wish that I should go to Hastinapura and kill the low sons of Dhritarashtra, I

---

196 Pavana - Wind-God.
197 Saugandhika Forest - The forest where Bhima finds the flower that Draupadi wanted.
198 Kubera - The god of Wealth.
199 Rakshasa – Demons.

will do that. Or I will grind that city with rocks. O immensely strong one! I will perform whatever deed you desire. On hearing these words of the great-souled one, Bhima was delighted and replied to Hanuman with happiness in his heart, "O bull among apes! You have already done everything for me. O mighty-armed one! May you be fortunate. Forgive me. I desire your favours. With a protector as valorous as you, all of us Pandavas have found a protector. With your energy, all of us will triumph over our enemies." Having heard these words, Hanuman told Bhimasena, "From brotherhood and out of my well wishes towards you, I will do that which will bring you pleasure. O brave one! O mighty-armed one! When you rush into the enemy's battle formations, armed with arrows and spears, and utter a roar like that of a lion, I will add my own roars to that of yours. Seated on Vijaya's[200] flagstaff, I will let loose terrible roars that will rob the enemies of their lives." Having said this, he disappeared.[201]

---

200 Vijaya - Arjuna's name; the undefeatable.
201 The Mahabharata 3 Translated by Bibek Debroy

Shift In Supply

What do we understand by the word "supply"?

Consumers demand goods and sellers supply goods to meet the demand of the consumers. When we visit a shop to buy stationery, we are demanding stationery (goods), and the shopkeeper, providing us with this stationery is actually supplying these goods to us. The words "providing" and "supplying" are synonymous, providing being a non-economic term. Therefore, we can derive that supply is the quantity of a commodity that a seller is willing to sell at different prices over a given period.[202]

Specifically, the total quantity of a particular type of commodity offered for sale at various possible prices is called supply[203]. Now, let us extend our discussion a bit more. Remember our discussion about the stationery shopkeeper. From his behaviour as a producer, we can interpret that if given an opportunity the shopkeeper would want to sell his entire stock of stationery, however, he can only sell that quantity of stationery, which is demanded by the consumer. He cannot sell more or less of it. So, we must keep in mind that supply is the quantity that the seller wishes/ is willing to sell, not what he actually ends up selling. In other words, "Supply is the desired quantity of a commodity".

Supply has two aspects:

Individual Supply- The supply of a commodity by an individual seller for sale at different prices in the market is called individual supply.

Market Supply- The supply of a commodity by all the sellers of that commodity for sale at different prices in the market is called market supply[204].

---

202 All in One Economics CBSE Class XI
203 All in One Economics CBSE Class XI
204 All in One Economics CBSE Class XI

To understand more clearly the difference between individual and market supply, it is useful to know about a supply schedule. In economics, schedule refers to a tabular representation. The supply schedule represents various quantities of a commodity sold in the market by a seller in correspondence to the price of the commodity in a row-column format.[205]

COLUMN A	COLUMN B	COLUMN C	COLUMN D
Price of Pencil (₹)	Quantity of pencil that Firm A is willing to supply	Quantity of pencil that Firm B is willing to supply	Market supply= (Quantity supplied by Firm A) + (Quantity supplied by Firm B)
10	2	5	2+5= 7
20	4	10	4+10= 14
30	6	15	6+15= 21
40	8	20	8+20= 28

*Note: The numbers in columns B and C are random and have no mathematical relation.

From the table, COLUMN B and COLUMN C represent Individual Supply, while COLUMN D represents Market Supply.

Having already stated that supply highlights the relationship between the price of goods and the quantity supplied, the same relationship can be represented diagrammatically using a tool called a supply curve.

The supply curve defines the positive relationship between the price of a commodity in correspondence to the quantity supplied. The supply is therefore an upward sloping curve in the XY-plane. Typically, the quantity supplied is measured on the X-axis and the price on the Y-axis. Deriving from the upward slope of the supply curve, one can easily infer that a greater quantity of a commodity is supplied at higher prices as it results in higher profit for the seller. Individual Supply Curve represents the supply of an individual firm

---

205 All in One Economics CBSE Class XI

in contrast to the Market Supply Curve, which is a horizontal summation of individual supply curves.

Having realised the relationship between the price and the quantity supplied, we can relate our understanding to the law of supply,

"The Law of Supply states that other things being equal, quantity supplied increases with increase in price and decreases with decrease in price".

At this point in our discussion, you might be thinking of a question, "How about changes in supply?"

Well, supply is dynamic in nature and subject to changes depending on various factors. If supply changes due to an alteration in the price of a commodity, then the resultant change in supply is defined by the term "Movement along a supply curve". If a change in supply results from changes in any other factors apart from the price of a commodity, then such a change is given by the term "Shift in the supply curve".

Movement along the supply curve has two forms:

1. Extension in supply: When the quantity supplied increases owing to an increase in the price, there is an upward rightward movement on the supply curve called extension in supply.
2. Contraction in supply: When the quantity supplied decreases owing to a decrease in the price, then there is a downward leftward movement on the supply curve called contraction in supply.

Shift in supply curve:

The supply curve shifts to a new position on the XY-plane only if the change in supply is caused by factors other than the price. We must remember that price in this case is assumed to be constant. Always under a shift in the supply curve, two supply curves are drawn to indicate the change in position of the original supply curve.

Shift in supply curve has two forms:

1. Increase in supply: Supply curve shifts to the right when the quantity supplied increases due to a favourable change in any of the other factors excluding price. In other words, an increase in supply refers to an increased supply at the same price or the same supply at a lower price.
2. Decrease in supply: Supply curve shifts to the left when the quantity supplied decreases due to an unfavourable change in any of the other factors excluding price. In other words, a decrease in supply refers to a decreased supply at the same price or the same supply at a higher price.

What are the factors which cause a shift in supply?

Factor Name	When does the factor result in an increase in supply?	When does the factor result in a decrease in supply?
Price of related commodities	• Decreased price of substitute goods • Increased price of complementary goods	• Increased price of substitute goods • Decreased price of complementary goods
State of technology	Technological progress	Technological deterioration
Cost of production	Increase in the price of factors of production	Decrease in the prices of factors of production
Government Policy	Decreased tax rates and increased subsidies	Increased tax rates and decreased subsidies
Number of firms in the industry	Increased number of firms	Decreased number of firms

Factor Name	When does the factor result in an increase in supply?	When does the factor result in a decrease in supply?
Business Confidence/ Expectation	Positive expectation of the business regarding the sales of their products/ elevated confidence levels	Negative expectation of the business regarding the sales of their products/ diminished confidence levels
Firm's Goal	Change in firm's goal from profit maximization to sales maximization	Change in firm's goal from sales maximization to profit maximization

Note: In addition to the above-mentioned factors there could be many more factors that affect the change in supply

From the above story, it can be deduced that Hanuman is a supplier and Bhima is a consumer. Bhima demands to see Hanuman's gigantic form. Hanuman fulfills Bhima's demand by expounding his enormous form.

Furthermore, as we continue to read the story in the Tirtha-yatra Parva, we realise that Hanuman requests Bhima to ask for a boon owing to his brotherhood. Even though Hanuman urges Bhima to ask for a boon, Bhima refuses to ask for anything stating that Hanuman had already done everything for him. Bhima only asks for blessings from Anjeneya, which cannot be classified as a boon. By asking for blessings, Bhima is representing his contentment. He is satisfied at the sight of Hanuman's humongous form. In the place of bestowing one favour on Bhima, Hanuman increases his favours from one to two. Instead of just promising to add to Bhima's roar in the war, Hanuman blesses Arjuna by promising to reside on his flagstaff. Clearly, this is an increase in the supply of blessings owing to the shift in Hanuman's goal from just giving a boon to granting the maximum support to his brother. In this scenario, Bhima's contentment remains constant and doesn't affect the change in supply.

The above example of the shift in supply curve can be shown diagrammatically using the Individual Supply Curve.

Jayārthashastra

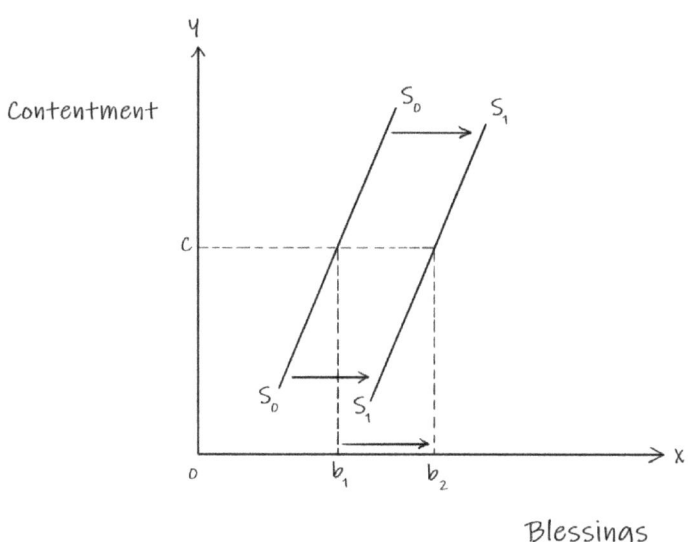

- On the X-axis, the number of blessings is measured
- On the Y-axis, Bhima's contentment is measured
- S_0S_0 represents the initial supply curve
    - the point where Hanuman agrees to add to Bhima's roar
    - In other words, at S_0S_0 Hanuman will only add to Bhima's roar in the war.
- S_1S_1 represents the new supply curve
    - Shifted from S_0S_0 due to change in Hanuman's goal
    - the point where Hanuman promises to sit on Arjuna's flagstaff
    - In other words, at S_1S_1 Hanuman will add to Bhima's roar as well as sit on Arjuna's flagstaff.
- b_1 represents the first blessing
- b_2 represents the first along with the second blessing
- C represents Bhima's contentment behaving like a price
    - In this case, it is constant

Although Bhima originally set out to find the Saugandhika Pushpa for Draupadi, his accidental encounter with Lord Hanuman turned out to be profitable for the Pandavas.

Yudhishtira's Inelastic Supply Of Dharma

"Colour is descriptive. Black and white is interpretive."

—*Elliott Erwitt*

The most iconic black and white movie I watched with my grandpa was the Telugu movie, "Pandava vanavasam" of 1965. I still remember the dialogue of Chitrasena (played by Dhulipala Seetarama Sastry) to Duryodhana (played by S. V. Ranga Rao) where he says in a majestic voice, "O Duryodhana! If you possess any shakti in you, then withstand my Maya". Whenever I hear this dialogue, the entire story of Ghosha yatra replays before my eyes from that movie. Reminiscing the magnificent acting of those evergreen stars, let us explore the story of Ghosha Yatra, but this time directed and produced by Jayarthashastra. Hopefully, it will break all the Box Office records...

Upon reaching the lake of the Kamyaka forest, the Pandava brothers decided to continue the rest of their journey on their own. They advised the people accompanying them to return to their abodes. Along with the virtuous Draupadi, Yudhishthira and his siblings continued their journey across the beautiful forests and mountains. As they continued to reside in the Kamyaka forest as part of their exile, many venerable rishis visited the Pandavas and their wife. The Pandavas treated each of their guests with utmost devotion and respect. Having offered hospitality to the rishis and Brahmanas as per the prescribed rites, they offered them food and served them.

One day, a renowned Brahmana visited Hastinapura, who was particularly well-versed in narrating stories. Upon being asked by Dhritarashtra, the Brahmana began to tell tales about the Pandava brothers. He elaborated on their miseries while highlighting their physical transformations owing to the harsh weather conditions. Dhritarashtra was devastated at the words of the Brahmana. As Dhritarashtra continued to express his heartfelt sympathy for the valorous Pandavas and Draupadi, Duryodhana and Shakuni eavesdropped on their conversation.

Duryodhana and Shakuni approached Karna and recounted Dhritarshtra's conversation before him. Duryodhana's rage amplified as he spoke to Karna. Karna sensed the growing anger in his friend and decided to calm him down. He said with a tinge of confidence in his tone, "O Duryodhana! Let us visit the Pandavas and witness their misery. Let us afflict them with great suffering by flaunting our prosperity. O bull among the Kauravas! The pleasure that one derives from beholding an enemy's suffrage is far greater than the pleasure derived from obtaining a son or a kingdom. Let your wives decked in precious ornaments and silk garments accompany us on our visit. Let them torment Draupadi with their grandeur. Afflicted by their prosperity, let Panchali[206] curse her fate and life".

---

206 Panchali - Draupadi.

Duryodhana experienced an elevated sense of satisfaction on hearing the Suryaputra's[207] words. However, with a heavy voice, he said, "O Karna! My father will never permit us to visit the Pandavas. He cares about the Pandavas like his own children; if he comes to know of our desires, he will never agree to our proposal. Although my heart yearns for that pleasure to see the Pandavas in misery, I am struggling to figure out a strategy by which King Dhritarashtra will allow us to visit the Pandavas. Therefore, O Karna, team up with Soubala[208] and find a means by which we can go to the forest. When I address King Dhritarashtra in the court tomorrow, you must proprose your plan before the King, grandfather Bhishma, and other advisers so that I can persuade them and obtain their permission to go to the forest.

At the break of dawn, Karna approached Duryodhana and informed him about the plan. He said, "O Duryodhana! Let us request the King to permit us to undertake an expedition to the Ghoshas[209]. This plan is the best and considered appropriate for a prince. The King will agree to it". Shakuni, having heard Karna's proposal keenly, was impressed with his idea.

As per Karna's plans, a cowherd named Samanga approached Dhritarashtra and spoke about the cattle. Immediately both Shakuni and Karna addressed the King, "O venerable one! The Ghoshas are in beautiful regions. It is the right time for branding the calves. This is also an excellent time for your son to go on a hunt. Therefore, you should permit Duryodhana to go".

Dhritarashtra was not convinced with these words. Out of fear, he addressed his son, Duryodhana, and said, "O son! The mighty Pandavas have lost the game of dice and are in exile. I am concerned that the powers of Bhimasena and Arjuna along with the fire-like wrath of Draupadi will burn you down. I am not in favour of sending you to the forest alone".

---

207 Suryaputra - Karna.
208 Soubala here refers to Shakuni. The son of Subala is Soubala and Shakuni is being addressed as Soubala.
209 Ghoshas - Herdsmen or the place where the herdsmen assemble.

Shakuni interrupted the King's speech by saying, " The great Pandava Yudhishtira lost the game and took an oath to reside in the forest for twelve years. All his brothers will abide by his oath and cause no trouble to us. Since we wish to undertake an expedition only to the Ghoshas and not to the abode of the Pandavas, I am positive that no trouble can befall upon my nephew. We shall sincerely complete the task of numbering, O King!" After much deliberation, Dhritarashtra permitted Duryodhana to go to the forest.

Duryodhana at once departed to the forest accompanied by a large army of brave soldiers, Karna, Duhshasana, Shakuni, all his brothers and wives. While headed towards Lake Dvaitavana, with all his mounts, King Duryodhana camped at a distance of one gavyuti[210]. . Having spent considerable time in the forest, King Duryodhana visited the ghoshas along with his comrades. He inspected thousands of cows and had them marked with numbers and branded. Furthermore, he ensured that the calves were also counted and branded. After the completion of this task, Duryodhana, Karna, Shakuni, and the others pleasured themselves amongst the cowherds.

Finally, the Kauravas arrived at the sacred lake of Dvaitavana. Coincidentally, on the same day, Yudhishtira performed a Sadhyaka Sacrifice[211] in the forest. After the successful completion of the yagna, Yudhishtira along with his wife, Draupadi also went to the lake. Duryodhana immediately instructed his servants and soldiers to construct luxurious dwellings for all the aristocratic Kauravas and their families. Upon his instructions , the servants and the soldiers quickly marched to the forest after arriving at Lake Dvaitavana. However, they were denied entry and obstructed by the Gandharvas[212].

---

210 Gavyuti is a unit of measuring distance. One gavyuti is equivalent to two kroshas (four miles) or one krosha (two miles).
211 Sadhyaka Sacrifice - A new sacrifice or a sacrifice which can be completed in a single day.
212 Gandharvas - Male nature spirits and husbands of the Apsaras. Some are part animals, usually a bird or horse. They have superb musical skills. They guard the Soma and play beautiful music for the gods in their palaces. Gandharvas are frequently depicted as singers in the court of the gods.

The servants and the soldiers returned to Duryodhana at once and informed him about the gandharvas. Duryodhana was angered at the actions of the gandharvas and he instructed his men to dislodge them at once. Duryodhana's men hurried to the forest and addressed the gandharvas, " O Gandharvas! We are here at the order of the mighty King Duryodhana. He has arrived here for the purpose of pleasure. He commands you to vacate this place immediately". The gandharvas laughed at these words and said, " Your King is truly an evil-minded man. He possesses no rights to command us. We are heavenly beings and are not subjected to his suzerainty. You are also unwise men who are here at the orders of your King. Return to your foolish Kaurava king or prepare to be dismissed to the abode of Yama". Frightened by the threats of the Gandharvas, the soldiers and other men returned to Duryodhana.

Duryodhana was provoked by the words of the gandharvas. He commanded his brothers and the soldiers to punish the gandharvas. All the brave men armed with weapons advanced to the forest even though they were restricted by the gandharvas peacefully. The gandharvas consequently approached Chitrasena requesting his support. Chitrasena[213] advised the gandharvas to fight the Kauravas and punish them. As instructed by him the army of gandharvas descended on the Kauravas.

As the gandharvas descended on the kouravas, they fled in all directions, however Karna fought bravely against the gandharvas, killing hundreds and thousands of them with his sharp iron arrows. Although he vanquished Chitrasena's entire army of gandharvas, the gandharvas again returned to the battlefield in thousands. This time, they had armed themselves with deadly weapons and descended on the Kouravas with great force.

Angered by the return of those gandharvas, Duryodhana along with Shakuni, Duhshasana, Vikarna and other sons of Dhritarashtra lodged themselves on their chariots and began killing Chitrasena's men. With Karna in the front,

---

213 Chitrasena - King of the Gandharvas who taught Arjuna the arts of singing and dancing while he was in heaven.

the Kouravas tormented the gandharvas with their valour. Suppressed by the Kouravas, the gandharvas succumbed and were frightened of the maharathas.

On seeing the pitiful state of his men, Chitrasena roared with rage. He disembarked from his abode, determined to kill the foolish sons of Dhritarashtra. With the help of his Maya weapons, Chitrasena left the Kouravas in a perplexity. It seemed as if each one of Dhritarashtra's sons was assailed and surrounded by ten gandharvas[214].

Being thus overcome by Chitrasena and his gandharva-army, the Kouravas fled the battlefield and approached Yudhishtira. They seeked refuge with him. Although many of the Kourava soldiers were defeated in battle, only Karna continued to fight with the gandharvas, displaying utmost dexterity. Along with him, the mighty Duryodhana and Shakuni continued to kill the gandharvas.

Desirous of killing Suryaputra, the gandharvas destroyed Karna's chariot. Holding a sword and a shield in his hand, the son of the suta jumped down from the chariot. He leapt onto Vikarna's chariot and whipped the horses, so that he might escape[215]. Similarly, the ghandarvas also surrounded Duryodhana's chariots from all sides, desirous of killing him. Within a few seconds, they destroyed his beautiful chariot and captured him alive. Duhshasana, Vivimishati, Vinda, Anuvinda[216] and the wives of the Kouravas also met the same fate as Duryodhana.

Witnessing the miserable state of the powerful sons of Dhritarashtra, the remnant soldiers of the Kuru army and Duryodhana's advisers went to Yudhishtira. Having heard about the Kouravas' battle with Chitrasena and his gandharvas, Bhimasena, the second eldest pandava uttered these words,

---

214 The Mahabharata 3 Translated by Bibek Debroy.
215 The Mahabbharata 3 Translated by Bibek Debroy.
216 Names of Kourava brothers.

"They came here for a different purpose, but something else has transpired. The gandharvas have accomplished what we should have undertaken. O son![217] This is the outcome of the king listening to evil counsel and indulging in deceitful gambling. We have heard, it is said that others bring down the enemies of one who is impotent. The gandharvas have performed this extraordinary act before our eyes. We are fortunate that, in this world, there exist men who wish to do that which is pleasant for us and while we were seated, they have taken up our burden and made us happy. We have been suffering from the cold, the heat and the wind and have become emaciated through our austerities. The evil-minded one was comfortable and wished to see us in this state. Those who followed the conduct of that evil-souled Kouravya, the adherent of adharma, are witnessing their own defeat. It is

---

217 The Mahabharata uses the word tata here.

Jayārthashāstra

because adharma was performed that this instruction is now being given. I am telling you. You can see that the Kounteyas[218] are not violent or evil."[219]

As Bhima continued to utter these words, Yudhishtira interrupted his speech by reminding that it was not appropriate to utter such harsh words. He advised Bhima, "O Bhima! Why are you speaking in this way to the terrified Kouravas who have sought refuge with us? They are confronted with difficulties. O Bhima! Dissension and quarrels occur among those who are related by blood. While enmity continues, the dharma of the lineage is not destroyed. If a stranger not related by blood seeks to harm a lineage, those who are good do not tolerate that stranger's violence. The evil-minded one[220]

---
218 Pandavas.
219 The Mahabbharata 3 Translated by Bibek Debroy.
220 Chitrasena.

knows that we have been residing here for some time. But he has ignored us and done something that is unpleasant for us. Through Duryodhana's forcible capture by the gandharva and through a stranger's oppression of the women, our lineage has been sullied. O tigers among men! For the sake of those who have sought refuge with us and to save the lineage, arise and get ready, without any delay. Let Arjuna, you, and the brave and invincible twins free Dhritarashtra's son, Duryodhana, from captivity. O tigers among men! These chariots are stocked with all the weapons. They have golden flags and are driven by Indrasena[221] and the other charioteers. O sons![222] Ride them and fight the gandharvas in battle. Ceaselessly endeavour to free Duryodhana. O Bhima! Every king will protect one who has come for refuge, not to speak of someone as capable as you. Who can ignore cries for help and the sight of hands joined in salutation, even if it happens to be a certain enemy? O Pandava! Out of granting a boon, obtaining a kingdom, the birth of a son and freeing an enemy from misery, the last is superior to the other three. What can provide greater satisfaction to you than that Duryodhana should be in distress now and that his life depends on the strength of your arms? O Bhima! O brave one! There is no doubt that I myself would have rushed to help him, had the sacrifice not been going on[223]. O Bhima! O descendant of the Kuru lineage! Try all the different means of conciliation to free Duryodhana. If the king of the gandharvas does not return him through conciliation, free Duryodhana through mild use of your valour. O Bhima! But if the Kouravas are not released through a mild battle, use every means possible to crush those who are contrary. They must be freed. O Bhima! O descendant of the Bharata lineage! I am only capable of giving you instructions, as long as the sacrifice is going on."[224]

---

221 Yudhishtira's charioteer.
222 Yudhishtira is addressing his brothers here. The word used is tata.
223 Yudhishtira is performing the sadhyaka sacrifice.
224 The Mahabbharata 3 Translated by Bibek Debroy.

Having heard Yudhishtira's words, Arjuna replied, "If the gandharvas do not free the sons of Dhritarashtra through peaceful means, the earth will drink the blood of the king of the gandharvas." Having spoken thus before Yudhishtira, the four pandavas ascended their chariots and rushed to the battlefield to save the sons and daughter-in laws of Dhritarashtra.

Inelastic Supply

Having already understood that supply is the quantity of a commodity that a seller is willing to sell at different prices over a given period, let us now expand our understanding to the elasticity of supply.

Just as elasticity of demand answers the question of "by how much does the demand change?" Similarly, the elasticity of supply answers the question of "by how much does the supply change?"

Elasticity of supply is defined as the responsiveness of the quantity supplied of a good to change in one of the variables on which supply depends.[225]

Predominantly, we characterise the elasticities of supply in these categories:

1. Price Elasticity of Supply
2. Point Elasticity of Supply
3. Arc Elasticity of Supply

Price Elasticity of Supply

Price elasticity of supply refers to the sensitivity/ responsiveness of the quantity supplied to a change in the own price of the commodity. Mathematically, we can express Price Elasticity of supply as a ratio of percentage change in the quantity supplied of a commodity to a percentage change in the price of the

---

[225] Tulsian's Business Economics and Business and Commercial Knowledge: A self-study Textbook by PC Tulsian and Bharat Tulsian

same commodity.[226] Since price elasticity of supply is a pure number, it is not represented with units.

$$\text{Price Elasticity of Supply } e_s = \frac{\text{Percentage change in quantity supplied}}{\text{Percentage change in price}}$$

$$= \frac{\frac{\Delta Q}{Q} \times 100}{\frac{\Delta P}{P} \times 100}$$

$$= \frac{\Delta P}{P} \times \frac{Q}{\Delta Q}$$

Here, ΔQ represents the change in the quantity of the good supplied Q to the market and ΔP represents the change in the market price P.

Point Elasticity of Supply

In simple terms, point elasticity of supply measures the elasticity of a particular point on the Supply Curve.[227]

---

195 All in One Economics CBSE Class XI

227 Tulsian's Business Economics and Business and Commercial Knowledge: A self-study Textbook by PC Tulsian and Bharat Tulsian.

Arc Elasticity of Supply

When the elasticity between any two points has to be measured on the supply curve, then the arc elasticity of supply is employed.[228]

There are primarily five degrees of price elasticity of supply:

1. Perfectly Elastic Supply
2. Perfectly Inelastic Supply
3. Unitary Elastic Supply
4. Elastic or Greater than Unitary Elastic Supply
5. Inelastic or Less than Unitary Elastic Supply

DEGREE OF PRICE ELASTICITY OF SUPPLY	RESPONSIVENESS OF SUPPLY	NATURE OF SUPPLY CURVE
Perfectly Elastic Supply	Supply expands or contracts infinitely without any change in the price	Supply curve horizontal straight line running parallel to the X-axis
Perfectly Inelastic Supply	Supply remains constant irrespective of the changes in the price	Supply curve is a vertical straight line running parallel to the Y-axis
Unitary Elastic Supply	Percentage change in supply equals the percentage change in price	Supply curve is a straight line passing through the origin, independent of the angle and slope/gradient
Elastic or Greater than Unitary Elastic Supply	Percentage change in supply is greater than the percentage change in price	Supply curve is a straight line cutting the Y-axis and intersecting the X-axis in a negative range. As Supply increases, the slope of the curve decreases, and hence the supply curve is a flatter line.

---

[228] Tulsian's Business Economics and Business and Commercial Knowledge: A self-study Textbook by PC Tulsian and Bharat Tulsian.

DEGREE OF PRICE ELASTICITY OF SUPPLY	RESPONSIVENESS OF SUPPLY	NATURE OF SUPPLY CURVE
Inelastic or Less than Unitary Elastic Supply	Percentage change in supply is less than the percentage change in price	Supply curve is a straight line intersecting the X-axis in a positive range. As Supply decreases, the slope of the curve increases, and hence the supply curve is a steeper line.

Elasticity of supply is fundamentally influenced by several factors, such as:

FACTOR NAME	WHEN IS THE SUPPLY ELASTIC?	WHEN IS THE SUPPLY INELASTIC?
Nature of Inputs Used	When inputs used in the production of a commodity are easily available	When inputs used in the production of a commodity are scarcely available
Risk-Taking	When the entrepreneur is willing to take risks	When the entrepreneur is reluctant to take risks
Nature of Commodity	Durable goods	Perishable goods
Time Factor	Longer time factor	Shorter time factor
Production Technique	Simple technology	Complex and expensive technology
Cost of Production	Decreased cost of production	Increased cost of Production

From the story of the Ghosha Yatra, the concept of inelastic supply perfectly matches Yudhishtira's behaviour as a firm. Yudhishtira's supply of support toward his brothers, the Kauravas is constant irrespective of the increase in the misery caused by the Kauravas to the Pandavas. In other words, Yudhishtira's good deeds stand independent of the circumstances befallen upon the Pandavas due to the Kauravas. The Kauravas first embarrassed the Pandavas in the court, then banished them into exile and made plans to torment them with their prosperity. Every consecutive action of Duryodhana and his comrades results in increased misery and hardships for the Pandavas, however, Yudhishtira's affection, forgiveness, and supportive nature is not influenced by any circumstances in his life. As described by the Mahabharata and other scriptures, Yudhishtira is truly an ideal man.

Hypothetically, even if the Kauravas continued to cause greater harm to the Pandavas, Yudhishtira would still offer support to Duryodhana in a time of crisis. The below graph presents Yudhishtira's inelastic supply curve of support. Traditionally, quantity supplied would be measured on the X-axis and the price would be measured on the Y-axis.

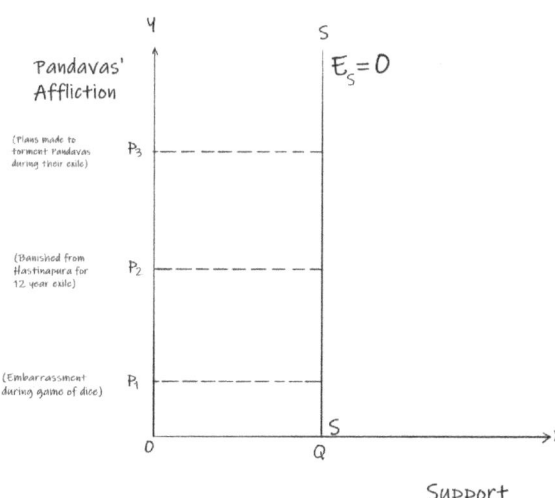

- On the X-axis, Yudhishtira's supply of good deeds, in this case, his support is measured
- On the Y-axis, the affliction faced by the Pandavas is measured
- Yudhishtira's support remains constant irrespective of the affliction caused by the Kauravas
    - At P_1, the Kauravas deceitfully defeat the Pandavas and disrobe their wife causing embarrassment

- At P_2, as part of losing the game of dice, the Pandavas are banished from the kingdom of Hastinapura for 12 years of exile followed by one year of Ajnatha vasa
- At P_3, the Kauravas headed by Duryodhana make plans to torment the Pandavas with their prosperity by visiting their refuge
- Notice that even though the price is increasing, Yudhishtira's dharma remains undisturbed and independent, thus resulting in a straight vertical line parallel to the y axis

• In other words, the ratio of percentage change in Yudhishtra's adherence to dharma to the percentage change in the affliction caused by the Kauravas is zero. Therefore, the price elasticity of Yudhishtira's supply is zero.

Thus, in one's life, the adherence to one's dharma is independent of life's circumstances.

The Quest For Satyavati's Supernormal Profit

"Photography is all about secrets. The secrets we all have and will never tell."

—Kim Edwards

With a bowl of butterscotch ice cream, I gazed at the pale blue sky for endless hours. Time had begun to turn as shapeless as the melting scoop of ice cream. I perched lazily on the couch beside the window. This was my summer vacation ritual. The ritual was quite simple… Sit, daydream, do nothing and relish the ice cream as if you had never seen one in your life. But that day, the ritual was modified… It's natural that when you gaze at the sky endlessly, your thoughts drag you into a memory lane. As my thoughts absorbed me into my memory lane, one particular photograph flashed before the curtains of my vision. It was one in which I wore a rose-pink-coloured frock with two pigtails, complementing the subtleness of the pink. I also carried the expression of a celebrity in that photograph, as I considered myself to be a photogenic luminary in those days.

As this picture flashed before me, I involuntarily rushed to my room and started desperately searching for it. The searching process demanded a great deal of effort as I had to search for the treasure hidden under a pile of papers. To my surprise, I found the photograph after investing two hours of hard work of diving into and sorting through the bundles of paper. The moment I held the photograph *in my hand, I felt as if I had earned my normal profit for all the efforts. On the contrary, below the photograph, I also discovered my mom's childhood photograph. She was sporting the same kind of frock with similar tiny pigtails. My mom was accompanied by her pet cat, Nattu. I burst into laughter as that was the first time that I had seen my mom as a child. My adventure was complete... I had earned my supernormal profit!*

'Normal Profit' and 'Supernormal Profit'... Well, let us understand them through Bhishma's vow.

After instating Bhishma as the heir apparent, Shantanu once set out along the banks of the river Yamuna to hunt deer. While he was thus pursuing deer in the forest, a divine scent bewitched his senses. Shantanu immediately altered his course and followed the divine scent. When he reached the source of the fragrance, he was taken aback to see a maiden before his eyes. The lady seemed to belong to the fishermen's tribe. She appeared radiant and celestial with her dark, yet enticing eyes. Shantanu asked the lady, "O timid one! Who are you and whose are you? What are you doing here?"[229]

The dark-eyed lady replied, "O great-souled one! I belong to the fishermen tribe. I am Satyavati. I am here on my father's instructions to ply a boat as per the dharma prescribed for us.[230]" Shantanu was enraptured by Satyavati's beauty and wished to marry her. He approached her father, the king of the fishermen tribe, and requested him to give Satyavati's hand in marriage to him.

The king of the fishermen tribe was glad at the proposal made by King Shantanu but he imposed one condition before the king. He declared, "O King! If you wish to marry my daughter, Satyavati, then you must promise me that you will instate the son born to her as the king of your celebrated lineage. Grant me this boon, O king and I shall happily give you my daughter's hand in marriage". King Shantanu was overwhelmed at the words of the fisherman. Though the feeling of love and admiration had overflown within his body, he was hesitant to grant this ambitious boon to the fisherman. King Shantanu, engulfed by remorse, returned to Hastinapura.

Shantanu was always loyal towards his duties as a king, but in solitude he suffered loneliness and regret. He was always immersed in thoughts about Satyavati when was alone. On one such day, Devavrata approached his father, who was in a depressive state, thinking about his love. He gently asked his

---
229 The Mahabharata 1 Translated by Bibek Debroy
230 The Mahabharata 1 Translated by Bibek Debroy

father, "O father! You are a great king, who is looked upon by all his subjects. All the kings under your sovereignty obey your words. Then, why is it that you are always in grief and silent?

Shantanu replied, "Without a doubt, I am always meditating, just as you say. O descendant of the Bharata lineage! You are the only son in this great lineage of ours. O son! I sorrow because of the impermanence of this mortal life. O son of Ganga! If anything happens to you, this lineage of ours will cease to exist.[231] "

Devavrata was intelligent and began to think about his father's words. He approached an old adviser, who was always concerned about his father's welfare, and asked him the reason for his father's unhappiness. The adviser revealed to Devavrata the true story and the boon asked by the king of the fisherman tribe.

Devavrata at once set out to meet the king of the fishermen along with other Kshatriyas. He asked the fishermen king to give his daughter's hand in marriage to his father. The king of the fishermen tribe addressed Devavrata, "O supreme among the kurus! I would never refuse this proposal. It would be my honour to give Satyavati in marriage to King Shantanu. But I have one condition. Only the son born to Satyavati should be the king of Hastinapura". Hearing these words of the Matsya Raja[232], Devavrata, for the sake of his father uttered the following words, "O Matsya Raja! I promise you that only the sons born to Satyavati shall be anointed as the king of Hastinapura".

---

231 The Mahabharata 1 Translated by Bibek Debroy.
232 King of the fishermen tribe.

Jayārthashastra

The king of the fisherman tribe further added, "O Devavrata! I am certain that you will always abide by the vow you have made, but I doubt the integrity of your sons towards your vow". Devavrata replied, "O king of fishermen! O supreme among kings! Listen to these words of mine. In front of these lords of the earth, hear what I have to say for my father's sake. O lord of men! I have already relinquished my right to the kingdom. I will not destroy the doubt that has arisen about my sons. O fisherman! From today, I take the vow of brahmacharya. Even if I die without a son, I will attain the eternal world of heaven."[233] The fisherman was shocked at the words of King Shantanu. He happily agreed for the marriage of his daughter Satyavati and the great king Shantanu.

---

233 The Mahabharata 1 Translated by Bibek Debroy

Supernormal Profit

Bhishma addressed Satyavati, "O mother! Please ascend this chariot and let us go to our own home..."[234]

Let us now focus on Satyavati for the next part of our discussion

It is universal that remuneration for a firm or an entrepreneur is profit. A firm carries out its business activities intending to earn profits. Similarly, an entrepreneur establishes his business with the fundamental objective of earning profit. Just as there is rent for land, similarly it is profit for entrepreneurship.

Just as there is a minimum amount of wage or salary, which is paid to a person for his/her service, is there a minimum level of profit, which the firm has to earn to continue the successful operation of his business? Yes, there is. It is termed as normal profit. Normal profit is the minimum level of profit required to keep the firm in the existing business.[235] Normal profit may also be understood as the level of profit enough to cover the economic cost of the firm. If a firm earns anything less than the normal profit, then it is not going to continue its business in the market. It is essential to consider the profit of a firm as an incentive for its continued operation. In other words, normal profit is a part of the firm's total cost or an opportunity cost of entrepreneurship[236].

But what if the firm earns more than the normal profit? Well, any profit that the firm earns over and above the normal profit is termed as super-normal profit.[237] The word "super" suggests the excess income earned by the firm.

---

234 The Mahabharata 1 Translated by Bibek Debroy
235 NCERT Introductory Microeconomics Textbook in Economics for Class XII
236 NCERT Introductory Microeconomics Textbook in Economics for Class XII
237 NCERT Introductory Microeconomics Textbook in Economics for Class XII

It is useful to note that:

1. In the long run, the firm does not produce any output, if it earns anything less than the normal profit
2. In the short run, however, the firm produces an output even if it earns anything less than the normal profit.[238]

From the story above, it can be interpreted that Satyavati's normal profit is her becoming queen and enjoying the luxury of the palace at Hastinapura. On the other hand, due to the vow taken by Bhishma (Devavrata), her sons and grandsons are certainly the natural heirs to the throne. This is her super-normal profit.

The fisherman's second condition questioning the integrity of Bhishma's children towards the vow made by him is typical to a firm's behaviour in the long run. Having already established that the firm, in the long run, produces an output only if it earns a profit greater than the normal profit, we can relate that the fisherman agrees to give Satyavati in marriage to Shantanu only if the future of her sons and grandsons are secured.

---

238 NCERT Introductory Microeconomics Textbook in Economics for Class XII

Breaking-Even In Apad Dharma

"I've learned...the best classroom in the world is at the feet of an elderly person".

—Andy Rooney

My loving great-grandmother G Nagaratna, whom I fondly addressed as Apissa, was indeed a woman of ideals. She was my constant companion throughout life's endeavours. We cherished many moments together. As a strong believer in spirituality, she always reminded me that life's success shouldn't dominate one's stability; similarly, failures should not torment a person's peace. She often made me realise that it was important to accept life's challenges with a neutral mindset, without underestimating or overestimating its nature.

As a kid, I loved to hear the stories of the Mahabharata from her in our usual place: under the tree in the temple. Among many such stories, her favourite one was the fable of the fowler and the pigeon. I remember hearing this fable for the first time when I was seven years old. Till this day, the opening line of her narration, "I shall narrate a gem from my memory...An exquisite tale that I heard from my grandmother named the fable of the fowler and the pigeon... A story that reminds me of my grandma and her life..." has stayed with me.

Dedicating this chapter to my Apissa, I invoke her blessings and recount this magnificent tale of Lubdhaka and the bird.

After the completion of the Great Mahabharata war, Yudhishthira begins to sorrow over the death of his kinsmen and declares his desire to renounce the kingdom and retire to the forest. At these words of Yudhishthira, his family members and the great rishis Narada, Vyasa, Devala, Devasthana and Kanwa counsel him. Amidst the discussions between Yudhishthira and other rishis, Sri Krishna advises Yudhishthira to visit Bhishma and learn about Raja Dharma[239], Apad Dharma[240], and Moksha Dharma[241].

In the Apad Dharma Parva of the Shanti Parva, Yudhishthira is enlightened about the dharma that should be followed in the time of an adversity.

Yudhishthira folded his hands before the supreme Bhishma and asked him, "O Grandfather! I seek your guidance on the dharma that should be followed by someone who is protecting a person who has sought refuge".[242]

---

[239] Raja dharma refers to the duty of the kings and leaders.
[240] Apad dharma refers to the rules of conduct when one faces adversity.
[241] Moksha dharma refers to the behaviour and rules to achieve moksha (emancipation, release, freedom).
[242] The Mahabharata 8 Translated by Bibek Debroy.

Bhishma looked at Yudhishthira and replied with a smile, "O grandson! There is great dharma in protecting someone who has sought refuge. A pigeon once honoured its enemy when he sought refuge. As appropriate, it honoured him and offered him its own flesh"[243].

Yudhishthira was taken aback by Bhishma's reference to a pigeon and expressed his curiosity to learn more about that noble soul. He questioned Bhishma, "In ancient times, how did an enemy come and seek refuge with a pigeon? What objective did it attain after offering him its own flesh?"[244]

---

243 The Mahabharata 8 Translated by Bibek Debroy.
244 The Mahabharata 8 Translated by Bibek Debroy.

Bhishma replied, "O Yudhishthira! This sacred story was narrated by Bhargava[245] to King Muchukunda[246]. This story includes dharma, artha and kama. Listen to this fable, as I narrate it to you".

Thus, Bhishma began narrating the fable of the fowler and the pigeon.

In a distant forest, there used to be a cruel hunter, who earned a living from hunting birds. The people residing in the vicinity of that forest regarded him as the form of death as he killed the birds in the forest using his net. Being ignorant of dharma, this hunter practised hunting of birds for a long time.

One day, when he was in the forest, the rain flooded the forest, causing large trees to bow down. Although Lubdhaka[247] was agonised by the downpour, he wandered around the forest and happened to come across a large tree. Having realised that his village was situated at a far distance from that forest, he decided to rest below the sprawling branches of that tree for the rest of that night. As a formality, he folded his hands before the humongous tree and said, "I seek shelter from the gods residing here". He then laid out a few dried leaves on the ground and supported his head with a stone. After a while, the hunter of birds slumbered away.

A bird along with its family resided on the branches of that tree. The bird's wife, who had journeyed into the dense forest in the morning had not returned. The male bird lamented, thinking about the reason for the non-return of his wife. He wept in sorrow as he recounted reminiscent memories of his wife.

On the other hand, the female bird was captured by Lubdhaka and she heard the misery of her husband. She felt pity for the fate of her husband and advised

---

245 Parashurama.
246 An Ikshvaku (Suryavanshi) king, who was the son of King Mandhata and the brother of Ambarisha.
247 Lubdhaka means a hunter and also a greedy person. We have interpreted it as a proper name.

him thus, "I will tell you what is indeed beneficial for you. Having heard, act accordingly. O beloved one! In particular, one must provide succour to someone who seeks refuge. This fowler has resorted to your residence and is lying down. He is afflicted by the cold. He is afflicted by hunger. It is necessary to honour him. If someone who seeks refuge is allowed to perish, the sin is equal to that from killing a brahmana or a cow, who is the mother of the worlds. Following the dharma of different species, that of pigeons has been ordained for us. Therefore, follow dharma and artha and give up all love for your body. Engage in honouring him, so that his mind is cheered".[248]

The male bird was engulfed in tears as it heard its wife speak these words from the cage, where she was imprisoned by Lubdhaka. The male bird addressed the fowler as per the prescribed rites, "Welcome. What can I do for you? Since this is like your own house, you should not suffer from any misery. Therefore, tell me quickly what I should do. What do you desire?[249]

Lubdhaka replied, "The cold is constraining me. You should free me from the cold". The bird immediately spread some dry leaves on the ground and departed to arrange for a source of fire. The bird found burning charcoal in a distant place and it returned with it to kindle a fire. Having kindled a fire, it spoke to Lubdhaka, "Be assured and without fear. Heat your limbs"[250]. Lubdhaka gradually recovered from the cold as his limbs were warmed due to the fire. Later, he addressed the bird once again, troubled by hunger. He said, "The hunger is killing me. I desire that you should give me some food". The bird replied, "I do not possess any riches with which I can destroy your hunger. We, residents of the forest, survive on what grows here"[251]. Having spoken thus to the slayer of birds, the pigeon was in a perplexed state. It thought deeply about the importance of honouring the guest and then said, "Wait for a while.

---

248 The Mahabharata 8 translated by Bibek Debroy.
249 The Mahabharata 8 translated by Bibek Debroy.
250 The Mahabharata 8 Translated by Bibek Debroy
251 The Mahabharata 8 Translated by Bibek Debroy

I will satisfy you". The bird kindled a fire and again addressed the hunter, "O hunter! I am firmly resolved to honour my guest with utmost devotion and dharma". Having circumambulated the fire, it penetrated the flames.

When Lubdhaka saw the actions of the bird, he was astonished and thought, "What have I done? Alas. Shame on my reprehensible and violent deeds. There is no doubt that I have committed great and terrible adharma". When he saw the bird descend into the blazing flames, he said, "Shame on my great stupidity and the deceitful conduct I have always engaged in. Having abandoned auspicious deeds, I have sought to capture birds. I have resorted to violence. There is no doubt that, by offering me its own flesh, the great-souled pigeon has instructed me. I will abandon my sons and wife and give up my own beloved life. The pigeon, extremely devoted to dharma, has instructed me about dharma. I will offer up my own body and avoid all objects of pleasure. I will shrivel it up, like a little bit of water during the summer. I will endure the torment of hunger and thirst. I will become lean, as if I am made up of veins. To ensure the world hereafter, I will observe many different kinds of fasting. Alas! By giving up its own body, it has shown me how guests must be treated. Therefore, I will follow dharma. Dharma is the supreme objective. O supreme among birds! Dharma is seen to be that which has been followed by that foremost practitioner of dharma.'[252] Having said these words out of compassion, Lubdhaka departed on mahaprasthanam[253]. He freed the imprisoned pigeons[254] and departed.

The she-pigeon wept in grief after she was released by Lubdhaka. It lamented over the sacrifice of her husbands. Remembering its loyalty to the pigeon, it also descended into the blazing fire. There, the she-pigeon saw her husband adorned with colourful garments and ornaments, majestically perched on a chariot. Together with its wife, the pigeon ascended to heaven. Lubdhaka witnessed the pigeons rising to heaven and was determined to attain moksha[255].

Break-Even Point

The word "Break-even point" is an indispensable part of the business, economics, investing and cost accounting vocabulary. In general terms,

---

252 The Mahabharata 8 translated by Bibek Debroy.
253 A great journey. A person leaves on mahaprasthanam when he departs from home and wanders around, awaiting death.
254 There were other captured pigeons also.
255 Freedom from cycles of death and rebirth (samsara).

break-even point is a point at which the total cost that a firm spends on the production of output is equal to the total revenue earned from the sale of the output. At the break-even point, there is no net loss or net gain, one is said to have 'broken even'.

Having understood the general idea of the break-even point, let us now understand it through the different disciplines.

In business terminology, break-even point refers to the sales volume at which there is no profit, no loss and the business is broken even. It also refers to the amount of revenue that a business earns from the sale of a certain production level necessary to cover both the total fixed and variable costs incurred within a specific time period.[256]

In investing terminology, the break-even point is said to be achieved when the market price of an asset is the same as its original cost[257].

In accounting terminology, the break-even point is calculated by dividing the fixed costs of production by the price per unit minus the variable costs of production[258].

In microeconomics, the break-even point of a firm can be explained both in terms of the short run (a time period in which the firm can only alter its variable factors of production in order to implement change to its production and not its fixed factors of production) and the long run (a time period in which the firm can alter both its variable factors of production as well as the fixed factors of production in order to implement change to its production).

It should also be noted that the break-even point of a firm is always defined with respect to its supply curve. So, in the short run, the break-even point of a

---

256 https://www.bankrate.com/glossary/b/break-even-point/
257 https://www.investopedia.com/terms/b/breakevenpoint.asp
258 https://www.investopedia.com/terms/b/breakevenpoint.asp

firm is a point where the firm only earns a normal profit (the minimum level of profit that is just enough to cover the economic costs of a firm). Graphically, the break-even point is located at the minimum point of the firm's average cost curve [AVC] at which the supply curve cuts the average cost curve.

   a. In the short run, the break-even point of a firm is the minimum point of the SAC [Short-run Average Cost] curve at which the short-run supply curve cuts it from below.
   b. In the long run, the break-even point of a firm is the minimum point of the LRAC [Long-run Average Cost] curve at which the long-run supply curve cuts it from below.

At this point in our discussion, it would be useful to understand the break even analysis, an important tool used by all businesses.

Break-even analysis entails calculating and examining the margin of safety for an entity based on the revenues collected and associated costs. In other words, the analysis shows how many sales it takes to pay for the cost of doing business.[259]

In other words, the break-even analysis is an effective tool that helps a firm to envision the point at which its product or service will become profitable.

So, the break-even point is often a benchmark that represents a revenue sufficient to cover the cost of production. Earning a revenue less than the break-even point is a loss and similarly a revenue greater than the break-even point is a profit.

Let us now use our understanding of the break-even point to understand the fable of the fowler and the pigeon from a microeconomic dimension.

Let us first consider the story from the male bird's point of view.

---

259 https://www.investopedia.com/terms/b/breakevenanalysis.asp

From this entire episode with the hunter, the bird ultimately gained moksha, however it also had to bear the suffering in terms of entering the blazing fire and witnessing its wife held captive by the hunter. Therefore, when we analyse the bird's gain (moksha) and its loss (pain and suffering) from a rational perspective, we realise that for gaining moksha the bird had to undergo considerable suffering both at a physical level as well as an emotional level. Therefore, rationally we can say that there is no net loss or net gain and the bird has broken even by attaining moksha.

Now let us consider the same story from Lubdhaka's perspective.

Clearly, Lubdhaka's acquaintance with the bird in the forest enlightened him about dharma and transformed his life. That episode made him realise the nature of his sin and paved him a path to attainment of moksha. However, Lubdhaka's act of setting the female bird free can be interpreted as a loss from an economic perspective. Hypothetically, if he would not have set the bird free then he might have earned a monetary gain from its sale, however by choosing not to do so, the monetary income that he might have earned from the sale of the bird becomes no longer available to him. Therefore, again when we perceive this story from a rational viewpoint, we realise that in order to gain the knowledge of dharma, the hunter had to sacrifice his livelihood. In this scenario, there is no net loss or net gain and Lubdhaka has broken even.

Arjuna's Opportunity Cost

True success requires sacrifice.

—Rick Riordan

Before every exam, a student must choose between two options: Study hard with perseverance or succumb to the distractions. It is a decision of where to invest one's time. The moment a student invests time in distractions, the other option of studying becomes unavailable to a student.

As a student, I have realised this often. But, the determination to choose studying over distractions never seems to take charge, unless necessity demands it to. Days before the exam, it is so easy to choose studying over distractions, isn't it?

At this point, I remember a household saying, "Yuddakale Shastra Abhyasa", which means "A warrior who practices the art of using weapons just before the battle.". Due to circumstances, don't we sometimes become these warriors?

But have you ever thought of it like this: the opportunity cost of investing your time in gaining knowledge is the momentary pleasure you sacrifice by not choosing to relax before the exam?

Jayārthashastra

The Pandavas ruled over Indraprastha. One day, a brahmana whose cattle were stolen by thieves approached the Pandavas for help to recover his cattle, which were a part of his wealth. He pleaded for help and repeatedly requested the mighty warriors to pursue the thieves and bring back his wealth. Arjuna, the resplendent warrior heard his plea and instantly assured the brahmana not to worry.

However, Arjuna was in a dilemma. The thought that all the Pandavas' weapons were placed in the room, where Yudhishtira and Draupadi were spending their private time, left him in a perplexed situation. On one side was his duty to relieve the brahmana of his grievance, and on the other was his fear of violating the rule and being banished to the forest for twelve years. Arjuna again thought to himself, "If I fail to bring back the brahmana's cattle, adharma will knock at the door of King Yudhishtira, but a violation of the rule will cause remorse to my dear brother. There can be only two occurrences: either the arrival of adharma or the decay of my body. The arrival of adharma will scar the king's reputation across all three worlds. Therefore, dharma must be sustained even at the cost of the physical body."

With this thought in his mind, Savyasachi[260] entered the room where Ajathashatru[261] and Krishna resided. Without casting his gaze on the two of them, he stormed towards his Ghandiva[262] and seized his bow with valour. Draupadi and Yudhishtira were flabbergasted with Arjuna's actions and were unable to comprehend the situation.

Arjuna, accompanied by the brahmana pursued the thieves, who were tormented by his gallantry and the cattle were finally restored. Arjuna then returned to the city of Indraprastha and spoke to Yudhishtira, "O king Ajathashatru, please permit me to reside in the forest for twelve years and observe the rites of a brahmachari, because I have violated the rule that we had made in the presence of Devarshi Narada[263]."

On hearing Arjuna's words, king Yudhishtira was engulfed with grief and advised his brother, "O Arjuna! I am now fully aware of the reason, which forced you to enter the room where I was residing with Panchali[264]. Dear brother, you have not caused resentment to me. Further, it is said that a younger brother entering an elder brother's room is not a transgression. Therefore, listen to my advice and abstain from departing to the forest."

Arjuna replied with firm determination, "O Lord, it is you who has always preached that there cannot be pretentiousness in the adherence to dharma and following this noble teaching of yours is important. The reality is that I

---

260 Savyasachi: Another name for Arjuna. Arjuna was able to shoot arrows from both his left and right hand with the same accuracy. (Savyasachi=ambidextrous)

261 Ajatashatru: Another name for Yudhishtira. The word Ajatashatru refers to one who has no enemies. Yudhishtira had no enemies and hence he was Ajatashatru.

262 Ghandiva: The divine bow presented to Arjuna by Agni.

263 The rule that they made before Rishi Narada was that if any one of the Pandava brothers set their eyes on Draupadi when she was with any one of the other pandavas, then he would have to retire to the forest and live the life of a brahmachari for twelve years.

264 Panchali: Another name for Draupadi. Draupadi was the daughter of King Drupada. He ruled over the kingdom of Panchal. Thus, she was Panchali belonging to the kingdom of Panchal.

have violated the rule made among ourselves and I ought to be banished to the forest for twelve years for the same. Neither can reality be altered nor can I restrain from going to the forest. Please forgive me, O Lord."

Having obtained permission to go to the forest, Arjuna was sanctified and he departed to live in the forest for twelve years.

Opportunity Cost

Very often, each one of us comes across a situation, where we are forced to choose between two alternatives. By choosing one option, we are forced to forgo the benefits of the other option... Have you come across such an instance in your life?

The moment we choose between two alternatives, a feeling of guilt does creep into us. The guilt often reminds us of the benefits that the other option provides. However, the bitter reality is that once we resolve to our preference, the other option will no longer be available to us.

Opportunity cost of some activity is the gain forgone from the second-best activity.

For example, if a person has Rs. 10,000. He can either donate these 10000 rupees to his father to help in the family business or deposit the money into a bank, which will earn him 5% interest. If he invests the money in the business, then the opportunity to invest the money in the bank becomes unavailable. In other words, the maximum gain that the person can earn from the two activities is the 5% interest from the bank. Therefore, the opportunity cost of investing the money in the business is the interest forgone from the bank.

From the conversation between Yudhishtira and Arjuna, one can conclude that Arjuna was presented with two choices: staying back at Indraprastha or departing to the forest. The moment Arjuna firmly decides to go to the forest, the opportunity of staying back with his family is no longer available to him.

Tanushree Nagaveni

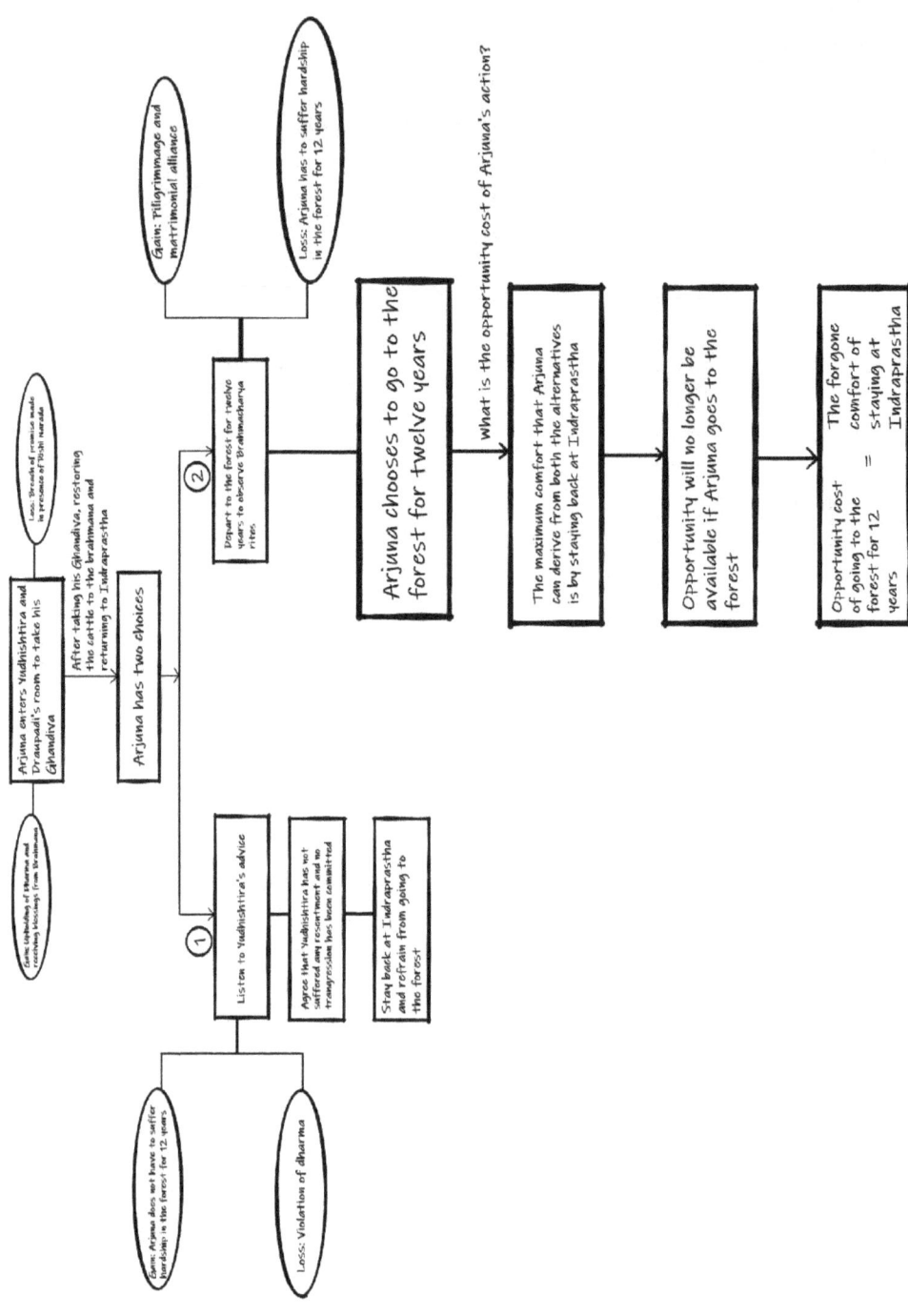

Therefore, the opportunity cost of going away to the forest is the luxury of the palace at Indraprastha, which Arjuna sacrifices.

The following flowchart explains the concept of opportunity cost with the help of the above story.

Having restored the brahamana's cattle, when Arjuna reaches Indraprastha, he has two choices before him. Arjuna can either abide by Yudhishtira's advice and stay back at Indraprastha or he can depart to the forest for twelve years and follow the Brahmacharya rites. But, when he chooses the latter option, he forgoes the comforts in Indraprastha. The opportunity of staying back in the palace is no longer available to him. Therefore, the opportunity cost of his action is equal to the forgone comfort of staying back at Indraprastha.

The Stable and Unstable Equilibrium in Amba's Life

"The graph to success is not always straight; it has curves and intersections".

—*Osunsakin Adewale*

I have always considered graphs to be a form of art. Gliding the pencil parallel to a ruler gives me immense satisfaction just as using a brush to illustrate my imagination on a canvas. My obsession with graphs grew infinitely with my introduction to economics.

Whenever I draw a graph, I tend to interpret many real-life scenarios by ascribing demand and supply with different attributes. Graphs are definite and have a certain system that gives them form and makes them easy to understand. Let's see how I used my ever-favourite graphs to illustrate the following story.

Jayārthashastra

Once, during the great Mahabharata war, Duryodhana asked Bhishma, "O foremost among the Bharata lineage! When you see Shikhandi in the field of battle, with arrows raised and ready to slay you, what is the reason for you not to kill him? You said earlier that you would kill the Panchalas and the Somakas. O Gangeya[265]! O grandfather! Tell me the reason for this".

Bhishma replied, "O Duryodhana! Together with the lords of the earth, listen to the reason why I will not kill Shikhandi when I see him in the field of battle. My father, King Shantanu, was a benevolent king and had dharma in his soul. After he met his destiny, I fulfilled my promise.

I consecrated my brother Chitrangada as the king of Hastinapura. When he died, abiding by the instructions of the late King Shantanu's wife Satyavati and in accordance with the decreed rites, I instated my younger brother Vichitravirya as the king. O Duryodhana! I desired to obtain brides for him and reflected on those who would be equal in beauty and lineage. Incidentally, at that time, I heard that the three daughters of the king of Kashi would be given away in a svayamvara[266].

All of them were unrivalled in beauty and their names were Amba, Ambika and Ambalika. All the kings of the earth had been summoned there. Amba was the eldest and Ambika was the one in the middle, while Ambalika was the youngest princess. On a single chariot, I went to the capital of the lord of Kashi. In the court of the King of Kashi, I saw the three ornamented maidens there and the kings, the lords of the earth, who had assembled there. Established in battle, I challenged all those kings. I raised those maidens onto my chariot, knowing that they were being offered as viryashulka[267] and told all the lords of the earth who had assembled there, 'Bhishma, Shantanu's son,

---

265 Bhishma.
266 A practice in which a girl of marriageable age chose a husband from a group of suitors.
267 Viryashulka is when the maiden is offered to the suitor who shows the most valour (virya), shulka meaning price.

is taking these maidens away by force. Use the limits of your strength to set them free'.

At this, all those lords of the earth arose, with weapons upraised. Enraged, they instructed their charioteers to yoke the chariots. O grandson! Those lords of the earth surrounded me from all directions. With a great mass of chariots, they attacked me from all sides. I repulsed them with a great shower of arrows. I vanquished all those kings and brought down their colourful and gold-embellished standards. On seeing the dexterity of my palms, they were shattered and retreated. After vanquishing those lords of the earth, I returned to Hastinapura. Having recounted my deeds to Satyavati, I handed over the maidens for my brother. She inhaled the fragrance of my head. With her eyes filled with tears, Satyavati told me, 'O son! It is through good fortune that you have obtained victory.'

With Satyavati's permission, a date was fixed for the marriage. The eldest daughter of the lord of Kashi spoke these bashful words, 'O Bhishma! You are knowledgeable about dharma and you are skilled in all the sacred texts. You should listen to my words and then act towards me in accordance with dharma. In my mind, I had earlier chosen the lord of Shalva as my groom. Without this being known to my father, he had also chosen me in secret. I desire someone else. O Bhishma! Especially because you are a Kourava, how can you, who have studied the sacred texts, make someone like that live in this household? Now that you know this, make up your mind about what should be done. O mighty-armed one! You should do what is appropriate. King Shalva is waiting for me. O mighty-armed one! You should take pity on me. O brave one! We have heard that you are famous in this world for being truthful to your vows'. After hearing Amba's words, I then informed Satyavati, the advisers, the brahmanas and the priests and allowed the eldest maiden, Amba, to leave.

On obtaining the permission, the maiden went to the capital of the lord of Shalva. She was protected by aged brahmanas and accompanied by her nurse. Travelling the entire distance, she went to that lord of men and told King Shalva these words. 'O mighty-armed one! O immensely radiant one! I have arrived here before you.' O Duryodhana! But the lord of Shalva smiled and told her, 'O one with the beautiful complexion! You have belonged to another one before this and I do not wish you as my wife. O fortunate one! Therefore, return again to Bhishma! After you have been forcibly abducted by Bhishma, I do not desire you. You were won by Bhishma and seemed to be delighted then. He defeated all the kings in a great battle. O one with a beautiful complexion! You have gone to another one before. I am a king who is instructed by dharma and am skilled in knowledge. How can I accept as my wife a lady who has gone to someone else before? O fortunate one! Go wherever you wish. Do not waste your time here.'

Amba was struck by the arrows of the god of love and told him, 'O lord of the earth! Do not speak in this fashion. I wasn't happy when I was abducted by Bhishma, the destroyer of enemies. O lord of Shalva! I love you. Love me back in return. I am an innocent maiden. Dharma does not approve of the abandoning of those who love you. I have come here after obtaining the permission of Gangeya, who never retreats from the field of battle. I have obtained his permission and have come here before you. The mighty-armed Bhishma does not want me. I have heard that all Bhishma's exertions were for the sake of his brother. O king! Gangeya has given my sisters, Ambika and Ambalika, whom he had also abducted, to his younger brother Vichitravirya. O lord of Shalva! I have never desired any man other than you. I swear on myself that I have not thought of anyone but you. O Indra among kings! I have come before you and I have not gone to any other man earlier. O Shalva! I am telling you the truth. I swear on my own self that this is the truth. O one with the large eyes! Love me'.

But though she spoke in this way, Shalva abandoned the daughter of the king of Kashi. She sought his favours with these and many other words. But the king who was the lord of Shalva did not show her his favours. Then the eldest daughter of the king of Kashi was overcome by anger. With tears in her eyes and with her voice choking with tears, she said, 'O lord of the earth! Having been discarded by you, I will go wherever I wish. I will go to the virtuous. It has been rightly said that where there is virtue, there is truth.' O Duryodhana! The maiden spoke in this way and lamented piteously. But the lord of Shalva abandoned her and Shalva repeatedly said, 'O one with the beautiful hips. Go. Go from here. I am frightened of Bhishma. You are Bhishma's property.' She was thus addressed by Shalva, who was not far-sighted".

Bhishma again addressed Duryodhana and said, "O descendant of the Bharata lineage! As she departed from the city, she thought to herself. 'There is no young woman on earth who faces such a difficult situation as me. I have been separated from my relatives. I have been treated badly by Shalva. I am incapable of returning to the city of Hastinapura. Bhishma granted me permission because I wished to go to Shalva. Will I blame myself or the unassailable Bhishma? Or should it be my foolish father who arranged for the svayamvara? Is it my own fault that I did not jump down from Bhishma's chariot? When that terrible war raged on earlier, should I have descended and run away to Shalva? The consequences are that I have to endure the fruits of this conduct, like a foolish person. Shame on Bhishma. Shame on my evil father, whose intelligence is foolish. He offered me as a viryashulka, as if I am a woman who can be offered at a price. Shame on me. Shame on King Shalva. Shame on the creator. It is because of everyone's bad sentiments that I now confront this calamity. In every way, a man must endure what destiny has determined. But Shantanu's son, Bhishma, is the chief reason for my hardship. I should exact vengeance on Bhishma, through austerities and fighting. It is my view that he is the reason behind my misery. But which lord of the earth is capable of withstanding Bhishma in battle?' Having reflected on these thoughts, she left the city.

She went to the hermitages of great-souled ascetics who were sacred in their conduct. Surrounded by those ascetics, she spent a night there. The one with the sweet smiles told them everything about herself and the details of what had happened, the abduction, the release and the abandonment by Shalva. A great brahmana named Shaikhavatya lived there. He was rigid in his vows and aged in his austerities. He was a preceptor in the sacred texts and in the aranyakas[268]. Shaikhavatya, the great ascetic and sage, spoke thus to the distressed maiden, 'O fortunate one! Now that this has happened, what can ascetics do for you? We are immensely fortunate ones who live in hermitages. We are great souls engaged in austerities.' But she told him, 'Show me a favour. I wish to wander around and perform extremely difficult austerities. Because of my stupidity, I must have performed deeds in earlier bodies. I must have acted in evil ways and this must certainly be the fruit. O ascetics! I am not interested in returning to my relatives. I have been rejected. I am unhappy.

---

268 The Aranyakas are specific sacred texts, composed in the forest (aranyaka) and meant to be studied there.

I have been wronged by Shalva. O ascetics! O those who are devoid of sin! I wish to be instructed here. You are the equals of the gods. Be compassionate towards me.' Shaikhavatya then consoled the maiden with examples, sacred knowledge and reasons. Together with the other brahmanas, he comforted her and promised that he would act accordingly".

Bhishma said, "O grandson! Then all the ascetics engaged themselves in their respective tasks. The ones who followed dharma wondered about the maiden and thought, 'What will we do?' A few among those ascetics said, 'We should take her back to her father's residence.' Others thought that I should be censured. Some others thought of going to the lord of Shalva and asking him to take her back. Others said no to this, because she had been rejected by him. All the ascetics, rigid in their vows, again said, 'O fortunate one! This having occurred, what can we, learned ones do? O fortunate one! Listen to these beneficial words. There is no need for you to wander around. O fortunate one! Depart from here and go to your father's residence. The king, your father, will know what should be done next. You possess all the qualities. Go and dwell there happily. You have no refuge other than your father. Roaming around is extremely difficult, especially for someone who is delicate'. The brahmanas spoke these words to the ascetic lady. 'On seeing you alone in this deserted and dense forest, kings will solicit you. Therefore, do not set your mind on this'.

Amba replied, 'I cannot go again to my father's residence in the city of Kashi. There is no doubt that I will be disrespected by my relatives. It was different when I dwelt in my father's residence as a child. I will not go where my father is now. O foremost among brahmanas! I wish to practise austerities under the protection of ascetics, so that I do not confront great ill fortune, in this world or the next'.

When those brahmanas were reflecting on this, the ascetic rajarshi Hotravahana[269] arrived in that forest. All the ascetics honoured the king.

---

269 A saintly king who was the grandfather of Aṃbā.

They worshipped and welcomed him and offered him a seat and water. After he had seated himself and had rested, in his hearing, those residents of the forest again spoke to the maiden.

On hearing the story of Amba, the daughter of the king of Kashi, her maternal grandfather trembled and arose. He placed the maiden on his lap and comforted her. He asked her about the entire story of the reasons behind her hardships. In detail, she told him exactly what had happened. Then the rajarshi was overcome by great grief and misery. The extremely great ascetic thought in his mind about what should be done next. He trembled and in great grief, told the distressed maiden, 'O fortunate one! Do not go to your father's residence. I am your mother's father. O daughter! Depend on me. I will dispel your sorrows. O daughter! You have become desiccated. I think you have had enough. Listen to my words and go to the ascetic Parashurama, Jamadagni's son. Rama[270] will remove your extremely great unhappiness and sorrow. If Bhishma does not listen to his words, Parashurama will kill Bhishma in battle. Go to the foremost among the Bhargavas[271] whose energy is like that of the fire of destruction. That great ascetic will establish you on a smooth path'.

She repeatedly shed many tears. She lowered her head before Hotravahana, her grandfather, and said, 'I will follow your instructions and will go. But will I be able to see that arya, famous in the world? How will Bhargava destroy my terrible misery? I wish to learn about this and I will go there after that'.

Hotravahana said, 'O child! You will see Parashurama, Jamadagni's son, in the great forest. He is engaged in terrible austerities. He is devoted to the truth. He is extremely strong. The sages, those who are learned in the Vedas,

---

270 Parashurama.
271 Parashurama.

the gandharvas[272] and the apsaras[273] always worship Rama on Mahendra, the foremost among mountains. O fortunate one! Go there. He is aged in austerities and is firm in his vows. After saluting him by lowering your head, tell him these words of mine. O fortunate one! Tell him once again about what you desire. On hearing my name, Rama will do everything that you wish for. O child! Rama is my friend. He is affectionate towards me and is my well-wisher. The brave one is Jamadagni's son. He is supreme among those who wield all weapons.'

While King Hotravahana was speaking to the maiden in this way, Akritavrana[274], Parashurama's devoted follower, appeared. All the sages arose in their thousands as a mark of respect and so did King Hotravahana from Srinjaya, aged in years. As is appropriate, those residents of the forest asked about each other's welfare. Then they seated themselves around Akritavrana and conversed about delightful subjects, beautiful and celestial ones. O Indra among kings! They were happy and delighted. When they had finished, the great-souled rajarshi Hotravahana asked Akritavrana about Parashurama, foremost among maharshis. 'O Akritavrana! Where is it possible to see Jamadagni's powerful and mighty-armed son, foremost among those who have knowledge of the Vedas?'

Akritavrana said, 'O lord! O king! Rama always speaks about you. It is my belief that Rama will be here tomorrow morning. You will see him when he comes here, desiring to meet you. O rajarshi! Why has this maiden come to the forest? Who does she belong to and what is her relationship to you? I wish to know this.'

Hotravahana replied, 'O lord! She is my daughter's daughter. She is the beautiful daughter of the king of Kashi. O unblemished one! She is the eldest

---

272 Gandharvas are celestial musicians and semi-divine.
273 Apsaras are celestial dancers who serve Indra, sometimes regarded as the wives of Gandharvas.
274 Akritavarna was a wise sage, and a disciple of Parashurama.

and, with her sisters, was at the svayamvara. She is famous by the name of Amba. Ambika and Ambalika are younger to her. O brahmarshi! For the sake of these maidens, all the Kshatriya kings gathered in the city of Kashi and there was a great festival. Then the immensely valorous and greatly energetic Bhishma, Shantanu's son, slighted the kings and abducted the three maidens.

The pure-souled Bhishma vanquished the lords of the earth and went to Hastinapura with the maidens. The lord then handed them over to Satyavati, for the sake of a marriage with his brother Vichitravirya. On seeing that arrangements had been made for a marriage, in the midst of the ministers, this maiden told Gangeya, "In my mind, I have chosen the brave lord of Shalva as my husband. When I have thought of someone, you should not give me to someone else." When he heard these words, Bhishma consulted with his ministers. Bhishma made up his mind and with Satyavati's permission, gave her leave to go to Shalva, the lord of Soubha[275]. O brahmana! The maiden was delighted at that time and went and told him, "I have been given up by Bhishma. Act towards me in accordance with dharma. O Shalva! In my mind, I have chosen you earlier." However, suspicious of her conduct, Shalva rejected her. Deciding to undertake austerities, she came to this hermitage. I recognized her when she recounted her lineage. She thinks that Bhishma alone is responsible for her unhappiness'.

Amba said, 'O illustrious one! It is just as Srinjaya King Hotravahana has said. O one rich in austerities! I do not wish to go back to my own city. O great sage! I will be insulted there. O supreme among brahmanas! I will do what the illustrious Parashurama asks me to. O illustrious one! It is my view that this is what I should do'.

Akritavrana said, 'O fortunate one! O woman! O child! There are two hardships. Which of these do you actually wish to redress? O fortunate one! If it is your view that the lord of Soubha should be urged, then, desirous of your welfare, the great souled Rama will ask him accordingly. Or if you wish to see

---

275 Shalva (Soubha was the capital city of the Shalva Kingdom).

Bhishma, the son of Ganga, vanquished in battle by the intelligent Bhargava Rama, he will do that also. O one with the beautiful smiles! We will think about what should be done after hearing your words, and those of Srinjaya.'

Amba replied, 'O illustrious one! When he abducted me, Bhishma acted out of ignorance. O brahmana! Bhishma did not know that my mind was set on Shalva. Before deciding, you should bear this in mind too. Having decided in accordance with what is right, then determine what should be done. O brahmana! Decide what needs to be done about both Bhishma, tiger among the Kurus, and the king of Shalva. I have told you exactly about the reasons for my unhappiness. O illustrious one! In accordance with the reasons, decide on a course of action'.

Akritavrana said, 'O Amba! What you have said about dharma is correct. Now listen to these words of mine. O timid one! If Bhishma had not taken you to Hastinapura, on the instructions of Parashurama, Shalva would have bowed down his head and accepted you. But you have been won over and abducted. Therefore, King Shalva has a doubt about you. Bhishma is insolent about his manliness and victory. I think it is appropriate that action should be taken against Bhishma'.

Amba replied, 'O brahmana! That has always been the great desire in my heart, if only I could kill Bhishma in battle. Whether you think that the fault lies with Bhishma or King Shalva, chastise the one because of whom I have faced this extreme misery'".

Bhishma addressed Duryodhana, "While they were conversing in this way, the day passed. O best of the Bharata lineage! It was night and a pleasant and cool breeze blew. Then Rama appeared, like the blazing fire in his energy. O Duryodhana! He was surrounded by his disciples. The sage had matted hair and was clad in bark. The unblemished one with an indomitable soul held a bow in his hand and a sword and a battle axe. He approached King Hotravahana of Srinjaya. On seeing him, all the ascetics and the immensely ascetic king arose, hands joined in salutation. So did the ascetic maiden. They eagerly honoured Bhargava with madhuparka[276]. Having been shown homage, he seated himself among them. Jamadagni's son and rajarshi Hotravahana of Srinjaya conversed about earlier times. When this conversation was over, in due course of time, the rajarshi spoke these sweet words, full of meaning, to the immensely strong Rama, foremost among the Bhrigus. 'O Rama! This is my grand-daughter. O lord! She is the daughter of the king of Kashi. Listen to her and decide on an appropriate course of action.'

Rama replied, 'Tell me your supreme account.' She approached Rama, who was like a blazing fire. The beautiful one lowered her head at Rama's feet. She touched them with hands that were like the petals of lotuses and stood before him. Her eyes were filled with tears and she wept in grief. She sought refuge with the descendant of the Bhrigu lineage, the one who is everyone's refuge.

Parashurama said, 'O daughter of a king! You are like Srinjaya to me. Tell me about the grief in your mind and I will act in accordance with your words.' Amba replied, 'O illustrious one! O one who is great in his vows! I have sought refuge with you. I am immersed in this ocean and mud of sorrow. O lord! Save me.'"

Bhishma said, "Rama saw her beauty, her youthful age and her extremely delicate form and began to think. 'What is she going to say?' Flooded by compassion, Rama, supreme among those of the Bhrigu lineage, thought in this fashion for a long time. Rama spoke to the one with the beautiful smiles. 'Tell me.' She told Bhargava everything, exactly as it had happened. After having heard the words of the princess, Jamadagni's son made up his mind and told the beautiful one, 'O beautiful one! I will send word to Bhishma, foremost among the Kurus. When he has heard my words, in conformity with dharma, that lord of men will act accordingly. O fortunate one! If Bhishma does not act in accordance with my words, I will use the energy of my weapons

---

276 An offering made to guests, consisting of honey and curd.

to burn him down in battle, together with his advisers. O princess! Or if you are so inclined, I will force the brave lord Shalva to a course of action.'

Amba replied, 'O descendant of the Bhrigu lineage! When Bhishma heard that my mind had earlier turned towards King Shalva, he discarded me. I went to the king of Soubha and spoke words that were difficult to speak. But doubting my character, he did not accept me. Bhishma, the one who is mighty in his vows, is the root cause of my hardship. He used force to overcome and abduct me. O mighty-armed one! Bhishma is the reason behind this unhappiness. Kill him. O Rama! Therefore, fulfil this desire of mine. Kill Bhishma'".

Bhishma said, "O Duryodhana! Having been thus asked to kill me, Parashurama spoke to the weeping maiden, who kept urging him repeatedly. 'O descendant of Kashi! I do not voluntarily take up weapons, except for the sake of those who are learned about the Brahman. What else can I do for you? Both Bhishma and Shalva will listen to my words and obey my instructions. I can do that. Do not grieve. But I cannot take up weapons in any way, unless I am instructed to do so by brahmanas. That is my resolution.'

Amba replied, 'O Rama! Dispel the grief that Bhishma has unleashed on me. Without any delay, kill him.' Rama said, 'O daughter of Kashi! If you speak the word, no matter how revered he is, Bhishma will follow my instructions and lower his head at your feet.' Amba replied, 'O Rama! If you wish to do that which brings me pleasure, kill Bhishma in battle. Since you have made your promise, it is proper that you should make that pledge come true.'"

While Rama and Amba were arguing in this way, Akritavrana spoke these words to Jamadagni's son, 'O mighty-armed one! You should not give up the maiden who has sought refuge with you. O Rama! Kill Bhishma, who roars like an asura, in battle. If Bhishma challenges you in battle, he will either be vanquished, or he will act in accordance with your words. The task of this maiden will then be done. O brave one! The words that you have spoken will come true. Confront him in a battle and fight with him.'

'"Rama replied, ' I remember the promise I made in earlier times. I will do what can be achieved through conciliation. I will take this maiden and myself go to Bhishma. Insolent in war, if he does not act in accordance with my words, it is my certain resolution that I will kill that insolent person'.

'Bhishma said, "Having arrived in Hastinapura, the great Parashurama sent word to me, saying that he had arrived. On learning that the immensely strong lord, the store of energy, had arrived on the outskirts of my kingdom, I was delighted. With a cow in front of me and surrounded by brahmanas, sacrificial priests who were the equals of the gods and other priests, I went there. On seeing me arrive, Jamadagni's powerful son received the homage and spoke these words to me. 'O Bhishma! What were your thoughts when you abducted the daughter of the king of Kashi against her wishes? You then abandoned her later. You have dislodged her from dharma. Who can now go to someone who has been touched by you? O descendant of the Bharata lineage! Because she has been abducted by you, she has been refused by Shalva. Therefore, following my counsel, take her back and let the princess abide by her own dharma. You do not deserve to treat her with such neglect.' On seeing that his mind wasn't that agitated, I spoke to him. 'O brahmana! There is no way that I can give her to my brother again. O Bhargava! She has told me that she has given herself to Shalva earlier. Having obtained my permission, she went to the city of Soubha. Because of fear, compassion, avarice or gain, I cannot abandon the dharma of kshatriyas. That is the vow that I follow.'

Rama's eyes dilated with anger and he said, 'O Bhishma! If you refuse to act in accordance with my words, I will kill you today, together with your advisers.' His eyes were wide with anger. I repeatedly tried to pacify him with sweet words. But I was incapable of pacifying him.

His eyes red with anger, Rama told me, 'O Bhishma! You know that I am your preceptor. O Kouravya! O lord of the earth! Yet, to bring about my pleasure, you are refusing to take back the daughter of Kashi. I am not interested in peace with you. Take her back and save yourself and your lineage. Since you have tainted her, she will not find a husband.'

When he spoke in this way, I told Rama, the destroyer of enemy cities, 'O brahmarshi! Since this cannot be done, what is the point of striving towards it? Because you are my preceptor, I have been affectionate and have greatly honoured you. But you are not acquainted with the conduct of a preceptor and I will therefore, fight with you. You will witness the valour of my arms and my superhuman bravery. Given this, I will do whatever I can. I will fight with you in Kurukshetra. Prepare yourself for the duel. O Rama! You will be killed by hundreds of my arrows. Sanctified by my weapons in that great battle, you will obtain the worlds that you have earned for yourself'.

Desirous of fighting, Parashurama went to Kurukshetra. I entered Hastinapura and told Satyavati everything. I performed the propitiatory rites and was blessed by my mother. The brahmanas pronounced sacred words of benediction. Applauded with benedictions of victory, I left Hastinapura. I arrived in Kurukshetra, the field where the battle would be fought. Like me, the powerful Rama also swiftly reached Kurukshetra.

A battle then ensued between him and me. As we sought to defeat each other, it lasted for many days and both of us were injured. Overcome by anger, the Lord Parashurama manifested the supreme weapon known as brahma. To counter it, I also used the supreme brahma weapon. The two Brahma weapons encountered each other in mid-air, without reaching either Rama or me. For the welfare of the world, when Rama withdrew his weapons because of the words of his ancestors, even I acted in accordance with the words that had been spoken to me by the knowledgeable ones. I was severely wounded. But I went up to Rama and honoured him. Rama, the great ascetic, smiled affectionately at me and said, 'O Bhishma! In this world, there is no Kshatriya like you who roams the earth. Go. In this fight, I have been extremely satisfied with you.' In my presence, Bhargava summoned the maiden. In the midst of those ascetics, he spoke these miserable words, 'O beautiful one! In the sight of all the worlds, to the supreme extent of my capacity, I have shown great manliness. But in battle, I have not been able to establish my superiority over Bhishma, supreme among those who wield weapons, even though I exhibited my supreme weapons. This is the ultimate of my power. This is the ultimate of my strength. O fortunate one! Go wherever you wish. What else can I do for you? Seek refuge with Bhishma. There is no other recourse for you. Unleashing his great weapons, Bhishma has vanquished me.' Having spoken in this way, the great-minded Rama sighed and was silent. The maiden then spoke to the descendant of the Bhrigu lineage. 'O illustrious one! It is just as your illustrious self has said. The intelligent Bhishma is invincible in battle, even to the gods. You have performed my task to the best of your capacity and the best of your endeavours. In this battle, you have been unrestrained in valour and have used many weapons. But in the end, he could not be surpassed in battle. Under no circumstances, will I go back to Bhishma again. O one rich in austerities! O extender of the Bhrigu lineage! Instead, I will go where I can myself bring Bhishma down in battle.' Her eyes red with anger, the maiden spoke in this way. Thinking about my death, she made up her mind to engage in austerities. O descendant of the Bharata lineage! After taking leave from me, Rama, supreme among the Bhrigu lineage, went with the sages to Mahendra, from where he had come.

Praised by the brahmanas, I ascended my chariot and, having entered the city, told my mother, Satyavati, everything that had transpired. O great king! She congratulated me. I instructed wise men to watch over the maiden's doings and from one day to another, they reported to me her goings, words, and deeds.

The maiden resorted to a circle of hermitages that was on the banks of the Yamuna and engaged in superhuman austerities. She gave up food. She became thin and coarse. She became covered with dirt and mud. Rich in austerities, she lived on air for six months and was like a pillar. Later, the beautiful one went to the banks of the Yamuna and stood in the water for one year, without taking any food. After that, for another year, she survived on a single leaf every day. She was terrible in her anger and stood on the tips of her toes. She continued in this way for twelve years and heated up heaven. None of her relatives were capable of restraining her. O king! O Kouravya! The maiden from Kashi roamed around, as she willed, in the hermitage of Nanda, in the sacred hermitage of Uluka, the hermitage of Chyavana, the region of the brahman, Prayaga, the sacrificial region of the gods, the forests of the gods, Bhogavati, the hermitage of Koushika, the hermitage of Mandavya, the hermitage of Dilipa, and the hermitage of Pailagargya. O king! O lord of the earth! The maiden from Kashi bathed at these tirthas and performed terrible austerities.

All the ascetics saw that she was firm in her resolution to perform austerities. O Duryodhana! They tried to stop her and asked, 'What do you wish to accomplish?' The rishis were aged in their austerities and the maiden replied to them, 'I have been abandoned by Bhishma and have been dislodged from the dharma I would have obtained through a husband. O ones rich in austerities! I have consecrated myself for his death. I have resolved that I will achieve peace only through Bhishma's death. It is because of his deeds that I have obtained this eternal and infinite misery. I have been deprived of the world of a husband. I am neither a woman, nor a man. O ones rich in austerities! I will not desist until I have slain Gangeya in battle. This is the resolution in my heart and I am engaged for this purpose. I am disgusted with my state as a woman and I have made up my mind to become a man. I wish to exact vengeance on Bhishma. I should not be dissuaded again.' The god who wields the trident, Uma's consort, manifested himself. In the midst of the maharshis, he showed his own form to the beautiful one. He satisfied her with a boon and she asked for my defeat. The god replied to the intelligent one, 'You will kill him.' At this, the maiden spoke to Rudra. 'O god! How can a woman like me be victorious in battle? O Uma's consort! You have promised Bhishma's defeat. O Shiva! Act so that your promise comes true, so that I can kill Bhishma, Shantanu's son, in battle.'

Mahadeva spoke truthfully to the maiden. 'O fortunate one! I do not utter false words. What I have said will come true. You will attain manhood and will kill Bhishma in battle. When you enter another body, you will remember everything. You will be born as a maharatha in Drupada's lineage. You will be an extremely honoured warrior who is swift in the use of weapons. O fortunate one! Everything will be exactly as I have said it will be. You will become a man after some time has passed.' Having thus spoken, Mahadeva disappeared, while all the brahmanas looked on. In the sight of those maharshis, the unblemished one, the one with the beautiful complexion, gathered wood from the forest. She constructed an extremely large funeral pyre and set fire to it. O great king! When the fire was blazing, with rage igniting her senses, she said, 'This is for Bhishma's destruction.' O king! On the banks of the Yamuna, the eldest daughter of Kashi entered the fire…"

"Later, she was born in the lineage of the Panchala king, Drupada as Shikandi. However, due to the unfolding of certain circumstances in her life, she exchanged her gender with a yaksha named Sthunakarna[277]. O Duryodhana! Later, Drupada gave Shikhandi to Drona as a student. O great king! This was a son who had been a woman earlier. Shikhandi, the son of a king, together with Parshata Dhrishtadyumna[278] and all of you[279] learnt the four parts of Dhanurveda. Thus, Drupada's offspring is both a woman and a man. He became a supreme warrior. The eldest daughter of the king of Kashi was known by the name of Amba. She was born in Drupada's lineage as Shikhandi. When he appears before me with a bow in his hand, desiring to fight, I will not glance at him even for an instant and will not strike. This has always been my vow and it is renowned throughout the earth. O descendant of the Kourava lineage! I will not shoot arrows at a woman, one who has earlier been a woman, one who has the name of a woman and one who has the form of a woman. Because of this reason, I will not kill Shikhandi. I know the truth about Shikhandi's birth. Therefore, I will not kill him, when he seeks to slay me. Bhishma would rather kill himself than kill a woman. When I see him stationed in battle, I will not kill him."[280]

The Case Of Unstable And Stable Equilibrium

The word 'equilibrium' is a special one as it finds shelter in many branches of study, whether chemistry, physics, economics or even philosophy. In general terms, it is a state in which opposing forces or influences are balanced. In economics, these opposing influences are the demand and supply that intersect each other, resulting in an equilibrium.

---

277 A prominent Yaksha in the Mahabharata, who dwelt in a forest close to the Panchala Kingdom.
278 Dhrishtadyumna was the son of Drupada—the king of Panchala Kingdom—and the twin brother of Draupadi. The word Parshata is another name for Drupada. So, Dhrishtadyumna is addressed as the son of Drupada, Parshata Dhrishtadyumna.
310 Kauravas and Pandavas.
280 The Mahabharata 5 Translated by Bibek Debroy.

In economics, equilibrium or more specifically market equilibrium is a situation of the market in which demand for a commodity is exactly equal to its supply corresponding to a particular price. Equilibrium may also be described as a situation where at a given price, quantity demanded is equal to the quantity supplied.[281] In other words, when demand=supply, the market has attained its equilibrium.

Predominantly, there are three types of equilibrium in economics

1. Stable Equilibrium
2. Unstable Equilibrium
3. Neutral Equilibrium

The equilibrium between demand and supply is attained at a price-quantity combination at which both buyers and sellers are satisfied about what they are buying and selling respectively and therefore they do not have an incentive to change their behaviour. Furthermore, changes in demand due to changes in the preferences of the consumers and changes in supply due to technological changes or variation in the prices of the factors of production (land, labour, capital, entrepreneurship) often occur which disturb the equilibrium. These changes in demand and supply will determine a new equilibrium price, however there is no guarantee that the new equilibrium price will be restored.[282]

Therefore, when the actual price shifts from the equilibrium price owing to disturbances, it is fundamental for an economist to critically consider whether any other forces would work so as to restore the equilibrium.

So, the equilibrium is stable, if following a disturbance in it, the equilibrium is established again, and unstable if the system tends to move away from the equilibrium situation.[283]

---

281 All in One Economics CBSE Class XI.
282 Modern Economics by Dr. H.L. Ahuja.
283 Modern Economics by Dr. H.L. Ahuja.

Fundamentally, the restoration of equilibrium is dependent on the behaviour of the buyers and the sellers.

Further, when there is disequilibrium whether it is changes in price or changes in the quantity through which adjustment takes place to restore equilibrium. Marie-Esprit-Léon Walras, a French Mathematical Economist and Georgist thought it is through changes in price that adjustment takes place. According to him, the behaviour of buyers is such that they tend to bid up the price when quantity demanded exceeds the quantity supplied at a given price and the behaviour of sellers is such that they tend to lower the price when the quantity supplied of the commodity is greater than the quantity demanded of it. With such changes in price, equilibrium will be stable.[284]

Let us understand the stable and unstable equilibrium through the story of Amba's revenge.

Case A: Unstable Equilibrium

The diagram on the right represents the unstable equilibrium in Amba's life. It should be noted that the demand curve D_0D_0 represents Princess Amba's demand for marrying Shalva. Corresponding to her demand curve, we measure her demand for a matrimonial alliance with Prince Shalva on the x-axis. The supply curve S_0S_0 represents Shalva's secret desire to marry Amba.

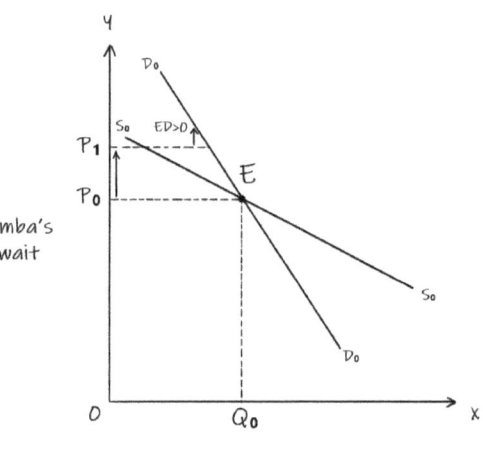

Demand for Shalva, Shalva's secret choice

---

284 Modern Economics by Dr. H.L. Ahuja.

Corresponding to his supply curve, his inclination towards her is also measured on the x-axis. The y axis represents her waiting period and hence labelled as 'Amba's await'. Traditionally, we measure the price on the y-axis and the quantity demanded/supplied on the x-axis.

From the diagram, we must also take into consideration that both the demand and supply curves are negatively sloped but the demand curve D_0D_0 is steeper than the supply curve S_0S_0. From the diagram, Amba's demand for Shalva (quantity demanded) is equal to Shalva's secret choice/inclination towards Amba (quantity supplied) at price P_0 (which in this case is her wait in the svayamvara for her turn to choose her groom).

If the market price is at the equilibrium price level P_0, then both Amba's and Shalva's await remains the same unless there are any external disturbances. Due to Bhishma's act of abducting all the three princesses of Kashi, the price (Amba's and Shalva's await) increases from P_0 to P_1, which is naturally above the equilibrium price P_0, then Amba's demand for Shalva exceeds Shalva's inclination for Amba. This situation is termed as excess demand in economics and is represented as ED>0 (where ED stands for Excess demand).

Given the behaviour pattern of a rational buyer, they would tend to bid up the price. Now, associating this behaviour pattern to our character Amba, we know from the story that she confesses her feelings for Shalva before Bhishma and leaves for Soubha, thereby increasing her wait but not losing her hope of marrying Shalva.

Therefore, the market price instead of returning to the equilibrium level P_0, will move away from it. Thus, the equilibrium at price P_0 in the above diagram is unstable.

Case B: Stable Equilibrium

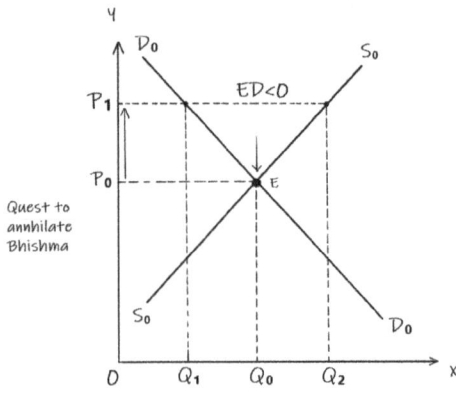

Demand for Bhishma's extinction, Parashurama's deed and Shiva's boon

If the demand curve (in this case Amba's demand curve representing her longing for Bhishma's extinction) is downward sloping and the supply curve (in this case Parashurama and Lord Shiva's supply curve representing their deeds and boon respectively) is upward sloping, the equilibrium between demand and supply is stable.

At price, P_1, the magnanimity of Shiva's boon exceeds Amba's demand for Bhishma's extinction (quantity supplied exceeds quantity demanded). This is because when Amba asks for a boon to kill Bhishma from Lord Shiva, she also questions Lord Shiva, 'How can a woman like me be victorious in battle?'.

Lord Shiva's answer, 'You will attain manhood and will kill Bhishma in battle. When you enter another body, you will remember everything. You will be born as a maharatha in Drupada's lineage. You will be an extremely honoured warrior who is swift in the use of weapons...' clearly indicates the magnanimity of the blessing. Not only is Lord Shiva blessing Amba to be the cause of death of Bhishma, but he is also blessing her to be a honoured warrior. Hence, this situation clearly represents that the quantity supplied is greater than the quantity demanded ($Q_2 > Q_1$). Therefore, at price P_1, excess demand is negative ED<0.

This means that at price P_1, Lord Shiva would not be able to give the boon to Amba as a disequilibrium exists. According to the typical behaviour of the firms to bid down the price until price is at P_0 in such scenarios (traditionally, termed as profit-maximizing behaviour), Lord Shiva's answer to Amba makes it clear that he brings down the price Amba must pay by blessing her to remember everything in her next birth and to attain manhood therefore. This effectively eases Amba's quest for Bhishma's annihilation because when she will be born again in Drupada's lineage, she will already be aware about the purpose of her life. As a result, the price reduces from P_1 to P_0. Once again, at P_0 Amba's demand and Lord Shiva's supply are at equilibrium.

Thus, with negatively sloping demand curve and positively sloping supply curve equilibrium when exists is stable as market price when disturbed moves towards equilibrium due to the assumed behaviour of buyers and sellers.[285]

---

285 Modern Economics by Dr. H.L. Ahuja.

Zero-Cost Profit for Draupadi

"Grandmothers are voices of the past and role models of the present. Grandmothers open the doors to the future".

—Helen Ketchum

I first heard the story of the Akshayapatra from my grandmother. It was essentially a tool that was used by my grandma to attract my attention and somehow feed me lunch; a meal that I hated the most.

If I declined from eating lunch, then my grandma would conveniently pause her story. So, I clearly had no choice but to eat my lunch in order to quench my curiosity of knowing what happened next in the story.

Now, when I reminisce about those after-school lunch moments, I realise that my grandmother was someone who owned her own Akshayapatra, one filled with endless stories…

During their Vanavasa, the Pandavas along with their virtuous wife Panchali[286] travelled across many regions. During their stay at these places, many venerable rishis and munis would visit them. As a result, they experienced immense difficulty in providing meals to all their guests. Panchali, therefore honoured Lord Surya and obtained the divine Akshayapatra[287] from him. The Akshayapatra was known to provide abundant amounts of food for the Pandavas as per their necessity until Draupadi commenced her meal. After Draupadi's meal, the Akshayapatra would cease to provide any more food.

The Kauravas on the other hand, were desperate to cause trouble to their brothers and hence they requested Rishi Durvasa to visit the Pandavas after Panchali had completed her meal. The Kauravas were aware of Rishi Durvasa's short temper and cursing nature, accordingly they wanted to utilise Durvasa's anger to cause hardship to the Pandavas.

One day, when the Pandavas and their wife had finished their afternoon meal, the Sage Durvasa, accompanied by one thousand disciples, approached them. Yudhishthira, the benevolent King received Durvasa and his disciples with utmost humility and devotion. He offered them appropriate seats and addressed them, "O venerable ones! Please return after performing your diurnal ablutions and observances". Durvasa Muni, not knowing how the king would be able to provide a feast for him and his disciples[288], proceeded with his disciples to a nearby stream to perform his ablutions. On the contrary, Panchali the beautiful queen of the Pandavas was in angst about the meal to be served to the Muni and his disciples. She frantically walked from side to side of the hermitage, her eyes fixed on the window. The Pandavas were miserable as they saw their wife in a helpless situation. Draupadi began to check all the vessels hoping to find some food, but her efforts were futile

---

286 Draupadi's name. Since she was a princess of the kingdom Panchal, she is often addressed as Panchali.

287 Akshayapatra is an inexhaustible vessel that holds a never-depleting supply of food.

288 The Mahabharata of Krishna-Dwaipayana Vyasa translated by Kisari Mohan Ganguly.

as there was absolutely no food in the hermitage. Fearing the wrath of rishi Durvasa, Draupadi began to sweat in fear. Her hands clinging onto the edge of her pallu turned cold. She was clueless.

At this instant, she realised that there were certainly no sources to provide Durvasa Muni and his disciples a feast. She remembered Lord Krishna. She said, "Krishna, O Krishna, of mighty arms, O son of Devaki, whose power is inexhaustible, O Vasudeva[289], O lord of the Universe, who dispels the difficulties of those who bow down to you, you are the soul, the creator, and the destroyer of the Universe. You are the preserver of the Universe and of all created beings. O Supreme and Infinite Being, O giver of all good, you are the refuge of the helpless. O Primordial Being, incapable of being conceived by the soul or the mental faculties or otherwise, you are the ruler of all and the lord of Brahma. I seek your protection. O god, you are known to be kindly disposed towards those that take refuge in you. Do cherish me with your kindness. O one with a complexion dark as the leaves of the blue lotus, and with eyes red as the corolla of the lily, and attired in yellow robes with, besides, the bright *Kaustubha* gem[290] in your bosom, you are the beginning and the end of creation, and the greatest refuge of all. You are the supreme light and essence of the Universe! Your face is directed towards every point. Under your protections, O lord of the gods, all evils lose their terror. As you protected me before from Dussasana[291], do extricate me from this difficulty".[292]

At Draupadi's plea, the lord of the universe, Krishna appeared before her. Draupadi bowed down to Krishna with utmost devotion and narrated to him the entire episode of Rishi Durvasa's arrival to their hermitage. Krishna

---

289 Lord Krishna's name meaning one who resides and shines brightly in all including the gods.
290 Kaustubha is a divine jewel or "mani" or "ratnam", which is in the possession of Lord Vishnu and a symbol of divine authority.
291 The second eldest son of Dhritarashtra and Gandhari. The younger brother of Duryodhana.
292 The Mahabharata of Krishna-Dwaipayana Vyasa translated by Kisari Mohan Ganguly.

patiently heard Draupadi and later said, "I am very much afflicted with hunger, can you give me some food without delay…" Draupadi was confused at Krishna's words and replied, "The Akshayapatra remains full till I finish my meal. But as I have already completed my meal today, there is no food in it now". Krishna replied, "This is no time for banter, O Panchali. I am distressed with hunger, go quickly, and fetch the vessel and show it to me"[293]. Draupadi placed the vessel before Krishna and when the supreme among the Yadus[294] investigated the vessel, he saw a grain of rice and a piece of vegetable sticking to its rim. Delicately, Krishna picked up the particle with his lotus-like fingers and placed it in his mouth. The Pandavas were astonished to behold Krishna relishing that grain of rice and vegetable. After swallowing that grain of rice and vegetable, Krishna said, "May it please the god Hari[295], the soul of the Universe, and may that god who partakes at sacrifices, be satiated with this"[296]. He addressed Bhima and said, "Approach the Muni and his disciples, who are offering ablutions in the nearby stream and invite them for lunch". At Krishna's words, Bhima went towards the stream to invite the rishis.

---

293 The Mahabharata of Krishna-Dwaipayana Vyasa translated by Kisari Mohan Ganguly.

294 Krishna, he belonged to Yadu lineage.

295 Name of Lord Vishnu.

296 The Mahabharata of Krishna-Dwaipayana Vyasa translated by Kisari Mohan Ganguly.

On the other hand, the rishis, who were performing ablutions in the water suddenly began to realise that their stomachs were full and that they were not feeling the slightest of hunger. It seemed to them as though their hunger was destroyed in seconds. When they came onto the banks of the stream, they stared at each other in bewilderment. The disciples turned towards Durvasa and said to him in a collective voice, "Having asked the king to make our meals ready, we have come here for a bath. But how, O regenerate *Rishi*, can we eat anything now, for our stomachs seem to be full to the throat. The repast has been uselessly prepared for us. What is the best thing to be done now?[297]" Durvasa carefully considered his disciples' views and replied, "By spoiling the repast, we have done a great wrong to that royal sage, king Yudhishthira. Would not the Pandavas destroy us by looking down upon us with angry eyes? I know the royal sage Yudhishthira to be possessed of great ascetic power. O Brahmanas, I am afraid of men that are devoted to Hari. The high-souled Pandavas are all religious men, learned, war-like, diligent in ascetic austerities and religious observances, devoted to Vasudeva, and always observant of rules of good conduct. If provoked, they can consume us with their wrath. Therefore, let us all run away quickly without seeing them again![298]"

At Durvasa's words, his disciples fled in all directions. When Bhima arrived near the celestial stream, he was surprised to find the Munis missing. He searched for them in the nearby places and learned from the ascetics that they had run away. Bhima then returned to the hermitage and informed Yudhishthira about Durvasa and his disciples. At Bhima's words, Yudhishthira and the other Pandavas were left in deep misery. When they were thus absorbed in deep misery, Govinda spoke, "Knowing your danger from that wrathful *Rishi*, I was implored by Draupadi to come, and (therefore) have I come here speedily. But now you do not have much to fear from the *Rishi* Durvasa. Afraid of your ascetic powers, all those venerable ones fled. Virtuous

---

297 The Mahabharata of Krishna-Dwaipayana Vyasa translated by Kisari Mohan Ganguly.
298 The Mahabharata of Krishna-Dwaipayana Vyasa translated by Kisari Mohan Ganguly.

men never suffer. I now ask your permission to let me return home. May you always be prosperous![299]"

The Simple Case Of Zero Cost

In economics, the term "market" does not simply refer to a place where goods are bought and sold, but it refers to an arrangement that facilitates the establishment of effective relationships between the buyers and sellers of commodities. It is essentially a series of activities that brings both the potential seller and buyer in close contact for the purchase and sale of a commodity.

There are fundamentally four components of a market, namely:

1. Commodity to be bought and sold
2. Buyers and sellers of the commodity
3. Area where the buyers and sellers meet
4. Close contact between the buyers and sellers

Several factors such as the number of buyers and sellers, nature of the commodity and the barriers to entry and exit of firms influence the form of the market.

Majorly, there are two forms of market:

1. Perfect competition
2. Imperfect competition

Imperfect competition is a form of market that includes monopoly, monopolistic competition, and oligopoly.

---

[299] The Mahabharata of Krishna-Dwaipayana Vyasa translated by Kisari Mohan Ganguly.

Perfect competition is a form of market where there are a very large number of buyers and sellers of a commodity. Homogenous products are sold at uniform price.[300] Homogeneity here implies that the product sold by all the firms in the market is identical in shape, size, quality, etc.

Imperfect competition on the other hand is a market structure that shows some, but not all the features of a competitive market. It may be classified into the following types:[301]

1. Monopoly: A market structure in which there is a single seller and there are no close substitutes of the commodity sold by the monopolist. [302]
2. Monopolistic Competition: A form of market in which there are many sellers of the product, but the products of each seller is somehow different from that of others.[303]
3. Oligopoly: A form of market in which there are a few big sellers of a commodity and a large number of buyers. Each seller has a significant share of the market. [304]

Among these classifications under the imperfect competition, let us focus on the monopoly form of market.

It is useful to note that just as the perfectly competitive firm tries to maximize its profit, the monopolist firm also seeks to maximize its profit.[305]

In this part of our discussion, we shall analyse this profit-maximizing behaviour of the monopoly firm to ascertain the quantity produced by the monopolist

---

300 All in One Economics CBSE Class XI
301 All in One Economics CBSE Class XI
302 All in One Economics CBSE Class XI
303 All in One Economics CBSE Class XI.
304 All in One Economics CBSE Class XI.
305 Modern Economics by Dr HL Ahuja.

firm and the price at which it is sold to the consumers. Let us assume that the monopolist firm sells its entire output without maintaining stocks. So, having established the profit-maximizing behaviour of a monopoly firm and the assumption of selling its entire output, it is now time to understand the simple case of zero cost under the short-run equilibrium of the Monopoly firm.

Imagine, a man named Mahadeva resides in the outskirts of the village named Minijenahalli. He is the owner of the only mango grove in the entire Minijenahalli. All the inhabitants of Minijenahalli loved the taste of those mangoes. So, they would crowd up in front of Mahadeva's mango grove every harvest season. Despite the enormous crowd, Mahadeva was able to prevent the theft of those juicy mangoes except through the purchase of those mangoes. Mahadeva was an old man incapable of climbing up the mango trees and plucking mangoes for his customers. Therefore, whenever a person purchased the mango from Mahadeva, he had to climb up the tree and pluck the mangoes on his own. Also, since Mahadeva's mangoes grew on a fertile land, which received sufficient rainfall, he did not have to water or nourish the trees in the grove. Thus, we can infer that Mahadeva is a monopolist who bears zero cost in producing mangoes.

From our previous discussion about profit, we know that the profit earned by a firm is the excess of total revenue earned from the sale of its goods after deducting its total cost of production. Profit is given by $\pi = TR-TC$. In the case of zero cost of production, it is implied that in the above equation TC is zero and the profit is maximum when the TR is maximum.

In the story of the Akshayapatra, we can regard the Pandavas along with Draupadi as a monopolist as only they possessed the Akshayapatra, which could provide an abundant quantity of food. Durvasa and his thousand students are in the place of a consumer whose demand for the afternoon meal can only be satisfied by the Akshayapatra. When these sages visit the Pandavas after Draupadi's meal, the Pandavas are in a dilemma.

The Akshayapatra is known to provide abundant quantities of food only until Draupadi finishes her meal. After Draupadi's meal, the Akshayapatra ceases to provide any more food. So, clearly the Akshayapatra does not allow for storing excess food like the assumption of a monopolist not maintaining any stocks. Now, when Durvasa and his thousand disciples arrive at Yudhishthira's hermitage, there is no food left to be served to the venerable rishis. At this moment, Draupadi prays to Lord Krishna, who manifests before her. From the story, we also know that Lord Krishna picks up the morsel of food left in the rim of the Akshayapatra and relishes it, thereby satisfying Sri Hari and all the rishis consequently.

Weaving an economic perspective to this scenario, we can interpret that Draupadi's profit (Preservation of grihastha dharma) is the excess of her total revenue (i.e., the contentment of Durvasa and his thousand disciples earned by satisfying their hunger through Krishna's deed) after deducting the cost of producing the food. Profit is given by $\pi = TR-TC$. Due to Krishna's deeds Draupadi's cost of production is zero. Therefore, her profit is maximum when her Total revenue is maximum. In this scenario, her Grihastha dharma[306] of feeding rishis when they visit her doorstep is preserved drawing from the satisfaction of the rishis.

We can thus say that her profit (Preservation of Grihastha dharma) is maximum (i.e., the prescribed grihastha dharma is followed without any compromise) when the total revenue (contentment of rishi Durvasa and his disciples) is maximum (i.e., they do not experience the slightest of hunger).

---

306 Grihastha dharma refers to the conduct and rules that one should follow in a married life along with duties of maintaining a home, raising a family, educating one's children, and leading a family-centred and a dharmic social life.

Yaksha's Hypothesis Of Independent Utility

"History is not a burden on the memory, but an illumination of the soul".

—Lord Acton

It was 12 AM and I was frantically flipping pages of the Indian freedom struggle in my 8th grade History textbook in one hand and the lesson Yaksha Yudhishthira Samvadha from my Sanskrit textbook in the other hand, while the ticking sound of the round kept amplifying at the turn of every page. Each ticking sound meant that I was one second closer to writing the history and Sanskrit exam. Excitement along with nervousness grew... not until my mind escaped from the chaos and found comfort in contemplating the unique confluence of Sanskrit and History.

To me, the marriage of Sanskrit and history is "itihasa"- thus it happened, just as the marriage of economics and Sanskrit is Jayarthashastra.

I can never forget the night of 26th November 2016. That was the day when the author in me came alive. An infinite desire to write a piece presenting the seamless weave of Sanskrit and social science was born that night. Reminiscing about that night, let us rewind to the story of Yaksha and Yudhishthira's conversation in the Araneya Parva of the Mahabharata.

Having rescued Draupadi from Jayadratha[307], the brave Pandavas returned to Dvaitavana[308] and resided in Markandeya's[309] hermitage. Once, when the Pandavas were seated in the beautiful forests of Dvaitavana, a brahmana approached Yudhishthira and spoke the following words, "O King! I placed my kindling and churning rod[310] against a tree. But, they got entangled in the antlers of a deer, which escaped, carrying away my kindling and churning rod. O King! Pursue that deer and bring back my kindling and churning rod, so that I can carry out my agnihotra"[311].

Upon hearing the brahmana's plea, the Pandavas pursued the deer armed with their supreme bows and arrows. Although they spotted the deer within close proximity, their arrows could not stab the deer. As they continued to follow the deer into the dense woods, they were exhausted and tired. In a spur of a moment, the deer disappeared leaving the Pandavas in a fatigue. Unable to move their limbs, owing to the extreme exhaustion, the brave Pandavas seated themselves under a sprawling banyan tree. Yudhishthira, gasping for air, spoke to Nakula, "O Nakula! Search for a water-body from above a tree". Nakula instantly climbed up a tree and surveyed the dense spread of trees and spotted a water-body hidden amid the canopies. When he informed Yudhishthira about the water-body, Dharmaraja immediately told him to fetch water for everyone. Nakula stormed through the forest and followed the sound of the cranes. As the sound of the cranes kept intensifying, Nakula's thirst for water too kept heightening. After wandering through the dense forest of Dvaitavana, Nakula finally arrived at the water-body, whose clear balmy waters left Nakula soothed. Just before Nakula could lose himself completely to the tranquillity of the waters, his thirst had overpowered his senses. He slowly went closer to the water-body and bent down to drink some water. Having curled his hands

---

307 Jayadratha - The king of Sindhu, married to Dushala; the only sister of the Kauravas.
308 Dvaitavana - A forest and a lake mentioned in Mahabharata located on the banks of the Sarasvati river.
309 Markandeya - An ancient rishi born in the clan of Bhrigu Rishi.
310 Used to light a fire through friction.
311 Agnihotra refers to a yajna of casting ghee into the sacred fire as per strict rites.

to form a cup, Nakula held the cold water in his palms. Although a few drops of water kept escaping from in between his fingers and palms in a perfect synchronization to the ripples of the water, Nakula's attention was focused on quenching his thirst. As he was about to sip the water from his palms, a faint voice interrupted his action. Involuntarily, the frequency of the dripping water from his hands increased. As he turned all around to find the source of the sound, the water in his hand emptied itself completely into the water-body leaving his thirst unquenched.

Unable to locate the source of the sound, Nakula began to keenly observe the vicinity of the water-body. He stood in an alert stature prepared to face the unexpected. . He heard the voice again, but this time a little louder. He tried to contemplate every syllable. The voice said in a hushed tone, "O son! I own this lake and you can only drink water from this lake after answering my question". Anxiety plummeted as Nakula heard the voice speak. Owing to the feeling of anxiety, his thirst for water amplified. Having ignored the voice, Nakula drank the water and within seconds he fainted and hit the ground.

Yudhishthira, on the other hand, waited patiently for the return of his brother. He kept wandering amidst the canopies, his eyes fixed towards the direction from where Nakula was expected to return. After several hours of waiting, he addressed Sahadeva, "O younger son of Madri! I am worried about Nakula's well-being. I request you to find your brother and ensure that he is fine. Also fetch water for all of us, O Sahadeva!" Sahadeva immediately journeyed to the lake, where he was surprised by the sight of Nakula lying lifeless on the ground. As he approached the water-body to drink water, he heard the same voice again. It said, "O son! I own this lake and you can only drink water from this lake after answering my question". Sahadeva, who was eager to quench his thirst, neglected the words of the voice and drank the water from the lake. Sahadeva also met the same fate as his brother, Nakula. Yudhishthira was alarmed when the twins did not return. He immediately instructed Arjuna to search for the twins and fetch them back along with water. Arjuna also met the same fate as his brothers, Nakula and Sahadeva. So did Bhima, who went in search of his younger brothers.

Disturbed by the absence of all his brothers, Yudhishthira, entered the forest, which was populated by ruru deer, boar and birds, in search of his brothers. When he encountered his brothers lying lifeless on the banks of the pond, he was devastated. Sorrow seemed to engulf him instantly. His limbs shivered at the mere sight of his brothers lying devoid of senses. The hair on his body stood up in shock. His ears turned red as the reality of his brothers' death sunk in. Yudhishthira, the valourous king fell on his knees and began lamenting over his fate. However, his intellect, unable to accept the truth of his brothers' death, began to think. He thought about the reason for the death of his brothers as he began to search for weapons or any marks on his brothers' bodies. He was confused by the fact that there was not a single mark on any of his brothers' bodies or a weapon anywhere near the lake.

He reached a conclusion that the death of his brothers was caused by a divine being. He again thought to himself, "Perhaps I will find out after drinking the water. Perhaps this is a deed that has been undertaken by Duryodhana, who cannot differentiate between what should be done and what should not be done. The faces of my brothers are healthy in complexion. These men are excellent and each one of them is capable of withstanding the shock of a flood of water. Who but Yama, the arbiter of destiny, can subjugate them?" Reflecting in this way, he entered the water. As he entered, he heard these words from the sky.[312]

The yaksha said, "I am a crane that lives on aquatic plants and fish. I have taken your younger brothers to the land of the dead. O prince! If you do not answer my questions, you will be the fifth. O son! Do not be foolish enough

---

312 The Mahabharata 3 Translated by Bibek Debroy

to do this. I have obtained possession of this earlier. O Kounteya! Answer my questions. Then drink and take the water."[313]

Uncertain about the true form of the creature, Yudhishthira said in apprehension, "It is impossible for a crane to defeat my brothers. Therefore, tell me who you are?" The Yaksha replied spontaneously, "O Pandava! I am indeed not a crane but a yaksha[314]. I have solely vanquished your brothers and sent them to the land of the dead". Yudhishtira's ears trembled at the words of the yaksha. He approached the water-body and observed the yaksha overcome by grief and misery. The Yaksha stared at Yudhishthira with his malformed eyed, gigantic yet tall form.[315] The Yaksha again addressed the brave son of Pandu, "O Ajatashatru![316] Despite my repeated efforts to prevent your brothers from drinking water, they ignored my words and paved way for their own destruction. Therefore, I advise you not to commit the same mistake as your brothers. Answer my questions and you may drink and take the water".

Yudhishthira folded his hands before the Yakshan and said, "O Lord! Ask me. I will answer your questions according to my wisdom".[317]

---

313 The Mahabharata 3 Translated by Bibek Debroy.
314 Yakshas are nature-spirits.
315 The Mahabharata 3 Translated by Bibek Debroy.
316 Ajathashatru is the other name for Yudhishtira which means, one who has no enemies (He even addressed Duryodhana lovingly as Suyodhana).
317 The Mahabharata 3 Translated by Bibek Debroy.

Jayārthashastra

Yaksha: "What causes the sun to rise and who remains close to him? Similarly, what causes the sun to set and what is the sun established in?"

Yudhishtira: "Brahma causes the sun to rise and the Gods remain close to him. While dharma causes the sun to set, the sun himself is embodied in truth".

Yaksha: "How does one become learned, attain greatness, obtain a second[318] and become intelligent?

Yudhishthira: "One becomes learned through the sacred texts. One attains greatness through austerities. One obtains a second through perseverance. One becomes intelligent by serving the elders".

---

318 The word used in dvitiyavana, meaning one who has a second. But the meaning remains obscure. However, dvitiya also means the second in a family, that is, a son. Perhaps the sense that how does one obtain a son?

Yaksha: "What is the divine trait of brahmanas? What dharma of theirs is like that of the virtuous? What are their human traits? Which of their traits are like that of those without virtue?"

Yudhishthira: "The study of the Vedas is the divine trait of the Brahmanas. Austerities are like that of the virtuous. Mortality is their human trait. Slander is like the conduct of those without virtue".

Yaksha: "What is the divine trait of kshatriyas? What dharma of theirs is like that of the virtuous? What are their human traits? Which of their traits are like that of those without virtue?"

Yudhishthira: "Arrows and weapons are their divine traits of the kshatriyas. Sacrifices are like that of the virtuous. Fear is their human trait. Desertion is like the conduct of those without virtue."

Yaksha: "Which is the single sacrificial chant? What is the sacrificial formula? What do sacrifices need? And what can sacrifices not transgress?"

Yudhishthira: "The breath of life[319] is the single sacrificial chant. The mind is the sacrificial formula. Sacrifices need speech. Sacrifices cannot transgress speech."

Yaksha: "What is the best among those that descend? What is supreme among those that are sown? What is the best among those that stand? What is supreme among those that speak?"

Yudhishthira: "Rain is best among those that descend. Seeds are supreme among those that are sown. Cows are best among those that stand. Sons are supreme among those that speak."[320]

---

319 Prana.
320 The critical edition uses the word pravadatam, meaning those who speak. Some other versions use the word prasavatam, meaning those who are born. Since

Yaksha: "Who experiences the objects of the senses, is intelligent, is worshipped by all the beings in the world and breathes, but is not alive?"

Yudhishthira: "A person who does not render offerings to the five— gods, guests, servants, ancestors and himself—breathes, but is not alive."

Yaksha: "What is heavier than the earth? What is higher than the sky? What is swifter than the wind? What is more numerous than men?"

Yudhishthira: "The mother is heavier than the earth. The father is higher than the sky. The mind is swifter than the wind. Worries are more numerous than men."[321]

Yaksha: "What does not close its eyes while asleep? What does not move when it is born? What has no heart? What grows through speeding?"

Yudhishthira: "A fish does not close its eyes while asleep. An egg does not move when it is born. A stone has no heart. A river grows through speeding."

Yaksha: "Who is a friend to one who is travelling? Who is a friend at home? Who is a friend to one who is sick? Who is a friend to one who is about to die?"

Yudhishthira: "A caravan is a friend to a traveller. A wife is a friend at home. A physician is a friend to one who is sick. Charity is a friend to one who is about to die."

Yaksha: "What travels alone? What is born again after birth? What is a cure for a cold? What is the greatest field?"

---

the answer is a son, the latter fits better than the former.
321 The critical edition uses the word nrinam, which means men, but some versions go with the word trinam which means grass. In the context of the above question, the word trinam is a better fit.

Yudhishthira: "The sun travels alone. The moon is born again after birth. Fire is the cure for a cold. The earth is the greatest field."

Yaksha: "In a single word, what is dharma? In a single word, what is fame? In a single word, what is heaven? In a single word, what is happiness?"

Yudhishthira: "In a single word, dexterity is dharma, generosity is fame, truth is heaven and conduct is happiness."

Yaksha: "Who is man's self? Who is a friend given by destiny? What is the support of his life? What is the best refuge?"

Yudhishthira: "A son is a man's self. The wife is the friend given by destiny. Rains are the support of his life. Generosity is the best refuge."

Yaksha: "What is supreme among objects that are lauded? What is supreme among riches? What is the supreme gain? What is supreme happiness?"

Yudhishthira: "Dexterity is supreme among objects that are lauded. Knowledge of the sacred texts is supreme among riches. Health is the supreme gain. Satisfaction is supreme happiness."

Yaksha: "What is supreme dharma in this world? What dharma always leads to fruits? What does not grieve when it is controlled? What alliance never breaks?"

Yudhishthira: "Non-violence is supreme dharma. The dharma of the three Vedas - Rig, Sama and Atharva always leads to fruits. The mind does not grieve when it is controlled. An alliance with the righteous never breaks."

Yaksha: "If abandoned, what makes one pleasant? If abandoned, what does not lead to sorrow? If abandoned, what ensures prosperity? If abandoned, what makes one happy?"

Yudhishthira: "The abandoning of pride makes one pleasant. The abandoning of anger does not lead to sorrow. The abandoning of desire ensures prosperity and abandoning desire makes one happy."

Yaksha: "When is a man dead? When is a kingdom dead? When is a funeral ceremony dead? When is a sacrifice dead?"

Yudhishthira: "A poor man is dead. A kingdom without a king is dead. A funeral ceremony performed without a learned brahmana is dead. A sacrifice without dakshina is dead."

Yaksha: "What is the right direction? What is spoken of as water? O Partha! What is food and what is poison? What is the right time for a funeral ceremony? Then you can drink and take the water".

Yudhishthira: "The virtuous are the right direction. The sky is water. The cow is food. A request is poison. A brahmana is the best time for a funeral sacrifice.[322] O yaksha! What do you think?"

Yaksha: "O scorcher of enemies! You have answered all my questions correctly. Tell me. Who is a man? Which man possesses all the riches?"

Yudhishthira: "The reputation of good deeds touches heaven and earth. As long as that reputation remains, one is said to be a man. One to whom the pleasant and the unpleasant, happiness and unhappiness and the past and the future are equal, is a man who possesses all riches."

Yaksha: "O king! You have explained who is a man and which man possesses all riches. Therefore, one of your brothers, whichever one you wish, will live."

---

322 Meaning brahma muhurta, those specific times of the day that are regarded as being presided over by the brahmana. They occur towards the early part of the day.

Yudhishthira: "O yaksha! Nakula is dark, with red eyes, mighty arms, and a broad chest. He is as tall as a shala tree. He will live."

Yaksha: "You love Bhimasena and you depend on Arjuna. O king! Why do you then wish Nakula, who is your stepbrother, to be alive? Bhima has strength equal to ten thousand elephants. Why do you discard him and wish Nakula to live? People say that Bhimasena is your beloved. Out of what sentiments do you wish your step brother to live? All the Pandavas depend on the strength of Arjuna's arms. But you discard him and wish Nakula to live."

Yudhishthira: "Non-violence is supreme dharma. It is my view that this is the supreme objective. I am attracted to non-violence. O yaksha! Nakula shall live. Men know of me as a king who always follows dharma. I will not deviate from my own dharma. O yaksha! Let Nakula live. Madri is like Kunti and I see no difference between the two. I wish the same for both my mothers. O yaksha! Let Nakula live."

Yaksha: "O bull among the Bharata lineage! Since you think that non-violence is superior to artha and kama, all of your brothers will be restored to life."[323]

Yudhishthira was astonished to witness his brothers coming back to life and standing upright on their legs. Their thirst and hunger were satisfied. It was as if they were awakened from a deep slumber. Without succumbing to the emotion of joy, resulting from yaksha's words, Yudhishthira immediately turned towards the yaksha and asked him, "O benevolent one! Who are you?"

The yaksha laughed and replied, "O Pandava! I am Dharma, your father. I disguised myself as a yaksha and arrived here with the objective of testing you. O son! You have passed my test and I am satisfied with your non-violence, and hence I desire to grant you a boon of your choice. Yudhishthira folded his hands in obeisance and asked, "O Father! It is my wish that the Brahmana's agnihotra should not be destroyed and that his kindling and churning rod

---

[323] The Mahabharata 3 Translated by Bibek Debroy.

should be restored to him". Dharma revealed that he had assumed the form of a deer and robbed the brahmana of his kindling and churning rod to test Yudhishthira. He was delighted by Yudhishthira's conduct and simplicity. Dharma blessed Yudhishthira with another boon of his choice. This time Yudhishthira said, "O Father! Bless us to be unrecognizable in the thirteenth year of our Ajñātavāsa (अज्ञातवास)". Dharma replied, "O Yudhishthira! Even if you and your illustrious brothers spend the Ajñātavāsa in your original forms, no one will be able to recognise you. With my blessings you spend the next one year in the kingdom of Virata. Return the kindling to the brahmana, because I stole it in the form of a deer to test you. Ask for a third boon, O son!"

Yudhishthira was humbled by his father's words. He respectfully addressed Dharma, "I have obtained the greatest blessing by witnessing your resplendent form. I will happily accept whatever boon you are satisfied to grant me. O lord! May I always be able to conquer avarice, delusion, and anger. May my mind always be inclined towards generosity, austerity, and truth. Dharma said, "O Pandava! You are naturally endowed with all the qualities. You are dharma yourself. But you will obtain what you ask for." Having said this, the illustrious Dharma, who sustains the worlds, disappeared.[324]

Hypothesis Of Independent Utility

In economics, the satisfaction that a consumer derives from the consumption of a given quantity of a commodity is termed as utility[325]. In other words, utility is the want-satisfying capacity of a commodity.

There are majorly two approaches to study utility:

1. Cardinal Utility Analysis
2. Ordinal Utility Analysis

---

324 The Mahabharata 3 Translated by Bibek Debroy.
325 All in One CBSE Economics Class XI.

Alfred Marshall propounded the Cardinal Utility Analysis. This approach involves measuring utility in terms of cardinal numbers and the unit of measurement used for utility is utils. Cardinal Utility Analysis is one of the oldest theories of demand as it explains a consumer's demand for a commodity and derives the law of demand, which establishes an inverse relationship between the price of a commodity and its quantity demanded of a product[326].

Professor Allen and Hicks propounded Ordinal Utility Analysis. It involves measuring utility in terms of the psychological satisfaction derived from the consumption of one good in comparison to the other commodity[327]. It involves ranking the commodities in terms of their preference.

Although Cardinal Utility Analysis is one of the first theories of demand, it has lately been criticised severely for its quantification of utility in numbers and hence many alternative theories have been introduced such as:

1. Indifference Utility Analysis
2. Samuelson's Revealed Preference Theory
3. Hicks' Logical Weak Ordering Theory

In our next part of the discussion let us focus on the cardinal utility analysis and its assumptions as given by Prof. Alfred Marshall

Having already established that Cardinal Utility Analysis primarily depends on the quantification of utility in terms of cardinal numbers, let us focus on the assumptions of cardinal utility analysis.

---

326 Modern Economics by Dr HL Ahuja.
327 All in One CBSE Economics Class XI.

Assumptions of Cardinal Utility Analysis:

1. The Cardinal Measurability of Utility
2. Constancy of the Marginal Utility of Money
3. Introspective Method
4. The Hypothesis of Independent Utilities

The Cardinal Measurability of Utility explains that utility is a measurable and quantifiable entity. In other words, a consumer can express his utility with the help of cardinal numbers. This assumption also allows for a consumer to compare the different levels of utility in terms of their size, that is, a consumer can say that 20 units of utility is greater than 10 units of utility. As part of this assumption, Alfred Marshall also highlighted that the marginal utility is measurable in terms of money. Marshall argues that the amount of money which a person is prepared to pay for a unit of good rather than he without it is the measure of utility he derives from that good. Thus, according to Marshall money is the measuring rod of utility, although economists from the cardinalist school measure utility in an imaginary unit called utils[328].

Another assumption of cardinal utility analysis is the constancy of the Marginal Utility of Money. Marginal Utility Analysis (MUA) explains that the marginal utility of any commodity decreases as the purchase or consumption increases, the cardinal utility analysis, however assumes that the marginal utility of money remains constant throughout an individual's expenditure on a commodity. Since, Alfred Marshall measures the marginal utilities of commodities using the measuring rod of money, it is essential that the marginal utility of money remains constant. As a measuring rod of utility, if money's marginal utility keeps on varying then the marginal utility values would be obscure and incorrect. Therefore, in Cardinal Utility Analysis, it is crucial for the marginal utility of money to remain constant.

---

328 Modern Economics by Dr HL Ahuja.

Changes in the price of a commodity	Changes in the real income of the consumer	Changes in the Marginal Utility of Money	Marshall's Assumption
Decreases	Increases	Decreases	Marginal Utility of Money remains constant irrespective of changes in price or real income of the consumer
Increases	Decreases	Increases	

Introspection is the method of judging the behaviour of the consumers. Through this method, it is possible to predict the behaviour of other consumers from one's own experience. That is, by peeping into our mind we are actually seeing into the head of other individuals as well.[329] From our experience, we are already aware that we derive less satisfaction as we consume additional units of a commodity. This experience can be utilised to conclude that others' marginal utility will also diminish as they consume additional units of a commodity. Therefore, the law of diminishing marginal utility is based on the assumption of introspection.

The hypothesis of independent utilities is also an important assumption in the cardinal utility analysis. As per the hypothesis of independent utilities, the utility that a consumer obtains from the consumption of a good is dependent on the quantity consumed of that good alone. In other words, the utility derived from the consumption of one good is not a function of the quantity of other goods. Therefore, the total utility that a person derives from all the goods purchased in the consumption bundle is a sum of the separate utilities of the individual goods present in the consumption bundle.

The concept, hypothesis of independent utility can be better understood from the conversation between Yaksha and Yudhishthira.

From the above story, we know that Yaksha asks a total of 18 questions to Yudhishthira. From this, we can derive that Yaksha's Utility is a function of the number of sub-questions asked in the main question along with its

---

329 Modern Economics by Dr HL Ahuja.

complexity. We must understand that the utility Yaksha derives from the answer of one question is not dependent on the number of sub-questions and complexity of any other questions. In other words, after listening or accepting the answer of one question, Yaksha's utility for the second question will not diminish owing to the general tendency of the diminishing marginal utility. He will derive that level of utility from each question, which he would have when he first heard the answer to that particular question. Deriving from the above explanation, we can say that Yaksha's utility does not diminish with the answer to every successive question. The total utility that Yaksha derives from his entire conversation with Yudhishthira is the sum of the separate utilities derived from the answers to the individual questions asked by Yaksha to Yudhishthira. Thus, this behaviour of Yaksha satisfies the assumption: Hypothesis of Independent Utilities.

The following table explains the above assumption with numeric values.

QUESTION NUMBER	NUMBER OF SUB-QUESTIONS	COMPLEXITY	YAKSHA'S UTILITY
1	2	3	9
2	1	5	9
3	4	4	9
4	4	4	9
5	3	2	10
6	4	5	9
7	1	2	8
8	4	5	10
9	4	4	9
10	4	2	9
11	4	4	9
12	4	5	10
13	4	3	9

QUESTION NUMBER	NUMBER OF SUB-QUESTIONS	COMPLEXITY	YAKSHA'S UTILITY
14	4	4	9
15	4	5	10
16	4	5	10
17	4	2	8
18	4	3	8
		Total Utility	164

In the above table, the second column shows the number of sub-questions present in the main question. The third column marks the complexity on a scale of 1 to 5 (5 being extremely complex and 1 being easy) and the fourth column presents Yaksha's utility from accepting the answers to his questions on a scale of 1 to 10. It should be noted that these values are hypothetical and are subject to change based on individual's discretion.

Notice that the last row in the above table indicates Yaksha's Total Utility from his conversation with Yudhishthira. The Hypothesis of Independent Utility holds that the sum of the individual question's utility is equal to his total utility.

$$TU = U_1 + U_2 + U_3 + U_4 + U_5 + U_6 + U_7 + ... U_{18}$$
$$TU = \Sigma U$$
$$TU = 164$$

(Note: TU represents Total Utility, U_1 represents utility of question 1 and so on for all the 18 questions)

Jayārthashastra

The graphs below present a pictorial representation of the above discussion.

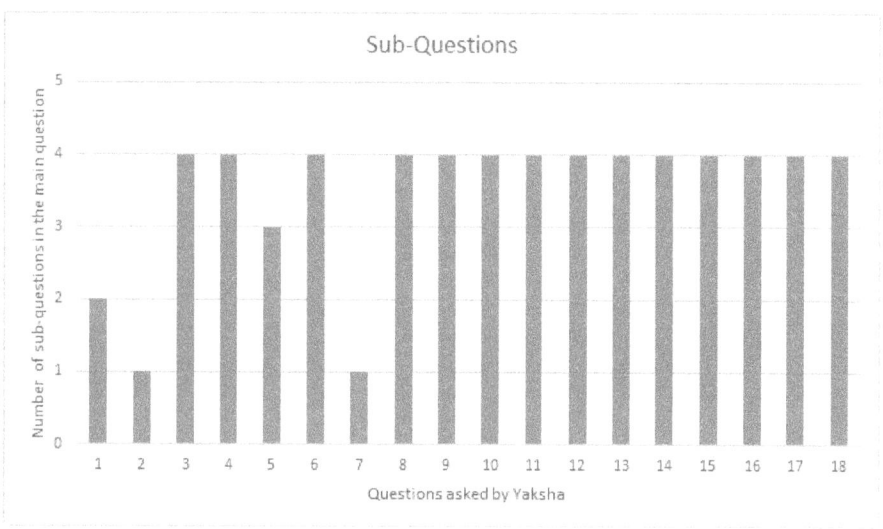

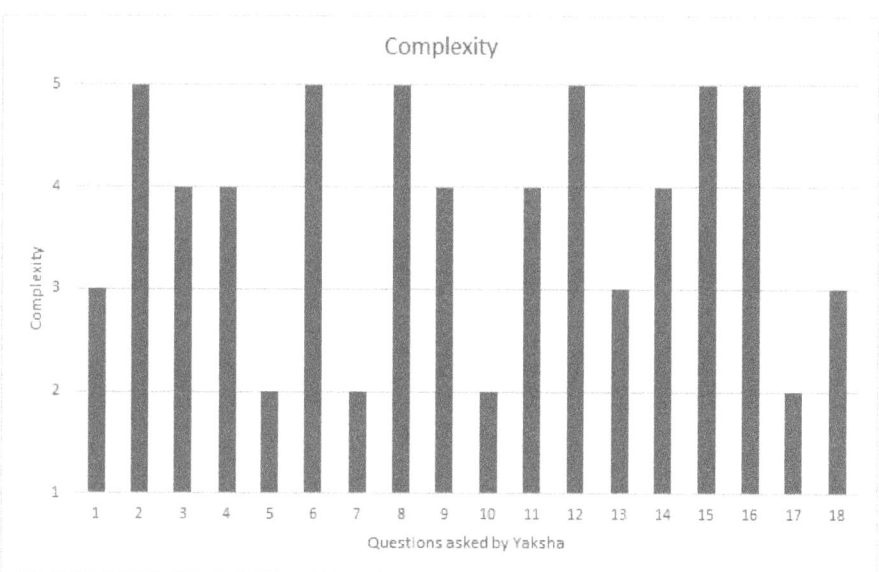

Tanushree Nagaveni

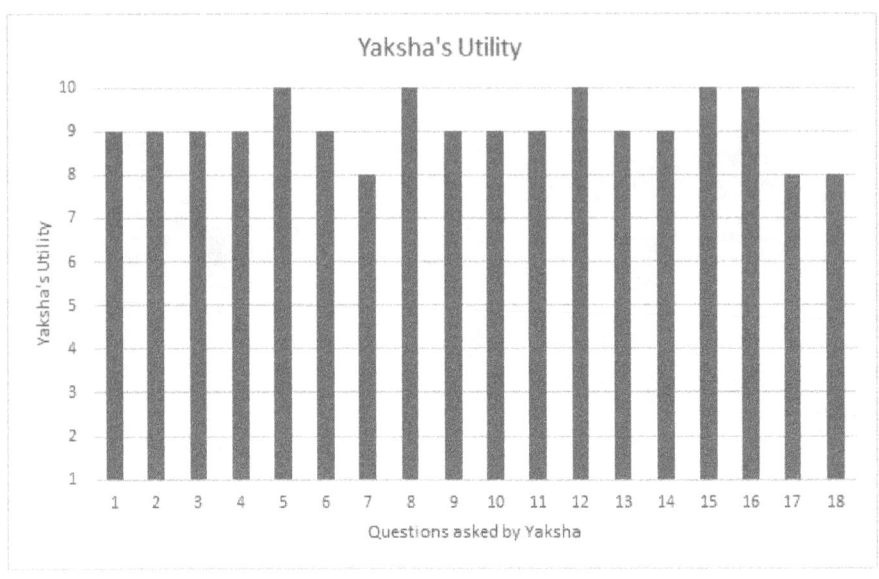

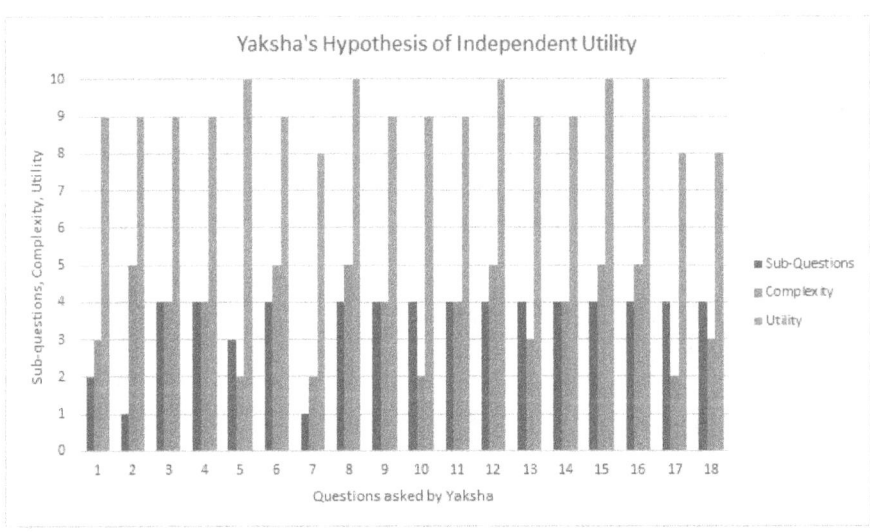

From the above explanation, it can be inferred that the assumption of Hypothesis of Independent Utility is indeed an indispensable assumption for the working of the Cardinal Utility Analysis.

The Folly Of Drona's Price Discrimination

What do you experience in the presence of a guru? Unconditional devotion, perseverance, determination, surrendering to the guru's knowledge…

A Guru is one who transforms you from an amorphous piece of rock into a beautiful sculpture. My experiences with my gurus have been ecstatic. As a student, I always embody utmost devotion and confidence in my guru to accept the knowledge that expounds in them. Throughout my learning journey with various teachers and mentors, I have observed one thing which makes a guru stand out from the rest… their infinite degree of patience and their zeal to inculcate the seed of knowledge in their students. Although my teachers are not always physically present before me, their blessings and wishes have guided me and continue to guide me through every step in my learning journey.

Anantha samsara samudhra thara naukayithabhyam guru bhakthithabhyam, Vairagya samrajyadha poojanabhyam, namo nama sri guru padukabhyam.

A verse that exalts the Sandals of the Guru, which have been analogized as "the boat to help cross the endless ocean of life"; a constant presence.

Tanushree Nagaveni

Drink the advice bestowed upon you by a guru and ponder over what is taught to you so that you can connect to your Guru's vision by nurturing the seed of knowledge sowed in you.

Ekalavya's devotion to Dronacharya has always been an inspiration to me as a student. Allowing the feeling of inspiration to soak in me again, I wish to recount the story of Ekalavya…

One day, when Dronacharya was teaching the various techniques of fighting to the Pandavas and Kauravas, a nishada[330] named Ekalavya, who was the son of Hiranyadhanu[331] approached Dronacharya and requested him, "O benevolent one! O Guru! Please accept me as your student." Dronacharya who was aware of dharma, considering it to be inappropriate to teach a nishada, refused to accept Ekalavya as his student.

Ekalavya prostrated before Dronacharya and invoked his blessings before leaving for the forest. In the forest, Ekalavya built a statue of Dronacharya out of clay. Every day, he worshipped the statue as if it were really Guru Dronacharya and began his practice of archery. Due to his extreme devotion and commitment, Ekalavya mastered the art of archery.

As time passed by, the Kuru princes were gaining proficiency in the art of using various weapons. On one such days, the Pandavas and Kauravas journeyed to the forest on a hunting expedition. A servant accompanied them carrying all the necessary items required for the princes. A dog also accompanied them. As the princes wandered into the deep wilderness of the forest, even the dog followed them. But, after a while the dog lost its way.

Finding its way through the dense forest, it stumbled upon Ekalavya, who had matted his hair, worn rags, and was rather dirty to look at. Frightened at his appearance, the dog barked. As it kept barking, Ekalavya displayed his mastery in *Dhanur Veda*[332]. Without looking at the dog, Ekalavya shot seven arrows into the dog's mouth. With sharp arrows sticking out of his mouth, the dog fled and whimpered before the Kuru princes. The princes noticed the arrows in the dog's mouth, and were astonished at the skill of the person who had accomplished this feat. They expressed respect for the person's talent in

---

330 Nishadas are usually hunters or fisherman who dwell in the mountains or forests.
331 Ekalavya's father and the leader of the forest dwellers.
332 Dhanur Veda is the science of archery. It is fundamentally a Sanskrit treatise on warfare and archery.

performing *Shabda Beda*[333]. They then began to search for the person who had performed this feat. After searching for hours in the forest, they finally came across Ekalavya. Arjuna noticed Ekalavya shooting arrows without any breaks. He felt ashamed of his skills and ability. Arjuna questioned the nishada in complete surprise, "Who are you? Who is your guru?" Ekalavya replied, "I am Ekalavya, the son of Hiranyadhanu. I am a student of Guru Dronacharya". Replying to Arjuna's question, Ekalavya pointed towards the clay statue of Dronacharya made by him. Arjuna was astounded by Ekalavya's gesture. He considered himself to be inferior to Ekalavya.

With this thought consuming his mind, Arjuna along with the other princes returned to Drona's hermitage. There they narrated the incident which they witnessed before Dronacharya. Arjuna approached Drona and asked him, "O venerated guru! You promised me that you would make me the best archer in the world, but you never revealed to us that you have a student, who is better than all of us". Dronacharya took a moment to analyse the predicament before him and finally spoke, "O Arjuna! I am well aware of the promise I made to you. I have not accepted Ekalavya as my student. But if he has accepted me as his guru, then he will have to pay me my *gurudakshina*[334]. Let us go and meet Ekalavya. Follow me, dear Arjuna".

Both the teacher and student went to the forest and reached the place where Ekalavya was practicing his archery. Dronacharya was surprised at the Ekalavya's proficiency in shooting arrows towards his goal.

When Ekalavya noticed Dronacharya watching his skills, he knew no bounds of joy. Tears began to roll down from his eyes. He dropped his bow and

---

333 A specific skill in archery, which involves shooting at an object just by the aid of sound without looking at the object. The word Shabda Beda informs us that Ekalavya had not seen the dog while shooting the dog. It is inferred that Ekalavya had only heard the bark of the dog and had not seen it.

334 Gurudakshina refers to the wealth or gifts offered to the *guru* by the disciple.

rushed towards his guru. He fell at the feet of Dronacharya and expressed his devotion towards Dronacharya.

Dronacharya immediately addressed Ekalavya, "Dear Ekalavya! Who is your guru? How did you learn Dhanur vidya?" Ekalavya replied, "O guru! I am a student of Dronacharya. Through my devotion to guru Dronacharya, I have mastered the art of Dhanurveda". Saying so he pointed towards the clay statue. Dronacharya was surprised at Ekalavya's words and said, "If you have accepted me as your guru, O Ekalavya, then you will have to pay me my *gurudakshina*". Ekalavya smiled and said, "O guru! What do you wish for?" Drona commanded, "Offer me your right thumb as *gurudakshina*, O son!" Always devoted to the truth, Ekalavya cheerfully cut off his own right thumb, with happiness on his face and peace in his heart, and gave it to Drona.[335]

---

335 The Mahabharata 1 Translated by Bibek Debroy.

Thus, Dronacharya's promise to Arjuna was safeguarded and Dronacharya ensured that Arjuna became the best archer in the world.

Price Discrimination

Now let us look at it through the microeconomic lens. I suggest you take a minute and observe the behaviour of Dronacharya, Ekalavya, and Arjuna. Since microeconomics relates primarily to the behaviour of individuals, it is necessary to be able to analyse the behaviour of individuals in the economy.

When I observe Dronacharya's behaviour in the story of Ekalavya, the only word that strikes my mind is "discrimination". Dronacharya discriminates between his two students based on the lineage of their birth. The *gurudakshina* he demands from Ekalavya is higher than what he demands from Arjuna. This behaviour of Dronacharya closely relates to the concept of price discrimination in microeconomics.

In simple words, price discrimination refers to the practice of a seller of selling the same goods at different prices to different buyers. A seller adopts price discrimination only when it seems possible and profitable for him to do so. For example, if a seller of a refrigerator sells the refrigerator to one buyer at Rs. 50,000 and at Rs. 80,000 to another buyer (all conditions of package material used, sale, and delivery are the same in the two cases) then clearly, he/she is practicing price discrimination[336].

Price discrimination as mentioned above is rare. It is very difficult for a seller to sell a homogenous product at different prices to different buyers. Therefore, the scope of price discrimination can be extended to include the sale of various varieties of the same goods at different prices which are not proportional to its marginal cost. According to Prof. Stigler, price discrimination may be defined as, "the sale of technically similar products at prices which are not proportional to the marginal costs".

---

336 Modern Economics by Dr. HL Ahuja

For example, let us consider the table below:

Products	Marginal cost	Price charged by seller to buyer
A	50	70
B	60	100

The marginal cost of both products A and B are Rs. 50 and Rs. 60 for the producer respectively. But the seller sells product A at Rs. 70, whereas product B at Rs. 100. In this case, the seller is practicing price discrimination because the price difference between the two products (100-70=30) is greater than the cost difference between them (60-50=10).

Price discrimination may be of the following types:

1. Personal: When a seller charges different prices from different persons.
2. Local: When a seller charges different prices from people of different places and localities.
3. According to use or trade: When a seller charges different prices for the same product based on its use.[337]

According to Prof. AC Pigou, price discrimination can also be of the following three types:

1. Price discrimination of the first degree.
2. Price discrimination of the second degree.
3. Price discrimination of the third degree.

Dronacharya's behaviour of demanding different *gurudakshina* from both his students can be explained in terms of price discrimination of the first degree.

---

337 Modern Economics by Dr. HL Ahuja

Price discrimination of the first degree involves maximum possible exploitation of each buyer in the interest of a seller's profits. Price discrimination of the first degree is also known as perfect price discrimination. Price discrimination of the first degree occurs when the monopolist can sell each separate unit at a different price. Thus, every buyer is forced to pay a price that is equal to the maximum amount he would be willing to pay rather than do without the good altogether. In this way, the seller leaves no consumer surplus for any buyer.[338]

By asking Ekalavya to give his thumb as a *gurudakshina*, Dronacharya forces Ekalavya to pay the maximum price that he can in order to retain his knowledge of *Dhanur Veda*. Ekalavya treasured archery more than anything and therefore he is willing to pay any price to be able to retain it. Once Ekalavya offers his thumb to Dronacharya, he loses his skill as an archer, and at the same time, Dronacharya gains profit as Arjuna will remain an unparalleled archer in the world.

There is no consumer surplus for Ekalavya and price discrimination of the first degree stands proved.

---

338 Modern Economics by Dr. HL Ahuja

Knight's Theory Of Profit and Arjuna's Pashupathastra

Eetha linga deva shiva aatha rangadhaama Vishnu||
Maathaado manku manuja ahankaara bittu||

Veedakke silukaniva veda naalku thandanava ||
Bhoodi maiyolu dharisihaneetha idda giriya poddanaatha ||
hare ranganaatha||

Vyaadhanaagi olidaniva maadhava madhusoodhanava||
Madananna uruhidavaneetha madana puthrana
padedavanaatha naatha||
Gangeya pothhaniva haange garuda gamananiva||
Thunga helavana katte linganeetha || hare ranganaatha|| shree
ranganaatha||

—Helavana katte Giriyamma

He is Lord Shiva; He is Lord Vishnu residing in Sriranga
Speak up, O ignorant man, desist from egoism.

He (Shiva) cannot be connected to the Vedas; He (Vishnu) brought back the four Vedas
He (Shiva) smears ashes on his whole body; He (Vishnu) carried the mountain

Tanushree Nagaveni

Hare Ranganaatha
As a hunter, he (Shiva) blessed Arjuna, He (Vishnu) Madhava annihilated Madhu (the demon)
He (Shiva) subjugated cupid, he (Vishnu) obtained cupid as his son
He (Shiva) carried Ganga, he (Vishnu) roams around on his mount the garuda
He is the linga of the lofty Helavana Katte
Hare Ranganatha, Shri Ranganatha

Sanchari comes from the root Sanskrit word "sanchara" which means to traverse or navigate. In the context of Bharatanatyam, sanchari is a tool that allows a dancer to elaborate the lyrical framework of a composition through imagination or self-interpretation (Manodharma). Often, sancharis are employed to narrate a story to the audience.

In my opinion, I consider sanchari as a journey that allows me as a dancer to explore different dimensions of a story. Sanchari allows me to step into the shoes of a character and experience the emotion that culminates in the character to the fullest.

Amongst all the sancharis that I have performed, the most memorable and unique one is the sanchari depicting the tale of Arjuna receiving the pashupatastra in the composition "Eetha linga Aatha Ranga" by the illustrious Helavana katte Giriyamma. When I first learnt this sanchari from my Guru Sri Vid. GS Nagesh, the feeling was ecstatic. Portraying Arjuna's character through certain hastamudras and facial expressions gave me a sense of empowerment. On the other hand, when I depicted Lord Shiva, I experienced divinity. Even to this day when I perform this sanchari, the surreal feeling never fails to embrace me in synchrony with the line "Vyadhanagi olidhaniva" in bowli raga.

Having explored the tale of Arjuna receiving the pashupata through sanchari, I now seek to explore it from the perspective of Knight's theory of profits.

Armed with his divine Ghandiva and his sword, Arjuna journeyed towards the snow-caped peaks of the Himalayas guided by the subtle northward breeze. Determined to achieve his goals, Arjuna's mind was fixed on austerities. Having traversed the dense forest filled with flowers and fruits, Arjuna finally reached the peaks of the Himalayas.

Having settled on those peaks, Arjuna then engaged in austerities in the heart of a beautiful forest. He clad himself in *darbha* grass, bark and deerskin and carried a staff. In the first month, he ate fruits once every period of three nights was over. In the second month, it was for double the period[339]. In the third month, he ate once every fortnight, surviving on decayed leaves that fell on the ground. When the fourth moon arrived and the moon was full, the mighty-armed son[340] of Pandu survived only on air. He raised his arms, and without anything for support, stood on the tips of his toes. Because of the frequent baths he took, the matted hair of that great-souled one whose energy was infinite became as lustrous as lightning and the lotus[341].

Petrified by the intensity of his penance, all the *maharishis* went to Lord Shiva. Having prostrated before *Mahadeva*, they collectively addressed him with the utmost respect, "This immensely energetic Partha has established himself on the peak of the Himalayas. He is engaged in difficult and terrible austerities and smoke is emerging in all directions. O lord of the gods! None of us knows what he wishes for. He is tormenting us. It would be better if he were to be restrained."

Lord Shiva replied, "In a happy frame of mind and without fatigue, swiftly return to wherever you have come from. I know the resolution that is fixed in

---

339 It is implied here that Arjuna ate after a period of six nights.
340 The word used is nandana, meaning beloved as well as son.
341 The Mahabharata 2 Translated by Bibek Debroy.

his mind. He does not wish for heaven, riches, or long life. I will accomplish today everything that he wishes for."[342] Thus, advised by *Maheshwara*, all the *maharishis* returned to their abodes, satisfied with *Rudra's* words.

After all the *maharishis* had departed, Lord Shiva assumed the form of a *kirata*[343]. Adorning himself with a bow and many arrows, he incarnated along with Devi Parvati in that beautiful forest.

As *Maheshwara* journeyed through the enchanting forest, he came across a son of Diti named Muka. Overcome by a strong wish to kill the son of Kunti, Muka had assumed the form of a boar. As the boar rushed towards Arjuna, tearing through the sharp blades of grass, the intelligent Pandava grasped his Ghandiva and strung the bowstring with all his might. Complimenting the dreadful twang of the supreme Ghandiva, Arjuna said, "I have come here, without causing you any injury. But since you nevertheless desire to kill me, I will first send you to Yama's abode today."[344] As Arjuna nocked the arrow on the Ghandiva, preparing to shoot at the wild boar, Lord Shiva who was in the form of a hunter suddenly interrupted the Partha, "I was the one whopursued this boar."." Neglecting these words of the hunter, Arjuna released his snake-like arrow. At the same time, even the hunter released his arrow decorated with colourful feathers towards the boar.

Both the hunter as well as Arjuna's arrows struck Muka's body at the same time. The shower of arrows did not cease. Multiple arrows pierced his gigantic body. Unable to bear the pain of those sharp venomous arrows, Muka assumed his true form and breathed his last.

Observing the hunter with his resplendent bow and the thousands of women behind him, Arjuna said, "O one with the golden complexion! Who are you,

---

342 The Mahabharata 2 Translated by Bibek Debroy.
343 Kirata refers to a hunter. In this case, Lord Shiva assumes the form of a hunter.
344 The Mahabharata 2 Translated by Bibek Debroy.

wandering in this deserted forest and accompanied by women? This animal had been chosen by me. Why did you pierce it? When the rakshasa had arrived here, I was the one who had picked him first. Whether you did this from desire or intending to insult me, you will not escape with your life. What you have done towards me today is not in accordance with the rules of hunting. O one whose refuge is the mountains! Therefore, I will kill you today."

The hunter laughed at Arjuna's words and said, "He became my target first. I was the one who chose him first. It was my shot that robbed him of his life. Insolent about your own strength, do not blame others for your own faults. O evil-minded one! You have insulted me. You will not escape with your life. Stay there. I will shoot arrows like thunder at you. Do the best you can and unleash your arrows at me."[345]

Having shouted at each other, Arjuna and the hunter began firing arrows at each other. Arjuna displayed his bravery by shooting thousands of arrows towards *Shankara,* but these arrows had no effect on the hunter. He stood firm on the ground, untouched by a single arrow. Arjuna was astonished at the sight before his eyes and he exclaimed, "Excellent! Excellent! Aha! This one with a delicate body makes a home on the peak of the Himalayas. But he receives the iron arrows[346] unleashed from the Ghandiva and is not moved. Who is he? Is he a god? Is he Rudra himself? Is he a yaksha or the lord of the gods? The thirty gods often frequent this best of mountains. Except for the god Pinaki, there is no one who can withstand the force of the net of thousands of arrows I have created. As long as it is anyone other than Rudra who stands here, be it a god or a yaksha, I will send him to Yama's abode with my sharp arrows." Arjuna then began shooting hundreds of arrows towards Shankara continuously. However, the illustrious god, the one who brings fortune to the worlds and holds the trident in his hand, cheerfully received them, like a mountain withstands a shower of rocks.

---

345 The Mahabharata 2 Translated by Bibek Debroy.
346 The word used is naracha, which means an iron arrow.

Within a few minutes, Arjuna's arrows were exhausted. When his hand reached out to his quiver to draw an arrow, he realised that the quiver given to him by Agni was empty. He trembled in fear, "What will I unleash from my bow now? My arrows have been exhausted. Who is this man who swallows up all my arrows? I will kill him with the curved end of my bow, like a terrible spear is used on elephants. Yama wields the staff and I will send him to his abode."[347] Arjuna struck the hunter with curved end of his bow, but the illustrious lord snatched the bow away from Partha's hand, leaving him in perplexity. Arjuna resorted to his sword. He held the sharp glistening sword with both his hands and flew up in the air. Having shrieked like a mad elephant, he descended towards the mountain-dweller. His mirror-like sword hit the hunter's head; however the blade shattered into thousand pieces. Vijaya was awe-struck. Overcome by anger, he threw the hilt with great force. He then began to fight with the rocks and trees. Yet, none of these rocks and trees managed to displace the hunter from his place.

Finally, both the hunter and Arjuna charged towards each other and struck each other with their fists. The resultant sound overpowered even the thunder. The fierce fist fight went on for hours, before Savyasachi finally grasped the kirata and pressed his chest. In response to Savysachi's life-threatening move, the kirata retreated with the powerful striking of the fist. Mahadeva finally held Phalguna's body and struck him with immense energy and force. As a result, Arjuna lost his senses and fell to the ground, his body covered with bruises. His breathing stopped momentarily and he had lost complete control over his body. Owing to a lack of breath, Arjuna remained unconscious for a while. Hara was satisfied with Arjuna. He then spoke to Arjuna, "O Phalguna! I am pleased with you because of your matchless deeds. There is no kshatriya who is equal to you in valour and endurance. O unblemished one! Your energy and valour has been equal to mine today. O mighty-armed one! O bull among men! I am pleased with you. Behold me. O large-eyed one! I

---

347 The Mahabharata 2 Translated by Bibek Debroy.

will give you eyes[348]. You have been a rishi earlier. You will triumph over all your enemies in battle, even if they happen to be dwellers of heaven.[349]"

On seeing Lord Maheshwara himself, Arjuna expounded with joy and he prostrated before the Lord. He knelt before Rudra and bowed his head in devotion. He then said, "O Kapardin![350] O lord of all the beings! O destroyer of Bhaga's eyes![351] O illustrious god! O Shankara! Pardon my transgression. O illustrious one! It was in a desire to see you that I came to this great mountain, beloved by you, lord of the gods, and the supreme abode of the ascetics. O illustrious god, worshipped by all the beings! Be pleased. O Mahadeva! Pardon my crime and my extreme bravery. Out of ignorance and insolence, I fought with you. O Shankara! I seek refuge with you. Pardon me." Vrishabhadhvaja[352] smiled, and grasping Phalguna's beautiful hands, said, "I have pardoned you.[353] You were Nara in an earlier body, the companion of Narayana. You spent many ayuta[354] years in fearful austerities in Badari[355]. There is supreme energy in you, like that in Vishnu, supreme among men. The universe is held up through the energy of the two of you, foremost among men. O lord! At the time of Shakra's consecration, you and Krishna oppressed the danavas and you took up the great bow that thunders like clouds. O Partha! This Ghandiva is fit for your hands. O supreme among men! It was that which I snatched from you, using my powers of maya. These two quivers will again be inexhaustible, as they used to be for you. I am pleased with you. Truth is your valour. O bull among men! Accept a boon from me. What is it that you desire? You are the one who

---

348 So that Arjuna can see Lord Shiva.
349 The Mahabharata 2 Translated by Bibek Debroy.
350 Kapardin is one of Shiva's names. Kaparda or kapardaka means braided or matted hair and Shiva is named Kapardin because his hair is matted.
351 At the time of Daksha's yajna, Shiva uprooted the god Bhaga's eyes.
352 Shiva's name, the one with a bull (vrishabha) on his banner (dhvaja).
353 The Mahabharata 2 Translated by Bibek Debroy.
354 An ayuta is ten thousand.
355 The hermitage at Badari or Badarika, one of the sources of the Ganga.

shows respect. There is no one on earth who is your equal. Nor is there anyone in heaven. O conqueror of enemies! The kshatriyas find their chief in you."[356]

Arjuna replied, "O illustrious god! O Vrishadhvaja[357]! O lord! If you wish to grant me that which I desire, I wish for the terrible and divine weapon known as pashupata[358]. It is known as brahmashira. It is fearful and is terrible in prowess. When the terrible end of a yuga approaches, it destroys the entire world. Through this weapon, I can burn down in battle danavas, rakshasas, spirits[359], pishachas, gandharvas and pannagas[360]. When unleashed with mantras, it releases thousands of spears, fearful clubs and arrows that have virulent poison in them. With it, I will fight in battle with Bhishma, Drona, Kripa and the son of the suta[361], who always speaks very harshly. O illustrious god! O destroyer of Bhaga's eyes! This is my first wish. Through your grace, let me be empowered in my pursuit."

---

356 The Mahabharata 2 Translated by Bibek Debroy.
357 Vrishadhvaja and Vrishabhadhvaja mean the same.
358 Pashupati is Shiva's name.
359 The word bhuta means beings, but it also means evil spirits.
360 Nagas and pannagas are serpents. They are different from snakes, because they possess extraordinary powers, including that of assuming any form at will.
361 Karna

Jayārthashastra

The illustrious god said, "O Pandava! I will give you the great pashupata weapon, dear to me. You will be capable of bearing, releasing and withdrawing it. The great Indra, Yama, the king of the yakshas[362], Varuna and Vayu do not know it. How can it be known to humans? O Partha! But it must not be suddenly released at any man. If it is released at someone who lacks in energy, it will destroy the entire universe. There is no one in the three worlds, mobile or immobile, who cannot be killed by it. It can be released through thought, eyes, words or the bow."[363][364]

On hearing the words of Lord Shiva, Arjuna immediately purified himself in the prescribed manner and went before Lord Shiva, who said in a divine

---

362 Kubera
363 These divine weapons were based on mantras, the physical form was immaterial.
364 The Mahabharata 2 Translated by Bibek Debroy.

voice, "Learn." Rudra taught Arjuna the mysteries of the Pashupata weapon and about its withdrawal. Arjuna accepted the pashupata with utmost dedication. Maheshwara then touched Partha and granted him permission to go to heaven. Partha Arjuna prostrated before the Lord, lowered his head in obeisance before looking at the Lord. Umapathi[365] also handed over the great Ghandiva to Arjuna. Along with Devi Parvathi he rose to the sky and disappeared before Arjuna's eyes.

Risk, Uncertainty, And Profits: Knight's Theory Of Profits

It is known to us that profit is the difference between the total revenue and total cost of production of a firm. The excess of total revenue that remains after covering all the costs of production is profit. It may be useful to understand that profit is in reality remuneration for entrepreneurship, the fourth factor of production. For a layman, the word profit remains restricted to "a reward that an entrepreneur or a businessperson earns for carrying out his business activities", however economists have added and continue to add a new dimension to "profit" through their distinct views about its nature, origin, and role.

While these views have strengthened the understanding of the "theory of profits", there is a lot of confusion associated with the theory of profits due to the lack of agreement among economists about the true functions of an entrepreneur.

While some economists regard profit as a remuneration provided to an entrepreneur for performing his function of coordinating and organising the other factors of production, other economists consider the entrepreneur to be a special type of labour and profits as a special form of wages. Some other economists have also described the entrepreneur as performing the functions

---

365 Reference to Lord Shiva as the husband of Uma (Parvathi).

of bearing risk and uncertainty as he controls the business and takes price and output decision. He earns profits because he bears risk and uncertainty[366].

The following are some of the popular theories of profits:

1. Profits as a dynamic surplus: Clark's dynamic theory of profits
2. Schumpeter's innovation theory of profits
3. Risk, uncertainty, and profits: Knight's theory of profits
4. Hawley's risk theory of profit: Profit as a reward for risk-bearing
5. Walker's theory of profit: Profit as rent of ability, etc

Let us now focus on the Knight's theory of profits. Proposed by F.H. Knight, the Knight's theory of profit is an important theory that associates profit with risk and uncertainty. F.H. Knight propounded that *"profit is a reward for uncertainty bearing"*. According to him, dynamic changes can result in profits only if these changes and their consequences are both unpredictable in nature. Only those changes whose occurrence cannot be predicted give rise to profit.

Drawing from the above discussion, profits will not arise if there are no changes or if changes are predictable beforehand. A lack of changes eliminates the possibility of uncertainty, likewise profits.

Why does the lack of changes eliminate the possibility of uncertainty?

Think of it in this way. If all the conditions of the future were to be known in the present itself, then the competition in the market will act to create an ideal state, where prices are equal to costs and therefore profits would not arise.

Thus, it is our ignorance about the future and uncertainty about future conditions that give rise to profits.

---

366 Modern Economics by Dr HL Ahuja

It is observable in daily life that entrepreneurs draw estimates about the future conditions, such as the demand for a commodity, and other factors that affect the market price and costs. Based on their estimates, they make a contract with the suppliers of other factors of production at fixed rates of remuneration in advance. Following the hiring of the other factors of production (such as land, labour, and capital), they initiate the production process. They realise the value of the output produced through the production process entailing all the other factors of production only after it has been produced and sold in the market. During the time between the production process and the sale of the output in the market, there may be many changes that could alter the forecasts made by the entrepreneur and in turn give rise to profits, either positive or negative.

Suppose, the conditions of the future that would prevail during the sale of the output produced is known to the entrepreneur while he is hiring the other factors of production at fixed rates of remuneration, there is absolutely no uncertainty about the future, and therefore no profits.

Thus uncertainty, that is, ignorance about the future conditions of demand and supply, is the cause of profits.[367]

It should be noted that positive profits accrue to those entrepreneurs who make correct estimate of the future or whose anticipations prove to be correct. Those whose anticipations prove to be incorrect will have to suffer losses[368].

Profit is thus a **residual and non-contractual income** that accrues to the entrepreneur because of the existence of uncertainty about the future. Since the entrepreneur is an unhired factor of production, who hires other factors of production, it is, therefore, the entrepreneur who bears uncertainty and earns profit as a reward for that[369].

---

367 Modern Economics by Dr HL Ahuja.
368 Modern Economics by Dr HL Ahuja.
369 Modern Economics by Dr HL Ahuja.

We have discussed how the uncertainty of the future results in profit, but now it is time to ask ourselves this question: "What causes uncertainty?"

Well, it is important to reiterate that changes are the primary cause of uncertainty. However, one must also note that there are two types of changes that cause uncertainty.

I. Innovations: The term "Innovations" here refers to the introduction of a new product or service, or a new method of production, etc. The entrepreneurs introduce these innovations themselves, which creates uncertainty among the rival firms or competitors and uncertainty for the entrepreneur himself as no one can be certain about whether an innovation will be successful in the future.

II. The second type of changes are external to a business, resulting from its business environment such as,
   a. Changes in the tastes, preferences, and fashions of the people
   b. Changes in Government policies and laws especially taxation
   c. Changes in wage and labour policies and laws
   d. Movements of prices because of inflation and depression
   e. Changes in the income of the people
   f. Changes in production technology, etc

All the above-mentioned changes cause uncertainty and in turn, result in either positive or negative profits.

At this point in our discussion, it is useful to note that F.H. Knight also regards profit as a reward for bearing non-insurable risks and uncertainties.

Every entrepreneur must face risks because of the changes continuously occurring in the economy. But it is important to note that not all types of risks result in profit. Only non-insurable risks (Those risks which cannot be covered up by some type of insurance policy) involve uncertainty and therefore give rise to profits for an entrepreneur.

The idea that profit is a reward for uncertainty bearing can be related to our story of Arjuna receiving the pashupatastra.

Like any other individual, when Arjuna decided to head towards the Himalayas to receive the pashupata weapon from Lord Shiva, he might have made forecasts about the nature of his penance. He might have also made certain decisions about the stages of his penance and about how he would progress in his austerities (from eating fruits every three nights once to gradually increasing the period to six nights, a fortnight until he could only survive on air). From this process of drawing premises, Arjuna would have comfortably gauged the determination and severity required to please Lord Shiva and obtain the pashupata weapon. Such thoughts might have mentally prepared Arjuna to undertake such severe austerities.

Since future conditions were not known to Arjuna, he might have anticipated that the only way to please Lord Shiva was through his austerities. However, the occurrence of certain unpredictable changes in the form of Muka assuming the form of a boar to attack Arjuna and Lord Shiva incarnating as a kirata to test Arjuna gave rise to his profit in the form of receiving the pashupatastra.

Over the course of the story, Arjuna responds to these unpredictable changes by killing the boar and fighting with Lord Shiva. During his fight with Lord Shiva, Arjuna fights with various weapons such as arrows, the curved edge of the bow, sword, rocks, trees, and his fists. His act of using different weapons resembles an entrepreneur introducing innovations. Like the behaviour of an entrepreneur, innovation in the use of weapons creates uncertainty for him as he cannot be certain about whether a certain weapon would yield the desired outcomes.

In this case, Arjuna also faces a non-insurable risk due to the dynamic changes occurring in his environment. The risk of losing his life during the fight is certainly a non-insurable risk for Arjuna, which creates uncertainty.

However, ultimately uncertainty and risk-bearing give rise to profit for Arjuna. His capability to adapt to the dynamic environment and his determination pleases Lord Shiva, therebyearning him the deadly pashupata weapon.

On the contrary, if Arjuna were to be aware of Shiva incarnating as a kirata, then he would have probably not fought with Lord Shiva as he might have considered it inappropriate to fight with the God. Such a scenario would eliminate any possibility of uncertainty and profits.

In conclusion, positive profits in terms of receiving the pashupata weapon accrue to Arjuna because of his correct anticipations about the nature and difficulty of his penance.

The Prisoner's Dilemma and the Game Of Dice

Let me ask you a question.

What event in the Mahabharata laid the foundation stone for the great war?

Think about it.

Well, I consider the game of dice to be instrumental in setting the stage for the Mahabharata war. Your answer could be different. But what if Yudhishtira never agreed to gamble with the Kauravas? Would the course of the story change? How will the Mahabharata end then?

Take a moment and think about the possibilities…

Now, ponder about the question earlier: what if Yudhishtira never agreed to gamble with the Kauravas? Do you think this is possible? Perhaps, only if Yudhishtira would have used the tools of game theory, specifically the prisoner's dilemma.

How?

After the completion of the Rajasuya yagna, King Duryodhana took leave from the Pandavas and Draupadi. He set out for Hastinapura. On having witnessed the extraordinary opulence at the great Rajasuya sacrifice, his mind was unhappy. As he travelled, he was inflamed at the prosperity of the Pandavas and evil thoughts were seeded in King Duryodhana's mind. On seeing the happiness of the Parthas, the submission of the kings, the love the worlds had for them, from children onwards, and the supreme splendour of the great-souled Pandavas, Dhritarashtra's son Duryodhana turned pale. As he travelled, he thought intently about the sabha and the unrivalled prosperity of the intelligent Dharmaraja.

Dhritarashtra's son Duryodhana was so inattentive, that he did not respond when Subala's son Shakuni repeatedly spoke to him. On seeing him so distracted, Shakuni responded, "O Duryodhana! Why are you travelling with all these sighs?" Duryodhana replied, "O uncle! I saw the entire earth brought under Yudhishthira's suzerainty, conquered with the power and weapons of the great-souled one with white horses. I witnessed the sacrifice of Yudhishtira, like that of the immensely radiant Indra among the gods. I am full of envy and am burning day and night. I am drying up like a shallow pond in the hot season.[370] Witness—when Shishupala was felled by the foremost of the Satvatas[371], there wasn't a single man who stood by his side. The kings were burnt with the flames of the Pandavas and pardoned the crime. Who can pardon that crime? Vasudeva's great deed was improper and succeeded only because of the power of the great-souled Pandavas. Various kings brought many jewels to King Yudhishthira and worshipped him, like vaishyas who pay taxes. On seeing the blazing prosperity of the Pandavas, I am afflicted with jealousy and am burning, though I am not made that way. I will throw myself into the fire, consume poison, or immerse myself in water. I cannot bear to be alive. On seeing the pure prosperity of Kunti's son, I consider destiny to

---

370 The expression in the text translates as the onset of shuchishukra and there is repetition. Shuchi means the months of Jyeshtha and Ashada and would have sufficed. Shukra means the month of Jyeshtha.
371 Yadavas, the foremost one being Krishna.

be supreme and endeavour to be meaningless. O Soubala[372]! In the past, I have made attempts to kill Yudhishtira. But he overcame all of them and prospered like a lotus in the water. Therefore, I consider destiny to be supreme and endeavour to be meaningless. The Dhritarashtras[373] are declining and the Parthas are always prospering. When I see their prosperity and that beautiful sabha and the derisive laughter of the guards, I burn as if with fire. O maternal uncle! Please allow me now to suffer in misery and tell Dhritarashtra about the envy that has pervaded me."

Shakuni said, "O Duryodhana! You should not feel any jealousy towards Yudhishtira, because the Pandavas have always benefited from their good fortune. In the past, you have tried to kill them with many means. But those tigers among men escaped because of their good fortune. They obtained Draupadi as a wife and Drupada and his two sons as allies, and the valorous Vasudeva as an ally in winning the earth. O lord of the earth! They obtained an undiminished share of paternal wealth and extended it through their own energy. What is there to lament in this? Having satisfied the fire, Arjuna obtained the great bow Gandhiva, two inexhaustible quivers and other celestial weapons. He subdued the lords of the earth with that foremost among bows and the valour of his arms. What is there to lament in this? He freed the danava Maya from being burnt by the fire. Arjuna, then made him build that sabha. On Maya's command, the terrible rakshasas named Kinkaras guard that sabha. What is there to lament in this? O king! You have said that you have no allies. That is not true, because your maharatha brothers are always there to help you. The mighty archer Drona with his intelligent son Ashvatthama, Karna the son of a suta, the maharatha Kripacharya, I and my brothers, and the valorous Soumadatti[374] are with you. With these as allies, conquer the entire world."

---

372 Shakuni.
373 The sons of Dhritarashtra, the Kouravas.
374 Bhurishrava, the son of Somadatta.

Duryodhana replied, "O king! If you permit, I will defeat the Pandavas with you and the other maharathas. When I have conquered them, the entire earth will be mine, and all the lords of the earth and the sabha with its great riches."

Shakuni said, "With the use of force, the masses of gods cannot defeat in battle Arjuna, Vasudeva, Bhimasena, Yudhishtira, Nakula, Sahadeva and Drupada and his son. They are maharathas, great archers, skilled in use of weapons and invincible in battle. O king! But I know the means through which Yudhishtira himself can be conquered. Listen and act accordingly."

Duryodhana replied, "O maternal uncle! If there is a way to defeat them without any danger to our well-wishers and other great-souled ones, please tell me."

Shakuni said, "Kunti's son loves to gamble with dice, but does not know how to play. If challenged to play, he will not be able to refuse. I am skilled in gambling with dice, there is no one on earth, or in the three worlds, who is my equal. Challenge Kunti's son to a game of dice. O king! With my skill in dice[375], there is no doubt that I will win for you the kingdom and the blazing prosperity. O Duryodhana! Tell King Dhritarashtra all this. And if your father permits, there is no doubt that I will vanquish Yudhishtira." Duryodhana replied, "O Soubala! You yourself say all this to Dhritarashtra, foremost among the Kurus, in the proper way. I will not be able to do it."

Having experienced the great Rajasuya sacrifice of King Yudhishtira, wishing to do well to Duryodhana and having already heard Duryodhana's words about what he desired, Shakuni went to Dhritarashtra with Duryodhana. Approaching Dhritarashtra, Shakuni uttered these words. "O great king! Duryodhana is pale, yellow, and thin. Notice that he is miserable and is always worrying. Why do you not examine and determine the exact reasons

---

375 Dyuta is the act of playing or gambling. Here, the text uses aksha as the word for a dice.

why your eldest son is so miserable with a grief that can only result from an enemy?"

Dhritarashtra asked, "O Duryodhana! What is the reason for your great grief? If it is something that I can hear, please tell me. This Shakuni tells me that you are pale, yellow, and thin and that you are worrying. I do not see any reason for your grief. O son!"

Duryodhana replied, "Like any miserable man, I do eat and dress. But I tolerate the passing of time because I bear terrible envy. He is truly a man who vanquishes his enemies and liberates his own subjects from the oppression of that enemy. O descendant of the Bharata lineage! Satisfaction and pride destroy prosperity, so do compassion and fear. Immersed in these, no one achieves greatness. Having witnessed Kounteya Yudhishthira's blazing prosperity, I no longer find pleasure and that is what turns me pale. It is true that the prosperity of Kunti's son is invisible to me now. But I see the prosperity of my enemies and my own destitution as if before me now. It is for this reason that I have become pale, miserable, yellow, and thin. Yudhishtira supports eighty-eight thousand snataka householders and each of them has thirty servant maidens. Besides this, ten thousand others always eat the best of food in Yudhishthira's house, served on golden plates. The king of Kamboja sends him black, dark, and red skins of the kadali deer, expensive blankets, chariots, women and cattle and horses in hundreds and thousands. A hundred she-camels roam there three hundred times. O lord of the earth! The kings brought diverse riches in great numbers to that foremost of sacrifices undertaken by Kunti's son. I have never seen nor heard of such an inflow of wealth as I saw at the sacrifice of the intelligent son of Pandu. O king! O lord! I cannot be at peace and continuously worry because I have seen that limitless flood of riches of my enemy. Vatadhana[376] brahmanas, possessing the wealth of cattle, stood at the gate in groups of one hundred. They brought three kharvas[377] of

---

376 A vatadhana is a brahmana, who has been born of a brahmana mother and a father who is a brahmana but an outcast.
377 A kharva is simply a very large number, 1 followed by 10 zeros, or 10 billion.

riches as tribute, but were turned back. When they brought beautiful golden kamandalus[378] and filled these with tribute, it was then that they were allowed entry. In Varuna's brass pots, the ocean brought him ambrosia (madhu) that was better than the one brought for Shakra by the wives of the immortals. There were one thousand pots, adorned with many jewels and golden. On seeing all this, I felt as if afflicted with fever. They obtained these by going to the oceans of the east and the south. They had also gone to the west. But no one can go to the north, except the birds. Listen to me as I describe an extraordinary incident there. Whenever one hundred thousand brahmanas had been fed, it was arranged there that a signal would always be given through the blowing of conch shells. O descendant of the Bharata lineage! I continuously heard the repeated blowing of conch shells. On hearing these great sounds, my hair stood up on end. O lord of men! Many kings crowded the place as spectators. O great king! Those kings brought all kinds of riches with them, when they came to the sacrifice of the intelligent son of Pandu. Like vaishyas, the lords of the earth became servers to the brahmanas. O king! The king of the gods, Yama, Varuna, or the lord of the guhyakas Kubera does not possess riches equal to Yudhishthira's wealth. Ever since I have witnessed the overwhelming prosperity of Pandu's son, my heart has been burning and I can find no peace."

Shakuni said, "O you whose valour is in truth! Listen to the means whereby you can obtain the unmatched prosperity that you have seen with the Pandava. O descendant of the Bharata lineage! I am skilled in playing with dice, supreme on earth. I know their heart. I know how to stake. I know the special art. Though Kounteya Yudhishtira loves dice, he has no knowledge. If challenged, he will certainly come. I will challenge him.'"

Having been thus addressed by Shakuni, King Duryodhana then instantly addressed these words to Dhritarasthra, "O king! Shakuni is skilled in dice. Through dice, he will win the wealth of Pandu's son. Please grant him permission."

---

378 Water pots used by ascetics.

Dhritarashtra replied, "I always follow the counsel of my immensely wise adviser, Vidura. I will consult with him and then decide on the course of action. He places dharma in the forefront, has foresight and has our supreme welfare in mind. He will look at both sides and tell us certainly what should be done."

Duryodhana said, "If you ask Vidura, he will restrain you. O Indra among kings! And if you are restrained, I will certainly kill myself. O king! When I am dead, may you find happiness with Vidura. Enjoy the whole earth. What do you have to do with me?"

Dhritarashtra heard those painful words, though they were affectionately uttered. Submitting to Duryodhana's desire, he instructed his servants. "Let artisans immediately build for me a beautiful and large sabha, with a thousand pillars and a hundred doors, which is fit to be seen. When it is scattered with gems and dice everywhere, quietly come and report to me that it has been built well and that it is fit to be entered."

In an attempt to pacify Duryodhana, Dhritarasthra, lord of the earth, summoned Vidura, because he never took a decision without asking Vidura. Knowing the evils of gambling, he was still attracted towards it because of his affection towards his son. Having heard this, the intelligent Vidura knew that the door to kali was nigh. On seeing that the path to destruction was about to be opened, he quickly came to Dhritarashtra. The brother came to the great-souled elder brother and bowing down, with his head touching the other's feet, uttered these words. "O king! O lord! I do not approve of the decision you have taken. You should act in such a way that discord does not arise among your sons because of this gambling."

Dhritarashtra replied, "O Kshatta! If the gods in heaven show us their favour, there is no doubt that there will be no quarrel between my sons and my other sons. Auspicious or not auspicious, benign, or malign, let this gambling match between relatives, occur, as it is certainly destined. When I and Bhishma, are there, no evil can possibly occur, even if fate has decreed it. Immediately ascend a chariot that is yoked with steeds with the speed of the wind. Go to Khandavaprastha and bring Yudhishtira. O Vidura! I tell you that there will be no going back on my decision. I think it is supreme destiny that has led to this." Having heard this, the intelligent Vidura thought that this should not be. Extremely unhappy, he went to Bhishma.

Knowing Vidura's views, Dhritarashtra, the son of Ambika, again privately spoke these words to Duryodhana, "O Gandhari's son! Forget the dice, Vidura does not approve of it. The immensely intelligent one will not speak in vain. I think what Vidura has said is for my supreme welfare. O son! Act accordingly, for I think that it will be for your welfare too. Vidura knows all the sacred texts, with their mysteries, that the illustrious and wise devarshi Brihaspati, preceptor of Vasava, taught to the intelligent king of the gods. O son! I always follow his counsel. The intelligent Vidura is considered as foremost among the Kurus, like the immensely wise Uddhava is acclaimed among the Vrishnis. Dissension brings destruction to the kingdom, so give up the idea. You have obtained what the supreme texts say are what a son should obtain from his father and mother. O son! You have obtained the rank of your father and grandfather. You have studied, you have become learned in the sacred texts. You have always been reared at home. You are the eldest among your brothers and you have been established in the kingdom. Do you not consider this fortunate? This great kingdom of your father and grandfather is prospering. When you rule it, you shine like the lord of the gods in heaven. I know you to be wise. Then what is the reason for this grief? Why is your misery swelling up? Tell me."

Duryodhana replied, "I am an evil man that I eat and dress, despite what I see. It has been said that a man who does not feel envy is a wretch. O Indra among kings! O lord! This ordinary prosperity does not please me. I am miserable on seeing the blazing prosperity of Kunti's son. The entire earth is subject to Yudhishthira's suzerainty. I am telling you that I am miserable, since I am still established here, alive. The Chaitrakis, the Koukuras, the Karaskaras and the Lohajanghas live in Yudhishthira's abode, like prostrate slaves. The Himalayas, the oceans, the regions along the shores that produce all the gems and all others are inferior to Yudhishthira's abode. O lord of the earth! Since I was the eldest and foremost, Yudhishtira offered me homage and appointed me to the task of receiving the gems. O descendant of the Bharata lineage! Of the riches that were brought there, supreme, and invaluable, one could not see the near end, nor the far one. My hands were too tired to receive all those riches. When those who had brought riches from distant places had left, I was still tired. Having brought gems from Bindusarovar lake, Maya constructed a platform of crystal. On seeing the place full of lotuses, I took it to be water. On seeing me draw up my clothes, Vrikodara laughed at me. He thought me to be devoid of riches and deluded by the superior wealth of the enemy. Had I possessed the ability, I would have killed Vrikodara there. The derision of a rival burns me. I again saw a similar pond full of lotuses. Thinking it to be made of crystal, I fell into the water. At this, Krishna and Partha laughed out loudly at me, and so did Draupadi and the other women. This pained my heart. My garments having become wet, the servants gave me others on the king Yudhishthira's orders and this too made me more miserable. O lord of men! Listen when I tell you about another trick. In trying to go out through what looked like a door, but wasn't a door, I hit my head against a crystal slab and got hurt. Then, on seeing this from a distance, the twins were amused. In great sorrow, they held me in their arms. Sahadeva then repeatedly told me, as if amazed, 'O king! This is the door. Pass this way.' I saw jewels there, whose names I had not even heard of earlier. That is the reason my heart is burning."

'Dhritarashtra said, "O son! You are the eldest and the son of my eldest wife. Do not bear hatred towards the Pandavas. He who bears hatred is always as unhappy as in death. Yudhishtira is inexperienced. He is your equal in goals and friends. He does not hate you. Why do you hate him? O son! You are his equal in birth and valour. Why do you covet your brother's riches? Do not desire out of delusion. Be calm and virtuous. If you wish to accomplish the glory of a sacrifice, let the priests arrange for the great sacrifice known as saptatantu. The kings will bring you great riches, gems, and ornaments, from affection and respect. O son! The terrible act of desiring another's property brings misery. He who is satisfied with his own, remains anchored in his dharma and is happy. The signs of wealth are lack of concern for another's prosperity, constant perseverance in one's tasks and the protection of what one has obtained. The man who is unmoved in calamities and always skilled and engaged in his own, vigilant, and humble, will always witness good fortune. Give at sacrifices, enjoy the pleasures you desire, sport in the company of women and be at peace."

Duryodhana replied, "You know. But you confuse me, like a boat tied to another boat. Are you not attentive to your own interests? Do you have hostile feelings towards me? Dhritarashtra's sons follow your command and I do not rule them. You always say that everything must be done for the sake of the future. If the leader has lost the path because he has been deluded by the enemy, how can his followers follow that path? O king! You are old in your wisdom; you follow the elders and you have control over your senses. You should not confuse us when we are engaged in our tasks. Brihaspati has said that the royal path must be different from that followed by the worlds. Therefore, a king must always be vigilant in protecting his self-interest. O great king! A kshatriya's path is one devoted to victory. As long as one follows one's creed, dharma and lack of dharma are irrelevant. A charioteer uses his whip to drive out in all the directions, wishing to attack the blazing fortunes of his enemy. Those who are skilled in weapons say that the weapon isn't only the one that cuts. A weapon is that which vanquishes the enemy, be it open or hidden. O king! Discontent is the root of prosperity. That is the reason I wish to be discontented. The supreme one is one who strives for prosperity. In attaining prosperity and riches, shouldn't self-interest be our way? Others take away what has been obtained before. That is known as the dharma of kings. It was during a period of truce that Shakra cut off Namuchi's[379] head, because he knew that enmity towards a foe is eternal. Like a snake swallows rats, the earth swallows up two—the king who does not strive and the brahmana

---

379 A demon killed by Shakra (Indra).

who does not live at home. O lord of the earth! No one is by nature another man's enemy. The enemy is that one whose pursuits are the same as one's own, and not anyone else. He who stupidly watches the ascendance of the enemy's party, leaves a disease unattended and cuts off his own roots. An enemy may be insignificant. But if he is allowed to grow in valour, he will destroy one, the way an anthill destroys the roots of a tree it has grown on. Do not be pleased at the enemy's prosperity. The wise ones should not bear the burden of this policy on their heads. A person who wishes for an increase in his prosperity, the way he has himself grown since birth, grows and prospers with his relatives. Valour brings swift growth. As long as I do not obtain the wealth of the Pandavas, I will always be in doubt. I will either obtain those riches, or lay down my life in the field of battle. O lord of the earth! If I cannot equal Yudhishtira, what is the point of being alive today? The Pandavas are always prospering and we are stagnating."

Shakuni said, "Challenge the enemy to a game of dice. I will rob Pandu's son Yudhishtira of the prosperity that you have seen, which has been burning you. Be clear that I will not fight in front of armies. Through the throw of dice, a skilful one can vanquish one that is not skilful. O descendant of the Bharata lineage! Know that the bow and arrows are my dice. The heart of the dice is the string of my bow. Know that the carpet[380] is my chariot."

Duryodhana said, "O king! This one, who is skilled in dice, is ready to win over the prosperity of Pandu's son with dice. O father! You should find that pleasing."

Dhritarashtra replied, "I always listen to the counsel of my brother, the great-souled Vidura. I will decide on the course of action after meeting with him."

Duryodhana replied, "O Kourava! There is no doubt that Vidura will make you refrain from the resolution. He is engaged in the welfare of the Pandavas and not mine. No man should engage in his task with another's counsel,

---

380 On which the game is played.

because two minds seldom agree on a course of action. Like a straw mat[381] during the rainy season, a fool that abhors fear stands and destroys himself. Neither disease nor Yama wait for prosperity to come. Therefore, let us act for the good while there is time."

Dhritarashtra replied, "O son! I never like a fight with those who are stronger. Enmity creates distortion, and that itself is a weapon, though it is not made of iron. O prince! You think that disaster will bring welfare, this terrible collection of quarrels. Once it starts, in one way or another, it will release bows, swords and arrows."

Duryodhana said, "The ancient ones created the rules of dice. It leads to neither evil, nor blows. Today, you should approve of Shakuni's words. Let your instructions be issued for the swift construction of a sabha[382]. Because the doors of heaven will become closer, it is appropriate for us to be engaged in this. Approve of this act with the Pandavas and we will then stand equal to them."

Dhritarashtra replied, "O Indra among men! I do not like the words that you utter. But do what brings you pleasure. Later, you will remember your words and suffer, because such words cannot bring prosperity to those who abide by dharma. A long time in the past, Vidura, who follows wisdom and learning, had foretold all this. The great calamity that will destroy the seed of the kshatriyas has now arrived and we are powerless."

Having uttered these words, the wise Dhritarashtra decided that destiny alone was supreme. Fate robbed the king of his senses and he instructed his men to obey his son's words.

On hearing these words, without hesitation, thousands of wise and skilled artisans swiftly built the sabha and stocked it with every kind of object. Then,

---

381 The word used for a straw-mat is a kata and there is probably an unintended pun, since kata is also a particular throw of the dice.
382 Assembly hall where the game will be played.

in a short space of time, they informed the king that the beautiful assembly hall was ready and that it had been adorned with multicoloured gems and beautiful golden seats. Then Dhritarashtra, lord of men, spoke to the learned Vidura, foremost among his advisers, "Go to Prince Yudhishtira and swiftly bring him here at my command. Say that he and his brothers should come here and see this beautiful sabha that I have built, with many gems and decorated with expensive beds and seats. We will then have a game of dice among well-wishers."

Knowing his son's mind and that fate could not be avoided, King Dhritarashtra, lord of men, acted thus. Vidura, supreme among learned ones, did not approve of his brother's words and thought them to be unjust. He spoke to him, "O king! I do not approve of this errand. Do not do this. I fear the destruction of our lineage. O Indra among men! When the sons are disunited, a quarrel is certain and I am concerned about this game of dice."

Dhritarashtra replied, "O Kshatta! Unless destiny turns adverse, I am not worried about a quarrel. The universe is under the control of the creator. The entire world does not run independently. O Vidura! Therefore, today, go to the king Yudhishtira at my command and quickly bring Kunti's invincible son, Yudhishtira, here.'"

On King Dhritarashtra's forceful command, Vidura started towards the wise Pandavas, on horses that were noble and strong, trained well, and possessed great speed. He proceeded swiftly and came to the king Yudhishthira's city and after being worshipped by the brahmanas, the immensely intelligent one entered. The palace was like Kubera's abode and Vidura went to Dharmaputra Yudhishtira. Ajatashatru, the great-souled king who was always devoted to the truth, welcomed Vidura with due homage and worship and then asked about the welfare of Dhritarashtra and his sons.

Yudhishtira asked, "O Kshatta! I do not see your mind to be happy. I hope everything is well. Are the sons obedient to their elders? Are the commoners obedient to his rule?"

Vidura replied, "The great-souled king is well with his sons. Surrounded by his kin, he rules like Indra. O king! Surrounded by his obedient sons, he is content. He is without worries and is firm in the desires of his own heart. The king of the Kurus has first asked me to enquire about your health and welfare and then say, 'I have built a sabha that matches yours. O son! Please come with your brothers and see it. O Partha! Assemble there with your brother and have a game of dice with your well-wishers. We will be delighted at your arrival and so will all the Kurus who are assembled there.

The great-souled King Dhritarashtra has assembled gamblers [383]there. You will see the rogues assembled there. I have come here for this. O king! Agree."

Yudhishtira said, "O Kshatta! Gambling can produce quarrels. Knowing this, which intelligent one will consent to gambling? What do you think is the right course of action for us? We are always obedient to your words."

Vidura replied, "I know that gambling is the root of all misery. I made every effort to restrain him. However, the king has sent me to you. O wise one! Knowing this, do what is best."

Yudhishtira asked, "Other than the sons of King Dhritarashtra, who are the other rogues who are there to play? O Vidura! I am asking you. Tell me. Who are the hundreds with whom one will have to play?"

Vidura replied, "O lord of the earth! There is Shakuni, king of Gandhara. That king is eager to play, has a skilled hand and knows the nature of the dice. There are Vivimshati, King Chitrasena, Satyavrata, Purumitra and Jaya."

Yudhishtira said, "It seems that some of the most feared rogues have assembled there. They are sure to play with the powers of maya. However, everything is

---

383 The word used is duradara. This means a gambler, which is probably what is intended. But the word also means the stakes used in gambling and the box in which dice are kept.

under the control of the creator. I will not refuse to play with those rogues. O Vidura! I do not wish to go and gamble on King Dhritarashtra's command. A father always has a son's welfare in mind. Therefore, tell me what I should do[384]. I have no desire to gamble with Shakuni. But if the confident one challenges me in the sabha, I will never refuse, because that has been my eternal vow."

Having thus spoken to Vidura, Dharmaraja instructed that all the arrangements for the journey should quickly be made. The next day, he set out with his army and his attendants, and with the honoured Draupadi and other women of the household. "Destiny robs us of reason, like a glare falling before the eye. As if tied in a noose, man follows the will of the creator." Uttering these words, King Yudhishtira set out with Kshatta. Partha, the destroyer of enemies, could not ignore the summons. He ascended the chariot given by Bahlika. Partha Pandava, the destroyer of enemies, dressed in royal garments, left with his brothers. Brahmanas walked ahead of him and his regal prosperity blazed. He was summoned by Dhritarashtra following what has been decreed by destiny.

Arriving in Hastinapura, he went to Dhritarashtra's palace. Pandava, the one with dharma in his heart, met Dhritarashtra and Drona, Bhishma, Karna and Kripa. As is proper, the lord also met Drona's son Ashvatthama. The mighty-armed one then met Somadatta, Duryodhana, Shalya, the valorous Shakuni and all the other kings who had assembled there before him, and Jayadratha and all the other Kurus. Surrounded by his brothers, the mighty-armed one then entered the abode of the immensely wise King Dhritarashtra and met Queen Gandhari, who was always devoted to her husband. She was surrounded by her daughters-in-law, like Rohini[385] by the stars. After showing homage to Gandhari and being welcomed by her in return, he saw his aged father Dhritarashtra, the wise lord whose eyesight was his knowledge. O king!

---

384 The sense is that Vidura is like a father and Vidura will have the welfare of the Pandavas in mind. Therefore, Yudhishtira will agree because of what Vidura says, not because of what Dhritarashtra wants.

385 The fourth of the twenty-seven nakshatras, Aldebaran.

The king inhaled the fragrances of the heads[386] of the descendants of the Kuru lineage and the four Pandavas, led by Bhimasena. O lord of the earth! On seeing the handsome Pandavas, tigers among men, all the Kouravas were extremely delighted. Taking their leave, the Pandavas entered their houses, full of jewels. The women came to see them, Draupadi at their forefront. On witnessing Yajnasena's blazing prosperity, Dhritarashtra's daughters-in-law were not enthused.

After having conversed with the women, the tigers among men went out. They performed physical exercises and the due rituals. After the daily rituals were over, they covered themselves all over with divine sandalwood. When their minds were pure, the brahmanas pronounced benedictions on them. Having eaten the best of food, they retired to their sleeping quarters. Women sang to them and the descendants of the Kurus went to sleep. After resting for some time, they discarded their sleep to the sound of praises of bards. Having happily slept during the night, they performed all the daily rites in the morning and entered the beautiful sabha, crowded by rogues.

Shakuni said, "O king! The carpet has been spread out in the sabha and these people have found the time. O Yudhishtira! The time for gambling and fixing the nature of the dice has come."

Yudhishtira replied, "O king! Dishonest gambling is evil. There is no kshatriya valour in that. Nor is there any good policy in it. Why do you then praise playing with the dice? O Shakuni! The learned do not praise deceitful gambling. Like a cruel person, do not defeat us through a crooked path."

Shakuni said, "He who knows the numbers and is knowledgeable about deceptions, is tireless in the art of gambling and is extremely intelligent in gambling, is the one who knows all the techniques. Through handling the dice, one can defeat the enemy. Blaming destiny is pointless. O king! Let us

---

386 This has been translated literally and the gesture is a sign of affection.

gamble and have no anxiety. Let us immediately decide on the stakes and not tarry."

Yudhishtira replied, "Asita–Devala are supreme among sages and always frequents the doors of the worlds. They have said that it is a sin to play with deceitful gamblers. It is best to win a battle through dharma, in which case, gambling is sanctioned. Aryas do not use mleccha language, nor use deceit in behaviour. Men who are truthful in their vows do not use trickery in a battle. We have always sought to protect deserving brahmanas with our strength. O Shakuni! Do not play beyond those limits and do not win in excess[387]. I do not desire happiness and riches through deceit. But even if a gambler plays without deceit, gambling is never praised."

Shakuni said, "O Yudhishtira! The learned triumph over non-learned only through trickery. That is how the wise triumph over the stupid, but people don't call it trickery. In approaching me for the game, if you think that I will resort to trickery, if that is your fear, then refrain from the game."

Yudhishtira replied, "O king! Once challenged, I will not withdraw. That is the vow I have taken. Fate is the powerful one and we are in the power of destiny. Who in this assembly will I play with? What is the counter-stake? Let the gambling begin."

Duryodhana said, "O lord of the earth! I will stake all my jewels and my riches. My maternal uncle, Shakuni, will gamble on my behalf." Yudhishtira replied, "To me, it seems unfair that one man should gamble in another's place. O learned one! You know this. However, if that is what you want, so be it."

When arrangements had been made for the gambling, all the kings, with Dhritarashtra at the forefront, entered the sabha—Bhishma, Drona, Kripa,

---

[387] The sense is that Yudhishtira uses his wealth for the sake of brahmanas. Therefore, Shakuni should limit his winnings.

the immensely intelligent Vidura. Others also followed, not at all pleased in their minds. Those immensely energetic ones, with necks like those of lions, sat separately and together, on many colourful seats. O king! With the assembled kings, that sabha was radiant, like resplendent heaven when the gods have assembled. O great king! They were all brave warriors, learned in the Vedas and their forms were like that of the sun. Then the gambling between the well-wishers started. 'Yudhishthira said, "O king! This is a beautiful chain of gems, inlaid in supreme gold. It represents a lot of riches and has been procured from the whirl of the ocean. O king! This is my stake. What is your counter-stake? Let it be placed in the proper order and I will win this gamble." Duryodhana replied, "I also possess many gems and riches. But they serve no particular end for me. I will win this gamble." Then Shakuni, who knew the heart of the dice, grasped the dice. And Shakuni told Yudhishtira, "I have won."

Yudhishtira said, "O Shakuni! You have won this gamble from me by using deceit. Let us now grasp the dice and play a thousand times. I have a hundred laden jars, each filled with a thousand gold coins. O king! That apart, my treasury has inexhaustible gold and much gold[388]. Those are the riches I now stake to gamble with you."

As soon as he had spoken, Shakuni told the king, "I have won." Yudhishtira said, "My royal chariot is covered with tiger skin and is worth a thousand. It is finely built, beautiful, makes a thunderous noise and is adorned with nets of bells. It gladdens the heart and brought us here. This sacred chariot, supreme among all chariots, roars like the clouds and the ocean. It is drawn by eight horses that are famous throughout the kingdom. They are noble and have the colour of ospreys. No one who walks the earth can escape their hooves. O king! These are my riches that I now gamble with you for."

Having heard this, Shakuni used deceit and told Yudhishtira, "I have won." Yudhishtira said, "O Soubala! I have one thousand elephants that are in must. They have golden girdles and are hung with golden garlands. They are spotted.[389] They are well trained, with fine tusks and are capable of bearing kings. They can withstand every kind of noise in battle. They have giant tusks like shafts[390] and each bull has with it eight she-elephants. All of these elephants have the shade of new monsoon clouds and are capable of battering down enemy cities. O king! These are my riches that I now gamble with you for."

Having heard these words, Soubala laughed at Partha. Shakuni told Yudhishtira, "I have won." Yudhishtira said, "I have one hundred thousand slave girls. They are young and extremely beautiful. They wear bracelets and armlets,

---

388 Gold is mentioned twice and two different words are used, hiranya and jatarupa. Since both words mean gold, the distinction between them isn't clear. However, since hiranya also means a golden vessel, as distinct from gold, that might be the distinction. Alternatively, hiranya also means silver, or any other precious metal.

389 The word used is padmini, which can also mean that they have lotus marks on them. However, for elephants, padmini means the elephants are spotted. The word padmini also denotes a female elephant.

390 The shaft of a carriage or a plough.

necklaces of gold coins and wear ornaments. They wear expensive garlands and ornaments, beautiful garments, and are anointed with sandalwood paste. They wear jewels and gold and all of them are dressed in sheer garments. They are skilled in singing and dancing. On my instructions, they wait upon and serve the snatakas, advisers and kings. O king! These are my riches that I now gamble with you for."

Having heard these words, Shakuni resorted to deceit and told Yudhishtira, "I have won." Yudhishtira then said, "I have thousands of male slaves. They are always dressed in fine garments and are skilled and ready to serve. They are wise, young, skilled, and intelligent and wear polished earrings. With plates in their hands, they feed the guests day and night. O king! These are my riches that I now gamble with you for."

Having heard these words, Shakuni resorted to deceit and told Yudhishtira, "I have won." Yudhishtira said, "I have as many chariots. They have pennants and are equipped with golden vessels. There are also well-trained horses, charioteers, and wonderful warriors. Regardless of whether they fight or do not fight, each of them receives one thousand as monthly salary. O king! These are my riches that I now gamble with you for."

Having heard these words of Partha, the evil one resorted to deceit. Shakuni told Yudhishtira, "I have won." Yudhishtira said, "I have gandharva horses that are spotted and have the colour of partridges. They have golden harnesses and were happily given by Chitraratha[391] to Arjuna. O king! These are my riches that I now gamble with you for."

Having heard this, Shakuni resorted to deceit and told Yudhishtira, "I have won." 'Yudhishthira said, "I have ten thousand chariots, carts, and horses. They are yoked to the best draught animals. I have thousands of soldiers from each varna. They drink milk and feed on rice and grain. There are sixty

---

391 Chaitraratha is the king of the gandharvas.

thousand of them and all of them have broad chests. O king! These are my riches that I now gamble with you for."

On hearing these words, Shakuni resorted to deceit and told Yudhishtira, "I have won." 'Yudhishthira said, "I have four hundred treasure chests made of copper and iron. Each of them has five receptacles filled with beaten gold. O king! These are my riches that I now gamble with you for." On hearing these words, Shakuni resorted to deceit and told Yudhishtira, "I have won."

Shakuni said, "O Yudhishtira! You have lost great riches of the Pandavas. O Kounteya! Do you have any other riches that you have not lost yet?" Yudhishtira replied, "O Shakuni! O Soubala! I know of unlimited riches that I possess. Why do you ask me about my wealth? I can stake ayuta[392], prayuta[393], kharva[394], padma[395], arbuda[396], shamkha[397], nikharva[398] and an entire ocean[399]. O king! These are my riches that I will play with you for."

At these words, Shakuni resorted to deceit and told Yudhishtira, "I have won." Yudhishtira replied, "O Soubala! I have many cattle, horses, milch cows, sheep, and goats, of many species, to the east of the Sindhu.[400] O king! These are my riches that I will play with you for." At these words, Shakuni resorted to deceit and told Yudhishtira, "I have won." Yudhishtira replied, "O king! The riches that I have left are my city, the country, the land of all the non-brahmanas and the non-brahmana subjects. O king! These are my riches that I will play with you for." At these words, Shakuni resorted to deceit and told Yudhishtira, "I

---

392 Ten thousand.
393 A million.
394 Ten million.
395 One thousand billion.
396 One hundred million.
397 One hundred billion.
398 A billion.
399 An entire ocean of riches.
400 The Indus River.

have won." Yudhishtira replied, "O king! These princes[401] are resplendent in their ornaments, their earrings, the golden decorations on their breasts and the other bodily decorations. O king! These are my riches that I will play with you for." At these words, Shakuni resorted to deceit and told Yudhishtira, "I have won." 'Yudhishthira replied, "This dark youth with the red eyes is Nakula, with long arms and the shoulders of a lion. He and everything that he possesses will be one stake." 'Shakuni said, "O King Yudhishtira! But Prince Nakula is dear to you. If he becomes part of our riches, what will you have left to gamble with?" Having said this, Shakuni then flung the dice and told Yudhishtira, "I have won." 'Yudhishthira replied, "This Sahadeva is the one who administers dharma. He is known in the worlds as a learned one. Though this beloved prince does not deserve it, I will play with him with one who is not loved.[402]" At these words, Shakuni resorted to deceit and told Yudhishtira, "I have won." Shakuni said, "O king! I have now won Madri's two sons, dear to you. But I think you regard Bhimasena and Dhananjaya as dearer." Yudhishtira replied, "O foolish one! Without regard to what is proper, you are following that which is not dharma. You are trying to create dissension among those who are one of heart." Shakuni said, "O king! O bull among the Bharata lineage! One who is intoxicated falls into a hole and remains there, like the trunk of a tree. You are our elder and our superior. I bow down before you. O Yudhishtira! When gamblers play, they utter mad ravings about what they have not seen, whether asleep or awake." Yudhishtira replied, "Like a boat, he carries us over to the other bank of battle. He is a powerful prince who defeats his enemies. The world knows that this warrior does not deserve it. O Shakuni! I will play with you for Arjuna." At these words, Shakuni resorted to deceit and told Yudhishtira, "I have won." Shakuni said, "Pandava Savyasachi, the foremost archer among the Pandavas, has been won and has become mine. O king! Now play with your beloved Bhima. That is all you now have left to throw." 'Yudhishthira replied, "He is our leader and guide in battle. He is like the wielder of the vajra[403], the enemy of the demons. He is great of soul,

---

401 The other four Pandavas: Bhima, Arjuna, Nakula and Sahadeva.
402 Shakuni.
403 Indra.

with slanted eyes and knitted brows. His shoulders are like those of a lion and his anger is long-lasting. There is no other man with strength like his. He is the slayer of enemies and foremost among those who wield the club. O king! Though this prince does not deserve it, I will play with you for Bhimasena."' At these words, Shakuni resorted to deceit and told Yudhishtira, "I have won." 'Shakuni said, "O Kounteya! You have lost a great deal of riches. You have lost your brothers, your horses, and your elephants. Tell us if there are any riches that you have not yet lost." 'Yudhishtira replied, "I myself am left, especially loved by all my brothers. If won over, until the time of destruction, I will do whatever deed I am asked to do."' At these words, Shakuni resorted to deceit and told Yudhishtira, "I have won." Shakuni said, "O king! You have allowed yourself to be won and you have committed the worst evil act. When there are riches left, it is evil to allow oneself to be won." Thus spoke the one who was skilled in gambling with the dice. He had won in the game, one by one, the brave warriors of the world. Shakuni said, "But you have your beloved queen, who has still not been won in the game. Use Krishna Panchali as a stake and using her, win back yourself." Yudhishtira replied, "She is neither too short, nor too tall. She is neither too dark, nor too red. Her eyes are red with love and I will play with you for her. Her eyes are like the petals of lotuses in the autumn. Her fragrance is like that of lotuses in the autumn. Her beauty serves that of lotuses in the autumn. Her beauty is like that of Shri herself. Such is her lack of cruelty, her wealth of beauty, and the goodness of her conduct, that every man desires her for a wife. She retires to bed last and she is the first one to wake up. She looks after the cowherds and the shepherds. She knows everything about what should be done and what should not be done. When covered with sweat, her face looks like a lotus or jasmine. Her hair is long. Her eyes are copper-red. O king! O Soubala! I will make the beautiful Draupadi of Panchala, my stake. Let us play." When the intelligent Dharmaraja uttered these words, all the elders assembled in the sabha raised words of "shame". The sabha seemed to shake and the kings talked among themselves. Bhishma, Drona, Kripa, and the others broke out in a sweat. Vidura buried his head in his hands and sat with a downcast face, thinking, and sighing like a serpent, like one who has lost his senses. But Dhritarashtra was delighted and failing to control his emotions, repeatedly kept asking, "Has he won? Has the stake been won?" Karna, Duhshasana, and their allies were happy. But tears began to flow down the eyes of others who were in the assembly hall. However, Soubala was insolent with success and proud of the victory. He instantly flung the dice and said, "I have won..."[404]

Prisoner's Dilemma

The game theory is a collection of tools that help in the study of strategic interdependence. Strategic interdependence refers to a situation in which one player's actions affect the other's outcomes and vice versa.[405] Players in this context, refer to strategic decision-makers within the context of a game.[406] A game in economic jargon refers to any set of circumstances that has a result dependent on the actions of two or more decision-makers (players).[407]

John von Neumann and Oskar Morgenstern developed the game theory to solve economic problems.

Among the many tools in game theory, the Prisoner's Dilemma is a popular game theory paradox. The game was nicknamed by the Canadian mathematician Albert Tucker. It is often said that the famous paradox was extracted from a Hollywood procedural crime drama where two prisoners are each offered a plea deal to rat on each other. The game illustrates the difficulty of acting together for the common or mutual benefit given that people pursue self-interest. The incentives that the Prisoners' Dilemma Game represents are common and have been useful in analysing problems in a wide variety of areas, from competition between firms in economics to social norms in sociology to decision making in psychology to animals competing for scarce

---
404 The Mahabharata 2 Translated by Bibek Debroy.
405 Taken from Game theory 101 The Complete Textbook by William Spaniel.
406 The Basics Of Game Theory (investopedia.com).
407 The Basics Of Game Theory (investopedia.com).

resources in biology, to computer systems competing for network bandwidth in engineering.[408]

Two thieves plan to rob an electronics store. As they approach the backdoor, the police arrest them for trespassing. The police officers suspect that the pair planned to break in but lack the evidence to support such an accusation. They, therefore, require a confession to charge the suspects with the greater crime. Having studied game theory in college, the interrogator throws them into the prisoner's dilemma. He individually sequesters both robbers and tells each of them the following: We are currently charging you with trespassing, which implies a one-month jail sentence. I know you were planning to rob the store, but right now I cannot prove it—I need your testimony. In exchange for your cooperation, I will dismiss your trespassing charge, and your partner will be charged to the fullest extent of the law: a twelve-month jail sentence. I am offering your partner the same deal. If both of you confess, your individual testimony is no longer as valuable, and your jail sentence will be eight months each. If both criminals are self-interested and only care about minimizing their jail time, should they take the interrogator's deal?[409]

The solution to the prisoner's dilemma can be understood using a game matrix.

---

408 Introducing Game Theory: A Graphic Guide by Ivan Pastine and Tuvana Pastine.
409 Game theory 101 The Complete Textbook by William Spaniel.

	Player 2 Quiet	Player 2 Confess
Player 1 Quiet	-1 , -1	-12 , 0
Player 1 Confess	0 , -12	-8 , -8

- From the above story, we know that there are two players.
- Player 1's strategies (remaining quiet or confessing) are listed in the rows
- Player 2's strategies are listed in the columns of the matrix.
- Player 1's payoffs are listed first for each outcome, followed by player 2's. [410]
- To interpret the matrix, suppose if Player 1 confesses and Player 2 remains quiet then the game will end in the bottom left set of payoffs. The number 0 represents that Player 1 will receive 0 months of jail time and the number -12 represents that Player 2 will receive 12 months of jail time.

Now, having understood the interpretation of the game matrix, you may think about which is the best strategy for each player?

To find out the best strategy we must consider each player's moves separately.

Now let us first consider Player 1's strategy.

---

[410] Game theory 101 The Complete Textbook by William Spaniel.

What should be Player 1's strategy if he knows that Player 2 will remain quiet?	What should be Player 1's strategy if he knows that Player 2 will confess?
Quiet Quiet -1, * Confess 0, *	Confess Quiet -12, * Confess -8, *
• Between his two strategies/moves, it is best if Player 1 confesses, since he prefers to minimize his jail time. • If Player 1 remains quiet, he will have to remain in jail for one month • If Player 1 confesses, then he will not have to remain in jail. • Also, 0>-1 • Since he prefers less jail time to more jail time, confession produces his best outcome.[411]	• Again, between his two moves, it is best if Player 1 confesses, since he prefers to minimize his jail time. • If Player 1 remains quiet, he will have to remain in jail for twelve months • On the other hand, if Player 1 confesses then he will have to remain in jail only for eight months. • Also, -8>-12 • So, if Player 2 confesses then even Player 1 should confess.
From the above two cases, we can easily conclude that irrespective of Player 2's moves, Player 1 should confess to get less jail time.	

Note:

- Since the discussion is about Player 1's strategy, Player 2's payoffs are indicated using an asterisk mark
- Player 2's payoffs are completely irrelevant to player 1's decision in this context—if he knows that she will keep quiet, then he only needs to look at his own payoffs to decide which strategy to pick. Thus, the asterisks marks could be any number at all, and player 1's optimal decision given player 2's move will remain the same.[412]

Now let us consider Player 2's strategy

---

411 Game theory 101 The Complete Textbook by William Spaniel.
412 Game theory 101 The Complete Textbook by William Spaniel.

What should be Player 2's strategy if he knows that Player 1 will remain quiet?	What should be Player 2's strategy if he knows that Player 1 will confess?
<table><tr><td></td><td>Quiet</td><td>Confess</td></tr><tr><td>Quiet</td><td>*, -1</td><td>*, 0</td></tr></table>	<table><tr><td></td><td>Quiet</td><td>Confess</td></tr><tr><td>Confess</td><td>*, -12</td><td>*, -8</td></tr></table>
<ul><li>Between her two strategies/moves, it is best if Player 2 confesses, since she prefers to minimize his jail time.</li><li>If Player 2 remains quiet, she will have to remain in jail for one month</li><li>If Player 2 confesses, then she will not have to remain in jail.</li><li>Also, 0>-1</li></ul>Since she prefers less jail time to more jail time, confession produces his best outcome.[413]	<ul><li>Again, between her two moves, it is best if Player 2 confesses, since she prefers to minimize his jail time.</li><li>If Player 2 remains quiet, she will have to remain in jail for twelve months</li><li>On the other hand, if Player 2 confesses then she will have to remain in jail only for eight months.</li><li>Also, -8>-12</li></ul>So, if Player 1 confesses then even Player 2 should confess.
From the above two cases, we can easily conclude that irrespective of Player 1's moves, Player 2 should confess to get less jail time.	

Note:

- Since the discussion is about Player 2's strategy, Player 1's payoffs are indicated using an asterisk mark
- Player 1's payoffs are completely irrelevant to player 2's decision in this context—if she knows that he will keep quiet, then she only needs to look at her own payoffs to decide which strategy to pick. Thus, the asterisks marks could be any number at all, and player 2's optimal decision given player 1's move will remain the same.

---

413 Game theory 101 The Complete Textbook by William Spaniel.

Having considered both Player 1 and Player 2's strategies, we have reached a solution:

Both players should confess. As a result, they both will spend eight months in jail. Now from the above matrix compare the <confess, confess> outcome with the <quiet, quiet> outcome. The <quiet, quiet> outcome yields a better payoff in terms of only one month of jail time for both players whereas the <confess, confess> outcome gives both the players eight months of jail each.

Now you may wonder why the players cannot coordinate on keeping quiet. But as we just saw, promises to remain silent are unsustainable. Player 1 wants player 2 to keep quiet so when he confesses, he walks away free. The same goes for player 2. As a result, the outcome is inherently unstable. Ultimately, the players finish in the inferior (but sustainable) outcome.[414]

The above-mentioned example is an example of strict dominance. We say that strategy x strictly dominates strategy y for a player if strategy x provides a greater payoff for that player than strategy y regardless of what the other players do. In this example, confessing strictly dominated keeping quiet for both players. Unsurprisingly, players never optimally select strictly dominated strategies—by definition, a better option always exists regardless of what the other players do[415].

Strict Dominance In Asymmetric Games

We can also use the strict dominance on games even when they are not symmetric like the prisoner's dilemma. For instance, let us consider the tale of the game of dice in the Dyuta Parva of the Mahabharata.

---

414 Game theory 101 The Complete Textbook by William Spaniel.
415 Game theory 101 The Complete Textbook by William Spaniel.

Jayārthashastra

	Shakuni	
	Honest	Deceit
Yudhishthira Refrain	9, -2	3, 0
Gamble	8, 5	-1, 6

Note: The cardinal values of the above-mentioned numbers are insignificant to the outcomes.

We must understand that unlike the previous example of the prisoner's dilemma, here both the players Yudhishtira and Shakuni have a distinct set of pay-offs. The solution for this game is <refrain, deceit> as it is the only reasonable solution.

Again, let us analyse Yudhishthira's strategy.

What should be Yudhishthira's strategy if hypothetically, he knew that Shakuni would play honestly?	What should be Yudhishthira's strategy if he knew that Shakuni would play deceitfully?
Honest Refrain 9, * Gamble 8, *	Deceit Refrain 3, * Gamble -1, *

• If Yudhishtira refrains from gambling with Shakuni, then he earns 9 • If he agrees to gamble with Shakuni knowing *"gambling is the root of all misery"*, then he earns 8. • Since 9 is greater than 8, Yudhishtira should refrain from gambling with Shakuni.	• If Yudhishtira refrains from gambling with Shakuni, then here he earns 3. • If he agrees to gamble with Shakuni knowing that he will employ deceit to win, then he earns only -1. • Since 3 is greater than -1, Yudhishtira should refrain from gambling with Shakuni.
Thus, irrespective of whether Shakuni plays honestly or deceitfully, Yudhishtira should refrain from gambling with Shakuni.	

Now let us consider Shakuni's strategy.

What should be Shakuni's strategy if he knew that Yudhishtira would refrain from gambling?	What should be Shakuni's strategy if he knew that Yudhishtira would gamble?
		Honest	Deceit
Refrain	*, -2	*, 0				Honest	Deceit
Gamble	*, 5	*, 6	
• If Shakuni gambles honestly, then he earns -2 after knowing that Yudhishtira would refrain from gambling with him. • If he employs deceit in his gambling, then he earns 0. • Since 0 is greater than -2, Shakuni should employ deceit.	• If Shakuni gambles honestly with Yudhishtira after he accepts the invite for the game of dice, then here he earns 5. • However, if he gambles deceitfully with Yudhishtira then he earns 6. • Since 6 is greater than 5, and considering that it would be impossible to win all of Yudhishthira's stakes without employing deceit in a dice game, where the numbers appearing on the dice are entirely random, Shakuni's optimal strategy to avenge Duryodhana's insult in the Rajasuya Yagna of the Pandavas would be to employ deceit.
Thus, irrespective of Yudhishthira's moves, Shakuni should employ deceit to keep up his promise to Duryodhana.	

Therefore, the solution for the above game would have been for Yudhishtira to refrain from gambling and for Shakuni to employ deceit. Ultimately, Yudhishtira would have earned 3 and Shakuni would have earned 0.

Yudhishthira's Mahaprasthana

Dogs are not our whole life, but they make our lives whole.

—*Roger Caras*

When I think back about my childhood, one of the memories that paint a smile on my face is the time I spent with Eden, my pet. All those silly games that I played with her and those times when I fed her my lunch box just to get away from my grandma. Truly, she is my partner in my crime and my one friend who is always there beside me. We have grown together and we continue to grow to strengthen our bond of love and affection.

Not to forget Raja, Ranu, Snuffy, Cruz, Googly, Tommy, Simba, and Vishnu, who are all my companions and buddies. Here is to many more years with Eden, Simba and Vishnu…

I dedicate this chapter to all my furry best friends.

Upon hearing the sad news about the death of Vasudeva and the destruction of the Yadavas, Yudhishtira finally made up his mind to depart from this world. He uttered these words before Arjuna, "O immensely wise one! Time cooks all creatures. I think all this has happened because of that. You should also consider that.[416]" Having heard the words of his elder brother, Arjuna said, "Time! Time!" and agreed with the words of his elder brother. Bhima, Nakula, and Sahadeva also agreed with Arjuna's words. Having decided to embark on their maha-prasthana they called for Yuyuthsu. Yudhishtira anointed Parikshit as the king of Hastinapura and assigned the responsibility of supervising the kingdom to Yuyuthsu. He then addressed Subhadra, the wife of Arjuna, "This son of your son will be the king of the Kurus. The last of the Yadus, Vajra, has also been made king. Parikshit will rule in Hastinapura and the Yadava in Shakraprastha. King Vajra should be protected by you and do not think of adharma[417] in your mind[418]." Having spoken thus to Subhadra, Yudhishtira along with his four brothers offered water to Krishna, Balarama, and others. He gave away jewels, garments, villages, horses and chariots, women, and hundreds and thousands of cattle to the brahmanas. Dharmaraja also honoured Kripacharya and requested him to accept Parikshit as his student. Kripacharya happily accepted Parikshit as his disciple. Yudhishtira also honoured his subjects and announced his decision to depart from this world. The subjects of Hastinapura were apprehensive at Yudhishthira's words. They pleaded before him, "This should not be done." However, Yudhishtira, who was an embodiment of dharma did not listen to them. Having obtained permission from the subjects of Hastinapura, Yudhishtira along with his brothers decided to depart.

Dharma's son, Kouravya, King Yudhishtira, took off the ornaments from his body and donned the bark of trees. O lord of men! Bhima, Arjuna, the twins and the illustrious Draupadi—all of them donned garments made from the barks of trees. They performed all the recommended beneficial

---

416 The Mahabharata 10 Translated by Bibek Debroy.
417 That is, taking Vajra's kingdom away from him.
418 The Mahabharata 10 Translated by Bibek Debroy.

rites. All the bulls among men then cast the sacred fire into water[419]. [420]As they embarked on their maha-prasthana, the residents of Hastinapura were in grief. They lamented as they saw their king, his brothers, and his wife renounce Hastinapura.

As they journeyed to holy places before reaching the Himalayas, a dog accompanied the Pandavas. Now they were five brothers, Draupadi and a dog, who joined them as the seventh. As part of their last pilgrimage, all the Pandavas, Draupadi and the dog climbed the Himalayas. As they toiled up the mountain path one by one fell exhausted and died[421]. Draupadi succumbed first. When Bhima saw her, he addressed Yudhishtira, "O scorcher of enemies! This princess never committed act of adharma. O king! Why has Krishna fallen on the ground?" Yudhishtira replied, "O supreme among men! She had a great partiality for Dhananjaya. She has reaped the fruits of that."

Sahadeva was the next to fall after Draupadi. On seeing his brother fall, Bhima again questioned Yudhishtira, "Without any pride, he served all of us. Why has Madravati's son fallen on the ground?" Yudhishtira replied, "He thought that there was no one who was his equal in wisdom. O son of a king! It is because of that sin that he has fallen.[422]" Nakula also met the same fate as Sahadeva. Upon seeing Nakula's fall, Bhima again questioned Yudhishtira, "He had dharma in his soul and his adherence to it never suffered. He followed the words of his brothers. In the world, Nakula was unmatched in his beauty. Yet, he has fallen on the ground[423]." Thus, addressed by Bhimasena, Yudhishtira replied, "Nakula possessed dharma in his soul and was supreme among all the intelligent ones. However, he held a view, like Diti offspring[424], that no one

---

419 The sacrificial fire that burns in a household, the casting away symbolizing the giving up of the house holder stage.
420 The Mahabharata 10 Translated by Bibek Debroy.
421 Mahabharata by C. Rajagopalachari
422 The Mahabharata 10 Translated by Bibek Debroy.
423 The Mahabharata 10 Translated by Bibek Debroy.
424 Diti's offspring are the daityas.

was his equal in beauty. In his mind, he thought that there was no one who was superior to him. O Vrikodara! Understand. This is the reason Nakula has fallen. O brave one! Anything ordained for a person is bound to happen.[425]"

Upon witnessing his brothers succumb one by one, Arjuna felt miserable. Unable to bear the grief of the death of his brothers, he too fell. On seeing that the invincible one had fallen and was about to die, Bhima spoke to the king. "I cannot remember any falsehood that this great-souled one has wilfully uttered. What is the transgression, as a result of which, he has fallen on the ground?" Yudhishtira replied, "Arjuna always said that he would burn down the enemy in a single day. Though he was proud of his valour, he wasn't able to accomplish that. That is the reason he has fallen. Phalguna disrespected all the other wielders of the bow. Those who desire their prosperity must always act as they have spoken." Having said this, the king proceeded. Bhima fell. Having fallen, Bhima addressed Dharmaraja Yudhishtira. "O, king! Look towards me. I am loved by you and I have fallen. What is the reason I have fallen? If you know, tell me." Yudhishtira replied, "You ate too much and you boasted about your vigour. O, Partha! You disrespected others. That is the reason you have fallen on the ground." Having said this, without looking back, the mighty-armed one proceeded with the dog. After walking for a considerable distance, he met Indra. Indra had arrived on a chariot and asked Yudhishtira to ascend on the chariot.

---

425 The Mahabharata 10 Translated by Bibek Debroy.

On seeing that his brothers had fallen, Dharmaraja Yudhishtira was overcome by grief and spoke these words to the one with the one thousand eyes. "My brothers have fallen here. Let them come with me. O lord of the gods! Without my brothers, I do not desire to go to heaven. O Purandara! The princess was delicate and deserved happiness. Let her come with us. You should grant us this permission." Indra replied, "You will see your brothers and sons, together with Krishna and all the others. They have gone to heaven, ahead of you. O bull among the Bharata lineage! Do not grieve. O bull among the Bharata lineage! They have cast aside their human bodies and have gone there. However, there is no doubt that you will go to heaven in this body."

Yudhishtira said, "O lord of the past and the present! This dog has always been devoted to me. He should go with me. Because of compassion, that is my view." Indra replied, "O king! You will now obtain immortality, prosperity like mine, all kinds of great fame, and the happiness of heaven. Abandon the dog. There is no lack of compassion in this."

Yudhishtira said, "O one with one thousand eyes! How can a person who is noble perform an ignoble act? O noble one! That is exceedingly difficult to do. I do not want prosperity that comes about by abandoning those who are devoted to me." Indra replied, "For those with dogs, there is no place in the world of heaven. Krodhavasha takes away their beneficial and good deeds[426]. O Dharmaraja! You should think about this. Abandon this dog. There is no lack of compassion in this." Yudhishtira said, "It is said that there is great sin in abandoning one who is devoted. In this world, this is equal to the killing of a brahmana. O great Indra! Ever since I have been born, I have patiently done that. Therefore, for the sake of my own happiness, how can I act in a contrary way now?" Indra replied, "If gifts laid out for a sacrifice, or oblations poured into it, are seen by a dog, Krodhavasha takes the benefits away. Therefore, you should abandon this dog. If you abandon this dog, you will obtain the world of the gods. O brave one! Having abandoned your brothers and your beloved Krishna, you will obtain that world through your deeds. When you have given all of them up, why are you not ready to abandon the dog? Why are you confused?"

Yudhishtira said, "In the world of mortals, there is no friendship or enmity with those who are dead. I am incapable of reviving them. That is the reason I abandoned those who are no longer alive. O Shakra! It is my view that surrendering someone who has sought sanctuary, killing a woman, stealing the possessions of a brahmana and enmity towards a friend—these four are equal to the sin of abandoning someone who is devoted."

Hearing Dharmaraja's words, the illustrious one, who was in the form of Dharma, was pleased[427]. He gently spoke these words, which were full of praise, to Yudhishtira, Indra among men. "O Indra among kings! You have been born in a noble lineage. You follow your father's conduct and possess

---

426 Literally, krodhavasha means someone who is prone to anger. Krodavasha was one of Daksha's daughters, married to the sage Kashyapa. Krodhavasha's descendants are sometimes described as deities, sometimes as semi-divine and sometimes as other species.
427 The dog changed into Dharma, Dharma having assumed the form of a dog.

intelligence. O descendant of the Bharata lineage! You possess compassion towards all beings. O son! On an earlier occasion, I had tested you in Dvaitavana. Desiring to fetch some water, your valiant brothers were slain. Forgetting about your brothers Bhima and Arjuna and showing equality between your mothers[428], you desired that Nakula should be brought back to life. Now, instead of giving up the devoted dog, you have decided to forsake the chariot of the gods. O lord of men! Therefore, there is no one in heaven who is your equal. O descendant of the Bharata lineage! Therefore, in your own body, you will obtain the eternal worlds. O best among the Bharata lineage! You will obtain a divine and supreme objective."

Dharma, Shakra, the Maruts, the Ashvins, the gods, and the devarshis made Pandava ascend the chariot. The siddhas, who could roam around at will, left on their celestial vehicles. They were sacred and radiant, auspicious in words, intelligence, and deeds. The king, the extender of the Kuru lineage, climbed on to the chariot, which ascended swiftly, covering heaven and earth with its energy.[429]

Revealed Preference Theory

Revealed preference is a very popular theory given by the American Economist Paul Anthony Samuelson in 1938. The revealed preference theory states that consumer behaviour is the best indicator of a consumer's preferences if their income and the product's price are both held constant. The revealed preference theory works on the assumption that consumers are rational individuals.

In economics, consumer behaviour had been understood through the concept of utility for a very long time. However, utility is incredibly difficult to quantify in indisputable terms, and by the beginning of the 20th Century, economists were complaining about the pervasive reliance on utility. Replacement theories were considered, but all were similarly criticized, until Samuelson's "Revealed Preference Theory," which posited that consumer behaviour was not based on

---

428 Kunti and Madri.
429 The Mahabharata 10 Translated by Bibek Debroy.

utility, but on observable behaviour that relied on a small number of relatively uncontested assumptions.

Revealed preference is an economic theory regarding an individual's consumption patterns, which asserts that the best way to measure consumer preferences is to observe their purchasing behaviour. Revealed preference theory works on the assumption that consumers are rational. In other words, they will have considered a set of alternatives before making a purchasing decision that is best for them. Thus, given that a consumer chooses one option out of the set, this option must be the preferred option.

Revealed preference theory allows room for the preferred option to change depending upon price and budgetary constraints. By examining the preferred preference at each point of constraint, a schedule can be created of a given population's preferred items under a varied schedule of pricing and budget constraints. The theory states that given a consumer's budget, they will select the same bundle of goods (the "preferred" bundle) as long as that bundle remains affordable. It is only if the preferential bundle becomes unaffordable that they will switch to a less expensive, less desirable bundle of goods.

The original intention of revealed preference theory was to expand upon the theory of marginal utility, coined by Jeremy Bentham. Utility, or enjoyment from a good, is very hard to quantify, so Samuelson set about looking for a way to do so. Since then, revealed preference theory has been expanded upon by several economists and remains a major theory of consumption behaviour. The theory is especially useful in providing a method for analysing consumer choice empirically.

Three Axioms of Revealed Preference

As economists developed the revealed preference theory, they identified three primary axioms of revealed preference—the weak axiom, the strong axiom, and the generalized axiom.

- Weak Axiom of Revealed Preference (WARP): This axiom states that given incomes and prices, if one product or service is purchased instead of another, then, as consumers, we will always make the same choice. The weak axiom also states that if we buy one particular product, then we will never buy a different product or brand unless it is cheaper, offers increased convenience, or is of better quality (i.e., unless it provides more benefits). As consumers, we will buy what we prefer and our choices will be consistent, so suggests the weak axiom.
- Strong Axiom of Revealed Preference (SARP): This axiom states that in a world where there are only two goods from which to choose, a two-dimensional world, the strong and weak actions are shown to be equivalent.
- Generalized Axiom of Revealed Preference (GARP): This axiom covers the case when, for a given level of income and or price, we get the same level of benefit from more than one consumption bundle. In other words, this axiom accounts for when no unique bundle that maximizes utility exists.

Example of Revealed Preference

As an example of the relationships expounded upon in revealed preference theory, consider consumer X that purchases a pound of grapes. It is assumed under revealed preference theory that consumer X prefers that pound of grapes above all other items that cost the same or are cheaper than that pound of grapes. Since consumer X prefers that pound of grapes over all other items they can afford, they will only purchase something other than that pound of grapes if the pound of grapes becomes unaffordable. If the pound of grapes becomes unaffordable, consumer X will then move on to a less preferable substitute item.

Yudhishthira's behaviour in the above story exemplifies the revealed preference. He prefers to go to heaven along with the dog. He prefers this choice above all the other available choices such as going to heaven without the dog or staying back with the dog without going to heaven. Since he prefers to go to heaven accompanied by the dog, he will alter his preference only if this choice becomes unaffordable, i.e. if this choice violates his Dharma.

Author's Bio

Born and brought up in Bangalore, Tanushree Nagaveni has been exploring the great epics Mahabharata and Ramayana since the age of three under the abled guidance of her gurus and is a recipient of the High Achievement Award for Cambridge IGCSE Sanskrit. Tanushree is also a professional Bharatanatyam artiste and a painter. Following her formal introduction to economics, her interest in presenting the amalgamation of ancient scriptures and modern economics led her to author her first book *Jayarthashastra*. While pursuing her undergraduate studies as an economics major at the Leavey School of Business, Santa Clara University, Tanushree continues to actively research the relevance of ancient Sanskrit literature in modern times.

www.ingramcontent.com/pod-product-compliance
Lightning Source LLC
Chambersburg PA
CBHW030819310126
38835CB00073B/273